ENGLAND SPEAKS

1925

In an old Seaport

IN AN OLD SEAPORT

ENGLAND SPEAKS

By PHILIP GIBBS

*Being Talks with Road Sweepers, Barbers, States-
men, Lords and Ladies, Beggars, Farming Folk,
Actors, Artists, Literary Gentlemen, Tramps,
Down-and-outs, Miners, Steel Workers,
Blacksmiths, the Man-in-the-Street,
Highbrows, Lowbrows
And All Manner of Folk of Humble and Exalted
Rank with a* PANORAMA OF THE ENGLISH
SCENE *in This Year of Grace*
1935

Illustrations by E. LANDER

DOUBLEDAY, DORAN & COMPANY, INC.
Garden City *1935* *New York*

PRINTED AT THE *Country Life Press*, GARDEN CITY, N. Y., U. S. A.

CONTENTS

CONTENTS

VI THE FRONT LINE OF INDUSTRY

ILLUSTRATIONS

ILLUSTRATIONS

I

The Gay Crowd

1. His Nibs

"THE ROYAL FAMILY," said my road sweeper, leaning on his broom, "is a very respectable lot."

I agreed, with an inward spasm of mirth.

"Human, if you know what I mean," he added, gazing thoughtfully at a bit of newspaper which awaited his attention in the gutter. "They feel kindly towards us, and we feel kindly towards them. See what I mean?"

"Perfectly," I said.

My road sweeper expressed his personal admiration for the King.

"He's all right! A nice fellow—not like that there Hitler in Germany who puts folk into concentration camps because they don't see eye to eye with him. His Nibs does his duty like the rest of us, like I do mine, and I don't envy him his job. That's why I'm loyal. That's why we're all loyal, barring a few Reds who come out like rats here and there. It's my opinion, of course, and you can take it or leave it."

I was willing to take it. It's not often that I find myself in disagreement with this old soldier—he finished the last war at Fremicourt with a whiff of gas—who waves a friendly hand at me every time I appear in the street which he keeps clean of refuse blowing out of garages and back yards round the corner.

He was one of those half-million people who went surging towards Buckingham Palace on Jubilee nights—he had to do a bit of elbow work, he told me—cheering themselves hoarse

and setting up a chant of "We want the King!" until suddenly
on the balcony the King appeared with the Queen and his
family, gazing down upon this vast sea of faces, hearing those
incessant cheers like waves beating up to them, astonished perhaps, even awestruck, by this tremendous demonstration of
popular affection.

2. Mass Emotion

England is not much given to self-expression. The English
people are, as a rule, too self-conscious, and foreigners find us
strangely inarticulate as a nation. They can't make us out, and
wonder whether we are very stupid or very deep, and generally
agree that we are both. We can't make ourselves out, and are
surprised now and then—amazed even—by such sudden out-
bursts of massed emotion when we thought ourselves unemotional, and by occasional manifestations of national unity when
we believed that we were all at sixes and sevens or inhibited by
our dislike of "ballyhoo," our shyness and secret reserves, our
sense of humour, and our distrust of emotionalism and self-
exhibition. Isn't that how, even now, we imagine ourselves to
be?

I remember the time when this idea of ourselves as unemotional people received its first knock. It was when I was a boy.
It was the night of Mafeking, when suddenly, as though at a
given signal, the young gentlemen of England, or at least those
gathered in the West End of London, allowed themselves some
hours of mad revelry with those who were still called "the lower
orders." Many elegant top hats were flung above the heads of
the crowds that night, careless of expense, many policemen's
helmets were used for a game of catch-as-catch-can. Little
ladies of the theatrical world danced on restaurant tables where
the cloths were wet with spilt champagne. Parties of gilded
youth—they no longer exist—dangled their legs from the tops of
hansom cabs and growlers. Coster girls, who still wore their
feathers down the Old Kent Road, linked arms in Dionysian
dances with their boys and were wild-eyed mænads in London
streets. It was a great shock to the soul of respectable England.
"Disgusting!" said the Forsytes. "Un-English and hysterical,"

said the clergy. "An unseemly and alarming phenomenon, not in accordance with our national character," wrote the leader writers of Nonconformist papers. It was a long time before such a thing happened again.

It happened again on the night of Armistice after a World War, when the lights went up again after years of darkness, as a signal that a long agony had ended. There were no class distinctions that night, no shyness nor self-repression among those English crowds who came into the streets cheering and shouting. It was the surging up of a mass emotion, mass joy, mass relief after long tension when a nation which had been through the greatest ordeal of its history was conscious of its own spirit and of something mystical beyond this noise-making. The soul of England speaks now and then but not often. When it does there are some people who think it very un-English and don't like it.

3. Cinderella Dances

This emotion over King George's Jubilee was rather unexpected. It took everybody by surprise: its sudden and continuing exuberance, and its nightly revelries when London, to the farthest suburbs where the pavement ends—is it twenty miles now?—danced till dawn. The weather was marvellous. Not for many years—two hundred, said one of the newspapers, outbidding all others—had there been such warm May days and such sultry nights.

"You know," said a girl inside a tobacco kiosk, from whom I bought a box of matches on the Underground, "I think it was meant."

"Meant?" I asked, not getting her meaning, and hearing the approach of an Inner Circle train.

"God," she said, lowering her voice.

It was a nice idea that God should give such good weather for King George's Jubilee. It was a pity a frost came afterwards, destroying all the English orchards and ruining many fruit growers.

The girl in the tobacco kiosk had had a fine time, she told me, in such a friendly way that I let a train pass.

"We had a wonderful time down Fulham way," she said with laughing eyes. "You've no idea! I danced the shoes off my feet till three in the morning. Of course I felt a bit tired next day. One always has to pay the price for a bit of fun, doesn't one?"

"Nearly always," I agreed regretfully. "But how did you get your music for the dancing?"

"Oh, it was marvellous! Down our street—Fulham, you know —there were two gentlemen with wireless sets. They put them in the front windows, and the dear old B.B.C. gave us dance music till midnight. Then the people wanted the old tunes— 'Dolly Gray' and all that. So we fetched a gentleman who played the concertina. He plays it grand, and we kept on dancing till we nearly dropped. I must say we enjoyed ourselves, although I did dance the shoes off my feet."

There were thousands of other girls in London—hundreds of thousands—who danced their shoes away in the streets and, like Cinderella, forgot the chimes of midnight. Behind Curzon Street—wasn't it?—there was a party in one of the big houses with a band to play for them. A crowd gathered outside, making use of this music, and presently the pretty ladies with bare arms and bare backs, with young gentlemen in boiled shirts and tailed coats, came out and joined the street dancers, without class consciousness, or at least with a sense of comradeship. Extraordinarily un-English—except when now and then the English take off their masks and forget their inhibitions.

4. London with the Lid Off

"There's a lot of Communism in London," said a friend of mine before the first day of the Jubilee. "All the little Reds and Pinks and Pacifists will probably make themselves objectionable. There's a lamentable lack of enthusiasm. Unemployment has something to do with it, of course. One can't expect loyalty and enthusiasm from men living on a dole, without work or wages."

Interest seemed to awaken suddenly when the streets along the route were draped in flags and floodlighting began. Thousands of country cousins came to town. Suburban populations surged to the West End after office hours to see the decorations and the lighting effects. London became magical where the floodlights lit up the Cathedral and the old Abbey and many buildings which seem commonplace by day but are white and glamorous when they are revealed against the black curtain of the night. Floodlights streamed across the parks, giving an unearthly green to the grass, waking up the sleeping flowers, and touching every branch and twig with liquid silver.

"Ow, ain't it lovely!" cried one of the girls in the crowd. "I didn't know this ugly old London could be changed into fairyland!"

She was a little shopgirl, I imagine, and had her hand tucked through the arm of a tall boy without a hat.

"Feeling romantic?" he asked with a sideways smile as he followed the tide of life across the bridge in St. James's Park.

Millions camped out in the parks, kept open for this purpose by the King's orders on the night before the first Jubilee procession, and it was the beginning of many nights out. London was at its best during those weeks. The parks were on fire with beauty. Their flower beds were filled with massed colour of tulips and irises; red May trees—red and white—were flowering richly and drenched the air with scent.

I talked to one of the ticket collectors who take money for the chairs—those deck chairs in which it is good to recline in London's summer time—if it happens—with the sun in one's face and a view across the lake to the towers of Westminster.

"Having a busy time?" I asked.

He looked down at me and laughed as he punched my ticket.

"Busy? Not half! Never had such a time in my life. I've been punching these tickets until three and four in the morning. I've had to empty my bag of coppers time after time."

"Surely people don't pay their tuppences at night?" I asked. "Especially nights of Jubilee."

He was astonished at the question.

"Why not? It's the right charge, isn't it? And they're not hooligans, are they? You couldn't find better behaved people—not if you went inside Buckingham Palace. Family parties, as respectable as you or I. There hasn't been a single flower broken in the beds, in spite of all the thousands sitting on the

grass and having picnics at midnight. Not a blooming flower,
as far as I can see!"

"Marvellous," I said. "Could it happen anywhere else?"

"Ah, now you're asking!" said my ticket collector. "In my
opinion our crowd give a lesson to the world, and as an old
soldier I've seen something of it. It makes one proud. We're a
law-abiding people. We don't ask for trouble and we don't
make it."

I sat among those people on the grass in St. James's Park for
the purpose of social study. They were, as my friend said, family
parties. They were well dressed and well shod and well behaved.
A girl was combing her hair as though she were a wood nymph
in her own glade. A young man in grey flannel trousers and an
old sports coat asked me politely whether I happened to have a
match. A young mother held a bottle to the lips of a hungry
babe.

"Now don't you go picking them flowers!" cried a middle-
aged woman to a small boy crawling towards a bed of tulips.

The only licence they allowed themselves was to ignore the
notices of *Keep off the grass*.

5. *The Laughing Crowds*

On the morning of the first procession, when the King went
to St. Paul's for his thanksgiving, I walked among the crowds
along the line of route with my wife and family. We were
lamentably late in starting for a flat in Pall Mall where places
were waiting for us.

"We shall never get there," I said with my usual pessimism.

"Oh, it will be quite easy!" said my wife with her usual
optimism.

I lost her and the rest of my family at Hyde Park Corner and
did not expect to see them until I could get home again. I was
wedged in a compact mass of my fellow citizens.

"Any chance of getting through?" I asked mildly.

A nice-looking girl smiled into my eyes.

"Why not walk on top of our heads?" she asked brightly.

They had been there for hours, these people, some of them

The Abbey
jubilee night
6th may 1935

WESTMINSTER ABBEY, JUBILEE NIGHT—MAY 6, 1935

since dawn, but they were perfectly good-natured—they must have had an angelic spirit, for once—when a policeman asked them to make a lane for a group of Important People who desired passage and had tickets for high-priced stands.

"Now, ladies," said the policeman, "just squeeze a little tighter for a moment. The gentlemen won't mind."

By some miracle they made a lane, and I followed the ticket folk into the middle of the road. I had no right to be there, ot course. The Guards were taking up positions, and I had to dodge their bayonets.

"Nice morning," said one of the officers.

Carriage traffic was still moving along the sanded roadway. I followed in the wake of a Rolls-Royce and tried to look as though I belonged to it.

"Get on the pavement," said a mounted policeman, looking me sternly in the eyes. I ignored him, feeling guilty of high treason to all those who had stood so long. Of course, I thought, I shall never get as far as St. James's Street, to say nothing of Pall Mall.

All the stands were filled with the seat holders. There were people on the roofs of the houses along Piccadilly. On the pavements the crowd was deep and dense. But there was curiously little noise among all these millions past whom I walked. Now and then a gust of laughter travelled lightly above their heads. Officers of the Guards were calling out commands in falsetto voices. There was the stamp of soldiers' feet and the grounding of rifle butts. I could hear the song of birds in the Green Park. There was not as much noise as one hears in a Turkish village— nor even in an English village on market day.

I reached the flat in Pall Mall as easily as though I had been walking down the garden path of my country cottage. To my amazement my wife and family arrived five minutes later.

"Good heavens!" I exclaimed. "How did you get here?"

"Oh, we just walked," said my wife with a little triumph in her eyes. "Quite easy!"

On the balcony was a group of friends and the hospitable man who had invited us. From that vantage point we were able to study the demeanour of an English crowd on a day of pageantry, as often I had seen it before. They were tightly pressed down

Pall Mall. They were densely packed to the left of us by the Duke of York's steps when the band of the Coldstream Guards was discoursing merry music.

A man's voice spoke over my shoulder. I knew him as a good friend and a great traveller.

"England," he said, "does this kind of thing better than any other country. Look at those people down there! They keep order for themselves. There's no need to push 'em about; and I'll bet the official time-table will be kept to the second, though it looks as though only a miracle could get these carriages through to St. Paul's before the King begins to say his prayers. Foreigners think we're unintelligent. And of course we are! But there must be some kind of a brain behind all this. Somebody must be pulling the wires behind the scenes and making them all work smoothly. Pretty marvellous!"

Gusts of laughter arose from the crowd. Cheers rose to our balcony.

"Is that the King coming?" asked an elderly man who was reading *The Times* inside the room until the procession arrived: he had read *The Times* every morning for fifty years and the habit had grown on him.

It wasn't the King. It was the usual dustmen going down the route to pick up the last bit of paper before all the King's horses and all the King's men would pass that way. They did their job under the fire of a million eyes and took all the chaff with self-possession. One of them pandered to the spirit of the mob by raising his slouch hat with grave dignity, like a monarch acknowledging the homage of the crowd. They roared with laughter at him. It was the same old joke. I had seen it a hundred times. We are very traditional in our sense of humour.

"This King business still seems pretty strong in England," said one of my American friends.

The crowds had come out to do homage to the King. It was a personal tribute of affection from the mob of middle-class folk down there in Pall Mall and as far away as the East End. I thought of the words of my road sweeper: "He's all right." And they had come out to see a bit of pageantry which the Londoner dearly loves. But there was more in it than that on this day of Jubilee. There was all English history in it. Bells were

ringing from the old Abbey and many churches, and in that
sound the past was calling—the past of a people who are not
without heroic memories, who, deep down in their hearts,
though inarticulate, have a pride in their own quality and spirit
through a thousand years of struggle and conflict and tremendous drama. They are steeped in the spirit of Shakespeare who
has entered their souls from the Old Vic. They remember a
few pages of history. The Prince of Wales came with his escort
of Life Guards, and with him came young Edward who fought
at Crécy and young Harry who stood on a field at Agincourt
and said, "Oh, that I had but one ten thousand of those men
in England who lie abed today!" Hadn't they seen George
Robey play Falstaff to that Prince of Wales? A little princess
with a baby sister came driving by and waved her hand to the
crowds; her name was Elizabeth. The Lord Chancellor's coach,
drawn by sturdy horses with hairy hoofs, came driving out of
Queen Anne's England. When the King and Queen passed, the
cheers rose like a storm. They were for a man who had done his
duty and stood by his people in war time and by the beds of
wounded men year in year out. He was a simple man without
any posture or play-acting. But with him came Alfred and
Richard Cœur de Lion and all that England means once in a
while to English folk, even if England does not do much for
them.

"I am most touched by the decorations in the slum districts,"
I was told by a County Court judge who drives most mornings
through mean streets behind Euston and the Harrow Road.
"They've twisted coloured streamers round the railings. They've
gone to a lot of trouble in putting up their bits of bunting. And
yet there's a lot of overcrowding and unemployment in this
district of mine. It might have made them bitter and disloyal.
Has it? Why, every street flutters with their flags! They're
English, even if they sleep six to a room."

6. The Merry Wives of Walworth

I listened to the voices of the crowd during these days of
jubilation. England is inarticulate, it is said, but standing among

these people I heard them speak, and they haven't changed much since Shakespeare knew them in the taverns of East Cheap and in the pit of his Globe Theatre.

I stood among them for the Trooping of the Colour on the Park side of the Horse Guards Parade. I had arrived late and could see very little of the show. None of us in our part of the crowd could see more than the outside edge of the square, except by standing in the road when a mounted policeman rode away from us to press back other people with the flanks of his gentle horse before returning to deal with us again. The "Bobbies" were more lenient, only pretending to be severe when the mounted man was near. There was a very humorous policeman opposite my section of the crowd. He was a good-looking young fellow with merry eyes under his helmet, and he exchanged ceaseless back-chat with two women who were close to him. They were both married women and buxom. One of them, with light red hair and blue eyes, had a small boy in her arms who was sleeping restlessly with the sun on his curls, which were the same colour as his mother's. She had the strawberry-and-cream complexion of red-haired women. The other was a dark, merry-eyed wench with two children standing by her side. She was out to enjoy herself. She was enjoying herself vastly in a dialogue with the young policeman, knowing that it was affording good entertainment to the crowd within earshot of her.

These two women had come straight out of the pages of Shakespeare. They were the Merry Wives of Walworth.

At least, the policeman said they came from Walworth—he knew their type, he said—though the dark-eyed woman scorned the idea of such a place.

"Walworth!" she cried, with a scream of laughter. "What makes you think that? I'll give you my address, if you like—and it won't be in Walworth. And I'll make a date with you when you're off duty, but not when my husband's at home. He doesn't like the Force. Don't think much of their morals, specially when they're off duty. I don't mind taking a bit of a risk myself. I'm not intimidated by a uniform, no, nor a helmet neither. Take a man's clothes off and he's the same, I say. But then I'm a married woman and honest, and I don't care who knows it.

But if you do happen to come snooping around you won't find me in Walworth. I've an open-air swimming bath in my garden. Mixed bathing and all that. A fountain with stone goddesses without noses. But they don't mind!"

"When's your washing day?" asked the policeman, keeping a wary eye on the mounted officer.

"Washing day?" asked the dark-eyed woman. "Every day's washing day with me. I keep clean behind the ears."

"I don't want to get mixed up with the blue bag," said the policeman. "I wouldn't like your husband to find me helping to rinse out the children's clothes. Next time I come to Walworth I wouldn't mind a quiet cup of tea in the back kitchen."

"Well, you don't expect me to give it to you in the back bedroom, do you?" asked the Merry Wife of Walworth.

"Now, lady," said the policeman, "don't you go raising any false hopes in my breast. I'm a sensitive man. And I'm very shy."

The red-haired woman laughed heartily and shifted her child's head from one shoulder to another.

"Be yourself, baby!" she cried to the policeman.

The mounted policeman was pressing his horse's flanks against the crowd further up the roadway. We took the opportunity of another three yards, so getting a glimpse of what was happening on the parade ground. What was happening was a trot past of household cavalry with their helmets and brass breastplates glittering in the sunlight.

"Now, ladies," said the young constable, "I've told you before and I'll tell you again. The curbstone is where you're supposed to line up. You'll only get me into trouble, you know, because I'm soft-hearted."

"Hold my hand while nobody's looking, dearie," suggested the dark-eyed Wife of Walworth. "I'm soft-hearted myself. And I'm getting a fine view of the soldiers. I once fell in love with a colour sergeant, and I've been partial to soldiers ever since. And there's the King—God bless him! He's waving his hand to me. Now, isn't that kind?"

Many women in the crowd were holding up mirrors which they used as periscopes. Behind me two elderly men were exchanging reminiscences.

"I remember waiting for six hours on parade at Delhi when the King was coming. King Edward, of course. A hundred and twenty in the shade. Hot? Well, not half! The men were falling out like flies."

"Them was good old days!" said the other man. "Once a soldier one likes a bit of pageantry. Now, my wife is a Scotch body and not more than four feet and a half in her bare feet. She hasn't seen much of Royalty, so I brought her out on the first day of the Jubilee and perched her on my shoulder, where she saw fine. Of course, I couldn't see much myself, but she told me all about it. Well, I gave her a happy day, and we've been married twenty years. Think of that!"

The red-haired woman nudged the young constable.

"Now, what's all this crowd for?" she asked. "Those people over there seem to be playing at soldiers. Enjoying themselves, I daresay!"

"Constable!" cried the dark-eyed one. "Ask the King to come out and have a chat with me. . . . But it's shocking how that young woman is carrying on. She's got two policemen to carry her. Now I call that greedy!"

A young woman was being carried out fainting. Several more followed her under the care of St. John's Ambulance men.

"If any of you ladies faint near me," said the young constable, "I warn you that my method is rough and ready. I stands fainting people on their heads. It cures them at once. Brings the blood back to the brain. Infallible!"

"If only I could faint!" cried the Merry Wife of Walworth with a squeal of laughter. "But I'm indelicate, I am. It's my health. I'm too robust. I'm like Mae West. She and me have much in common."

"Now, ladies," said the young constable, "will you get back there before I have to get cross with you?"

I crossed the Park in time to see the King ride back through a rolling thunder of cheering. Behind him were his four sons. The Prince of Wales was concealed beneath his bearskin, but the crowd recognized him and gave him a special ovation.

"That young man," said a voice in the crowd, "has the energy of ten dynamos. I can't think how he keeps going."

7. The King's Levee

The King was holding a levee in St. James's Palace. Many people who hadn't been invited—I was one of them—lined up to see the uniforms, which were magnificent.

"Who's that romantic-looking laddie in a turban?" asked a girl standing near me.

Her companion was ready with the information.

"Oh, I'm sure he's a Bengal Lancer! That's how they dress in the film picture."

The officers of the Royal Air Force came out in a bunch with their plumed caps and looked self-conscious, as well they might.

Some Indian Rajahs stood about chatting with English officers who had the legs of cavalry men.

On the Mall side of the palace the escort of Life Guards were sitting motionless on their horses. They were wearing their long red cloaks because of a shower of rain. The guests at the levee were still coming in.

A tall middle-aged man just in front of me was talking to an American lady. The sight of all these uniforms seemed to have reminded him of a time when he too wore some kind of uniform, mud-coloured. He was talking about a Zeppelin raid over London when he was home on leave.

"It was a clear night," he said. "I could see the Zepp quite clear, like a silver cigar. Millions of people were watching it from all parts of London. An aëroplane—ours, of course—was trying to get near it and fire into it. It hovered above while the Zepp opened fire with all its guns. We knew afterwards that the pilot of the aëroplane was Captain Robinson. They made him a V.C. for it. He plugged the Zepp with tracer bullets. It burst into flame and came down at Cuffley, and I'll never forget the cheer which went up from millions of throats."

"Now, I'm glad to have heard that!" exclaimed the American lady.

The man who remembered the war spoke about the King's drive through the East End.

"Not many kings could go among their people quite as fearlessly. Don't you agree?"

"I certainly do!" said the American lady. "But then you English people——"

"The King looked as happy as a sandboy," said the man in front of me. "And both he and the Queen noticed a cripple who lay on a stretcher. They smiled and waved to him. It's little things like that which keep the people sweet, you know. Why, these people in the East End were as loyal as if they'd all been major generals."

"They love him as well as respect him," answered the American lady. "But can you tell me who is that distinguished-looking man in a cocked hat?"

"It's an Admiral," said her friendly informant. "Good type! I must say I admire our naval men. The best in the world."

He was uplifted with patriotic pride. He was doing a bit of "boosting" to the United States.

8. *The Pessimist*

Outside St. James's Palace a morning later I had a conversation with a man who was not so pleased with things. He stopped in front of me, behind the line of people watching the changing of the Guard, and said something which I didn't catch.

"What did you say?" I asked, bending down to him. I saw that he was a little old man with a pippin face and eyes as blue as a queer cap he wore. In one of his hands was a billy can.

He gazed up at me with his blue eyes.

"I said the human animal is cunning and cruel."

I was startled by this charge against the whole human race, on a sunny day, with a band playing.

"Why did you say that?" I asked.

The little old man answered me politely.

"I was talking to a lady who passed with a little dog and told her that little dogs are more pampered than human beings."

I ventured to inquire into the cause of his bitterness.

"Oh, I'm not bitter!" he protested mildly. "Only I know what's true. I've been round the world a bit. I was a naval man, and now I'm without visible means of livelihood. Not that it matters—I'll soon be dead."

He smiled and gazed into the distance, as though looking at the far horizon.

"Don't you get a pension?" I asked.

"I took my bounty after naval service," he told me. "That went a long time ago. Now I have to sleep out at night. Course I could go into the workhouse, but I like my liberty. I gets three shillings a fortnight. Poor relief. I'm one of the down-and-outs, as they call them. Funny, ain't it?"

I didn't see the humour of it. I was sorry for the poor old man.

"Now them working men," he said irrelevantly. "Aristocrats compared with the like of me. Do you think they'd spare a copper for an old fellow beyond his days of work? Not on your life, sir! Some of 'em aren't so bad. I'll admit exceptions. But taking 'em as a class they're cunning and cruel. That's the nature of the human animal. Oh, he's very bad is the human animal. Shocking! . . . Well, good-morning to you."

I passed a bit into his hand, and he looked surprised.

"I didn't ask for it," he said. "But thank you kindly all the same. I'm sorry that young woman with the lap dog didn't listen to me."

He glanced towards the Changing of the Guard.

"Funny, isn't it?" he remarked with a chuckle. "Underneath those uniforms there's the human animal. Very cunning! Very cruel!"

It was just by the fountain in the wall put there to the beloved memory of Queen Alexandra, with the waters of charity flowing always below the lovely figures by Sir Alfred Gilbert, with the inscription Faith, Hope, and Love.

The little old man trotted away.

9. Glamorous Nights

The only criticism of the crowds I heard was from the friend who had invited us to his balcony to watch the procession. He is middle-aged, with silver hair and a sunburnt face whose colour he keeps to a fine tone by sitting on sunny days in the back yard of a London club which is a sun trap when the English climate provides such a chance. He is a cheerful, laughing man with a liver which was proof against a life in India. But one morning I found him looking haggard.

"My dear sir," he said, "this Jubilee will be the death of me. It's putting a strain on my patriotism."

I was astonished. He is one of the greatest loyalists I know; he accuses me constantly of being too fair to the Germans, and believes that England and the British Empire are under divine protection.

"I haven't slept for a week," he told me. "Every night the noise in St. James's Street is diabolical. They keep it up till dawn —singing, dancing, shouting, screaming. They're all young people and mostly intoxicated."

"By the spirit of youth," I assured him.

I couldn't believe in that charge of drunkenness. I believed that it was nothing more than high spirits and young revelry. I saw no sign of it myself. The thought worried me. I asked people about it, and they all denied having seen any drunkenness.

I obtained a view on this subject from the commissionaire outside a theatre at one of the points where the crowds were greatest every day during the Jubilee celebrations and every night so dense indeed that the theatre had to be barricaded lest the crowds should be forced through the doors.

"Any drunkenness?" I asked him.

"Drunkenness!" he replied with astonishment. "Why, that's old-fashioned. Cases of sickness, but what can you expect with the stuff they call beer nowadays? It would make anybody sick on an empty stummick. You can't get drunk on it if you tried. I drink bitter myself and keeps my stummick well lined with food, as old soldiers ought to do. In my opinion it's weak beer which is undermining the nation's character and physical health. How can we keep ourselves a strong nation—the bulldog breed—without the honest beer which made our fathers men?"

He glanced towards four or five young men in evening clothes who had gone out into the street between the acts and now strolled in again before the curtain was rung up.

"Look at those young fellows," said the commissionaire when

they had passed on their way into the stalls. "Anæmic, as you might say. Nervy. It would do them a power of good to drink strong beer. But they can't get it. Swipes, that's what we drink nowadays. Lemonade and soft drinks! How can a nation be great on lemonade—or tonic water? I'm asking you!"

I could not answer him, as the bell was ringing for the third act.

I sat in a desert of empty stalls. The Jubilee was bad for managers and dramatists who had been hoping to reap a harvest after the lean days of Lent. Few people could get to the theatres, and few wanted to go because of the greater drama in the streets. No omnibuses or taxicabs were allowed in the zone of floodlighting. Venturesome souls who made their way through the throngs to see a play could not get home again without great difficulty. I had charge of a lady in an evening frock and light shoes. "Let's get a taxi somehow!" she pleaded. There was no taxi within a mile. We walked to an Underground station. Outside was a crowd of ten thousand people. We lined up at the end of this seething, swirling mass of laughing humanity. They were all very much amused. They seemed in no hurry to get home.

"What a jest!" said a well-dressed girl. "And somebody said we take our pleasures sadly!"

"He lied," said her companion. "But I daresay we've missed the last train to Raynes Park. What are we going to do now, I wonder?"

10. England Speaks

Something happened on the night of the King's Jubilee which had never happened before in the history of mankind. A human voice—the King's—spoke to the whole world. Hundreds of millions of people, thousands of miles away from where he sat in a quiet room, listened to his words, clearly and finely spoken with an undertone of real emotion. He was speaking to the peoples of the British Empire as the Father of the Family, and these sincere and simple words were heard by men and women of every creed and colour, eager to show their allegiance to the British Crown and their affectionate loyalty to the man who wore it. But they were heard by people who serve under other flags and have other loyalties. The United States listened and were moved by emotion, as American citizens have told me. Germany listened.

"Yesterday," a German girl wrote to me from Berlin, "I have been listening with the greatest interest to the speech of your king. He has a very great sympathy here which you could see by the interest in the Jubilee of everyone."

It was perhaps a portent—this one human voice talking to all the world. One day a man may say something to all the world which may change its destiny.

That night in England, in thousands of villages far from the glare and traffic of London, surrounded by quiet fields and woodlands, the rural folk gathered and tramped to their hill-sides to see the lighting of bonfires which made a chain from peak to peak, not only in England but from Wales to the north of Scotland, as when the beacons were lit in the days of Eliza-beth when the Armada was sighted. The soul of England spoke again that night, and these rustic folk remembered the war in which many of them had served, and were glad of peace and proud, I know, of a country which, with all its faults and troubles and injustice here and there, stands still, they think, for liberty.

"I had a bit of a thrill," said one of them—a man I know who served in Palestine and who now works in my garden in the country. "I thought back to the wartime. One can't help feeling proud of what England means in the world. We're not bullied about by youngsters in different coloured shirts. We're free men, as you might say."

This sense of security was felt by other men, one of them a ship's steward coming home in time for the Jubilee from the other side of the Atlantic. He had been robbed in a New York saloon.

"It's better to be in England again," he said. "The banks are safe. The streets are safe. The pubs are safe."

I noticed at this time that the ordinary citizen in small shops and third-class railway carriages and other places where one hears the authentic voice of England was for once self-conscious about the spirit of his own country. This Jubilee demonstration of good-will and good order—this sense of happiness among the people—had surprised him and even made him talkative on the subject.

The man from whom I often buy an evening paper when I am in town is critical of public men and public affairs. He has a grouse against the government for not dealing more efficiently with the problem of unemployment. He is a bit of a socialist, he tells me, and hates anything like privilege or class benefit. He has hard things to say sometimes while handing out his papers to his clients in a London square. But on one of these evenings after the first Jubilee night he stared at me with the blue eyes of a naval man and spoke emotionally.

"This is a country and a half. Not a sign of Communism in spite of unemployment and all that. Well, I admit it's wonderful. It's a tribute to the King, but more than all it's a sign to the outside world that England is going strong and stands united and won't stand for any monkey tricks. Well, I'm a bit of a socialist, and I don't deny it. But I'm not against Royalty, and I'm not against decency. Take the Prince of Wales. What's wrong with him? I've respected him since a night he came to Homerton and sat down among our club fellows without any fuss or any side. A man and a brother. A leader of the younger crowd who would do well to follow him. Anyhow, this Jubilee show won't pass unnoticed in foreign countries. I can't see anything wrong with it. Why, the crowds were as peaceable and law-abiding and decent and good-natured as a school treat in a country park. I'm proud of England, and I don't mind saying so."

I liked to hear him say so, because it was a pride in our decent qualities and in human liberty and order. Among all the voices in the crowd during this time of jubilation I heard words of good-humour. It was not all loyalty or King-worship. Those young boys and girls who danced their shoes off were having a great circus. They passed the word along: "It's amusing to see the dawn over London. We're having some good fun down our way. Come and join in!" A lot of that, no doubt. But there were other instincts stirred. England had been through a time of trouble. Now the tide seemed to have turned a little. The cuts had been restored from wages clipped in a time of economy when England had gone off the gold standard. There had been threats and fears of wars, making people anxious. Well, England was all right. The winter had been long and dark. Now the fine weather had come, and the pipes of Pan were calling even down mean streets. England is still a little pagan when the cuckoo shouts its first note, when the first gleam of spring falls aslant factory walls or creeps into slum courtyards. Other nations had dictatorships, tyrannies, denial of free speech and liberties. But, after all, the English air is good to breathe for men who like their freedom. So I heard the voices in the crowd.

II

Those Less Gay

1. The Dark Crypt

I T WAS a night in June. I had been to the theatre with a lady and had sat in a private box (for which I didn't pay), looking more at the audience than at the play, which I had seen several times before. It was called *The Aunt of England* and was a family affair, written by my son and my brother, with more drama behind the scenes than appeared to the public when the curtain went up. The audience liked it. I heard them laugh in the right places—and once or twice in the wrong place. Down in the stalls I could see the faces of the first six rows. One lady there, who had come across from the Savoy Hotel with her husband—they looked to me like Americans—never smiled once from first to last, and had a curiously sullen look as though she hated this play. But perhaps she hated her husband or had a grievance against life. One old gentleman whose white shirt billowed above his waistcoat had a rich chuckle. He was enjoying himself and blew his nose emotionally when Thea Holme, that charming little lady, came down in the moonlight to meet her lover. Several other people snivelled at these romantic scenes of young love in the sixties.

"Good for Anthony!" I thought. The plot of this play had been discussed in family conference in a little old farmhouse with low beams. Now it had come to life in the Savoy Theatre, and a well-dressed audience seemed enchanted by it.

Haidee Wright, an actress of the old school, took her calls for her wonderful study of a grand old dame. The audience streamed out after the National Anthem, and at the same time crowds were surging out of other theatres and cinemas down the Strand. Women in evening clothes walked on to Trafalgar Square with their men, to take a breath of air on this glamorous night. Even at midnight there were little groups of these pleasure folk crossing the square or hailing taxis outside the National Gallery. I put my lady into a taxi and told her that I would be home in an hour or two.

"Don't have your pockets picked," she warned me.

"There's not much inside them," I told her.

The lights were still brilliant below a summer sky—one could have seen to read by the lions of the Nelson column—and advertisement signs flickered and flashed at the corner of the Strand.

I went past the Gallery to St. Martin's in the Fields, built by an architect of my own name—a pupil of Wren—as I like to remember. A man was still selling evening papers, and I asked him a question.

"Is the crypt of St. Martin's still open?"

He looked at me sharply for a moment. I was not in evening clothes and wore a light overcoat and a grey felt hat.

The man took my arm and gave it a friendly pressure.

"Yes, mate. You'll find the gate open on the other side of the church. You can't miss it, and it's open all night."

I thanked him. There was pity in his voice. He thought I was one of those who needed a free night's lodging under the church of St. Martin's, as, but for the luck of life, I might have been.

Inside the entrance to the crypt, at the top of a flight of stone stairs, was a policewoman, who gave me a friendly, searching look.

"Anything I can do for you?" she asked.

I told her I wanted to have a talk with her, but she was going off duty for half an hour and directed me downstairs, where, she said, I would find her colleague.

I was passed on the stairs by a young man who came in stealthily and went past me like a shadow. As I followed him down I saw him take a pillow from a pile on the stone floor and go deeper into the dimness of the great crypt. From that gloomy vault came a smell I knew. It's the worst smell in the world except that of dead bodies. It's the smell of a night shelter

"The Crypt
St. Martins"

THE CRYPT, ST. MARTIN'S

for down-and-outs, a kind of sour smell of damp clothes and unwashed bodies and sweaty feet.

At a small deal table sat another woman in police uniform. For nine years she has sat there night after night, until her face has become grey and her hair white, though there is no dimness in her eyes, which are filled with a spiritual light not seen much under police helmets.

I took a kitchen chair and sat by her side while she told me about this life in the crypt of St. Martin's and the people who come down the steps out of the streets of London. All the time we talked men were coming down every five or ten minutes. Some of them were young men, not too badly dressed, I noticed. Others were middle-aged and shabby but not in rags. Nice fellows, I thought they looked, and the kind of men who had once been clerks, or porters, or men who carry sandwich boards. There were no types of tramp whom I used to meet in doss houses before the war, with rags tied round them by bits of string and with broken boots. These men were all very respectable looking, I thought. They were polite and good-mannered and said "Good-evening" to the policewoman before taking up a cushion and carrying it away to one of the benches in the semi-darkness of the distance. One man's face startled me. He had a light beard round his face and had the look of Christ in a picture by Ary Scheffer.

The Prince of Wales sat here one night for an hour or more with the policewoman who is there every night. He talked with some of the men. They didn't know who he was. He didn't tell them.

"We get all sorts here," said Miss Costello, who was the policewoman. "Some of them are very well educated, speaking two or three languages and having been to good schools."

She said something which made my heart give a lurch because I found it terrible.

"Education is a positive handicap nowadays. It's a drug on the market. It would be far better if some of these men could handle a pick and shovel instead of a pen or a typewriter."

"That's a frightful thing to say," I told her.

"It's true," she answered.

The policewoman whom I had first met came down presently,

and we talked together in low voices. While we talked I was conscious of the presence of that sleeping crowd beyond me. Soft little sounds came from them—sighs, the shifting of bodies on hard benches, the faint murmur of a distant snore.

"Lots of these young men," said Miss Costello, "come drifting down from the north—the devastated regions up there. They have an idea that if only they can get to London they will find a job. Needless to say, many of them don't. They lurk about, getting an odd job now and then, sleeping out, or down here, after a free meal from the Silver Lady or someone else."

"What happens to them?" I asked, knowing the answer.

The policewoman looked at me and gave a long-drawn sigh.

"What can you expect to happen? Some of them get more and more demoralized. Some of them get more and more vicious. They go deeper down into hell."

We were alone when she talked to me about that hell.

"They sink into the mud," she said in a tragic whisper. "Mud and slime. Their souls get steeped in it. They fling it about. Some of the girls are even worse than the boys. Mud and slime. Filth. It's too awful. Sometimes it makes one despair."

The other policewoman wanted a Hitler in England. At least she wanted something like the German Labour Camps and the German discipline, which would take hold of all this unemployed youth, this demoralized and sinking youth, and save it from the utter waste of life.

"They need discipline," she said. "They ought not to be allowed to lounge around as they do. There ought to be some organization to take hold of these boys and give them a chance. Doesn't England care?"

Now and again strange visitors come to the crypt of St. Martin's, which seems to be known everywhere.

One night the policewoman—or is she a saint?—saw a young, well-dressed girl slip in and take a seat on one of the benches, where she sat very quiet.

She looked like a high-school girl waiting for a lesson in geography. After being questioned in a friendly way, she confessed that she had run away from home and cycled into London from the Midlands. She had heard of St. Martin's crypt and had left her bicycle in the porch after finding it.

One night she had her counterpart in a good-looking boy of the "middle class" who said that he had run away from home to get away from a stepmother who illtreated him. His father, he said, had been killed in the war.

"These lads," said one of the policewomen, "are very apt to kill off their parents for the sake of a story!"

When the boy was settling himself down for the night two gentlemen appeared at the top of the steps, and one of them said he was looking for his son. The boy's mother, he said, adored him and was desperately anxious.

It was the boy who had told about his "cruel stepmother," but he was not delivered up until the father's story was proved to be true.

Those are odd visitants to the crypt. The usual frequenters of this sanctuary are the down-and-outs, the men who have been caught between the wheels—the grinding wheels of this machinery of modern life—between the dole and the devil—a dole which they can't get and the devil they don't want.

Many of them—perhaps most of them—are there through no fault of their own except that they lack some touch of will power, some hereditary strength, some vital urge, which might enable them to overcome ill luck and make a place for themselves. Others have gone too far to help. The last state is methylated spirits. Then the devil gets them all right.

There is only one woman at a time to look after the sleepers below the church of St. Martin's. She seldom has any trouble with them. Now and again a man gets ill-tempered and starts quarrelling with some fellow who is sleeping near him. The right word or two generally keeps him quiet. Now and again some man with poison in his brain makes a nuisance of himself to his neighbour who wants to sleep.

"It needs a little tact sometimes," said Miss Costello. "But most of them are like lambs."

2. Young Wolves

Outside in Trafalgar Square all the clocks of London were striking midnight. I heard the deep booming strokes of Big Ben.

Many motorcars were streaming through the archway leading to the Mall. The traffic of taxis was swirling round the square in an endless roundabout—until presently it thinned out. A girl and her lover, both in evening clothes, stood leaning over the parapet which looks down to the fountains.

"Life is amusing!" said the girl, who had bare arms under her white furred cloak.

"It has its moments," agreed the man. "This is one of them. But isn't it getting a little late and a little chilly?"

They moved away. All the smart people were going, or had gone, home. Other people were arriving. There was a battalion of young men lining up in a queue as though waiting for something. They were waiting for food to be distributed free of charge by a benevolent lady named Mrs. Appleby, as I heard her called by some of these young men. Others had not yet lined up. There was half an hour or so to wait. They were seated on the long benches or leaning up against the parapet, mostly in groups of five or six. They were neatly dressed, some of them in grey flannel trousers and dark jackets. They talked together in quiet voices and seemed cheerful, I thought. Several of them were smoking cigarettes, and one boy on a bench asked me for a match, which he shared with three others. I opened my cigarette case and offered its contents to some boys who were not smoking.

"Thanks most awfully!" said one of them.

A single figure near me was leaning against the parapet, and I spoke to him. He looked a different type from the others. He was older and more sturdily built than these cigarette-smoking boys. His shirt was open at the neck, and he had a square-cut face with brown eyes. There was something in the timbre of his voice when we chatted together which made me think he was not English.

"You don't belong to London, do you?" I asked.

He hesitated for a moment and then answered, "I'm an Australian."

He had been in the war—"at the tail end," he said—and had seen something of London in wartime. Out in Australia afterwards he had been caught in the slump. There was a lot of unemployment. It occurred to him that he might get a job in the Old Country, and he had worked his passage back. But he hadn't struck any luck. For a time he had worked as a hawker, but he had been frozen out. The other men regarded him as a foreigner.

"The London hawkers belong to a close profession," said the Australian. "A stranger doesn't have a chance among them. One has to be born among them."

Lately he had done a bit of bill posting. But it was an uncertain job, on today and out tomorrow, and perhaps for several weeks, if luck ran out. He had been out of luck lately and had been sleeping in the parks.

"Can't you do better than that?" I asked. "Aren't there any free shelters? That crypt, for instance."

The Australian shrugged his shoulders.

"It's not a good atmosphere. I prefer the fresh air. Still, it's not a real rest. It gets one down after a night or two."

He spoke in an educated voice. He used good words. He was a thoughtful, pleasant-spoken fellow.

"Can't you get any help from Australians in London?" I asked him.

He shook his head.

"I haven't tried. One of these days I may pack up and get back to Australia. It wouldn't do me any good if it were known that I had been among the down-and-outs. It's better not to advertise one's bad times."

"What do you think of this crowd?" I asked, looking over to those boys on the benches.

He didn't think much of them. He spoke gravely about the plight of these unemployed lads.

"When once they take to this kind of life they find it hard to escape. It gets hold of them. It starts as a bit of an adventure. They find it rather amusing, like playing at Red Indians! Then they get into the tricks of it and it becomes part of themselves until they're just guttersnipes, or worse."

Half-a-dozen young girls came by. One of them, nicely dressed in blue, put her hand on the shoulder of one of the boys who had accepted a cigarette from me. It was a comradely touch. They were two children lost in the wood—this jungle of life—with many demons lying in wait for them.

Another girl—a pretty little slut—screamed out a foul and frightful oath, bloodcurdling.

My Australian spoke to me quietly.

"They use awful language! I'm used to that kind of talk, but sometimes when I'm in company with these young fellows I sicken at the constant stream of filth which comes to their lips. It's a habit."

"Don't you ever meet any decent men?" I asked.

He thought out his answer.

"Now and then one meets a nice fellow. They're mostly older than these young chaps. They're ex-soldiers, and clerks who have had the push, and countrymen, and seafaring men. One meets all sorts. If one loses a job nowadays it's hard to get another. They're caught like that through no fault of theirs. It's just the condition of things in the world today. It's hard to say whose blame it is, but there's something wrong somewhere."

Two policemen came hurrying up and stopped at one of the benches where six boys were sitting.

"Now then, hop it!" said one of the policemen sternly. "Get off there or I'll push you off. Then you can have a night in the cells."

Five of the boys left the seat rapidly and slithered away. The sixth sat on sullenly until the policeman gave him a sharp jog.

"Now then, constable," I said. "They're doing no harm. Why shouldn't they use that seat?"

He gave me a quick glance and then laughed and was quite polite.

"One must keep order, you know, sir! We can't have these young fellows sprawling all over the place."

"All right," I said. "You know best, I suppose."

"Well, we try to do the right thing, sir."

He saluted me in a military way, as though he took me for a retired colonel, and I felt glad that he hadn't taken me for a newly arrived down-and-out, in which case he would not have been so polite!

The Australian gave me some glimpses of this underworld which had surged up after midnight in Trafalgar Square.

"Some of these lads hunt in packs."

"How do you mean?" I inquired.

"Five or six of them band together. Perhaps one of them is on the dole. If so he is a great Lord among them. Then they work the streets."

"In what way? Picking pockets?"

"Cadging mostly. They tell a tale to little shopgirls and city girls in the lunch hour, or on their way from work. They pick up about three shillings or three and ninepence a day. That provides them with cigarettes and a drink or two. When they're out of luck they come here to get a free meal. Most of them do a bit of dog racing."

He gave me a lot of information about the life of this new underworld, not criminal as in the old days and still in some strata of London life, but due directly to the unemployment of youth. Men drifted down from the north and became casuals.

"There's one thing," he remarked, "and that's important: one can keep oneself clean in London. The County Council shelters provide shower baths and foot baths. Then there are delousing stations where one can get one's clothes fumigated. The Salvation Army doss houses have good washing arrangements, but of course one has to be a bit of an aristocrat to use places like that. A shilling a night is a lot to a man who hasn't a shilling. Same with eightpence!"

The battalion of youth was going forward slowly to a fixed point. Mrs. Appleby had arrived with her free meals. It was half an hour after midnight. The Square was deserted except for these men.

"Of course I've made a failure of myself, and I've no right to talk," said the Australian. "But speaking generally it seems to me wrong that England shouldn't look after these lads a bit. There's good material in them until they get past everything."

"Aren't they physically degenerate?" I asked him.

He denied that. He said they had surprising stamina. Some of them who still wanted work walked from one end of London to the other in search of it, as he had done himself, generally without success, and often on an empty stomach after a night out.

I slipped him a bit of silver and felt guilty in having so much luck myself.

"That will keep me off the queue tonight," he said. "Thanks."

I shook hands with him and wished him luck. He held my hand hard, and we looked into each other's eyes. He had dark brown gipsy-looking eyes, such as I had seen under slouch hats when the Australians went into Bapaume when there was a war on.

"Cheerio!" he said.

3. Down-and-out

In Great Peter Street, Westminster, I sat down at the dining table opposite a pale, haggard-looking man about thirty-eight years of age who was good enough to let me talk to him. There were about four hundred men, I should say, in the room with us, having lunch which worked out at an average cost of sixpence for three courses. It was good food, well cooked in perfectly clean kitchens, as I had seen. Upstairs the long dormitories were light and airy, with comfortable-looking beds, much unlike the coffin boxes which I used to see in such shelters before the war. This Salvation Army Hotel seemed to me extremely well run and was spotlessly clean.

I looked round the tables where the men were eating and studied their faces. There were good English faces among them, of the labourer type. All these middle-aged men must have served England in wartime. I may have rubbed shoulders with some of them when they were all our heroes. Now they looked rather beaten, and had lost the old gaiety with which they had gone up the Albert-Bapaume road singing "It's a different girl again." But there were many younger men, any age between eighteen and thirty. Some of them grinned at me as I walked between their tables, and one of them winked as though to say, "First time here, old bird? Well, it's not too bad!"

"Who are all these fellows?" I asked the man opposite the seat I took.

He glanced round at his fellows and smiled with a slight shrug of his shoulders in a shabby overcoat.

"The usual crowd! Casual labourers, out-of-works, young fellows who've not known what it is to work since they left school, clerks pushed out of their offices to make way for young girls, and others like myself."

He had been a ship's steward. Liverpool was crowded with ships' stewards who could not get a ship. Now he had come down to London with the idea of getting a job as a waiter. No hope left. He was getting too shabby even to ask for a job. One look was enough. Halfway through the swing door of a restaurant the manager pushed his thumb in the opposite direction. Too shabby. All the look of a down-and-out.

"That's how it goes," said my man. "There are various associations for providing men with clothes, like the Lord Roberts Ex-Service Welfare. But there's a snag in it. They won't give one a new rig out unless one can prove that there's a job waiting for one. And one can't get a job without decent clothes. It's the vicious circle!"

I was interested in a man on the opposite side of my table a little to the left. He was listening to our conversation but turned his eyes away when I met them for a moment.

"That's an ex-officer," I thought. "I should say he comes from one of the Dominions. I would like to get into talk with him."

"I seem to know your face," said the man who had been a ship's steward. I told him my name, and he happened to know it.

"War correspondent, weren't you?" he asked. "I used to read your stuff in the *Daily Chronicle*."

I nodded.

"Twenty years ago now. Hard to believe!"

"I wouldn't mind those days back," said the man, with a kind of laugh which was a kind of groan. "I was a youngster. Hadn't been broken."

He talked very frankly about the down-and-outs, of which he was one.

"Seventy-five per cent their own fault," he said, "barring the young fellows who can't get any work, whether they want to or not. London is the dumping ground of derelicts. They come down expecting work. Funny, isn't it? I was like that myself. If only I can get to London, I thought. So went on the tramp, wearing my boots out and blistering my feet. And what for? Why, London is crowded out with the likes of us. We're not wanted."

"Hard luck!" I said.

He nodded and smiled.

"That's life, except for the fortunate! This world crisis knocked a lot of us, of course. Killed shipping. I'm one of those who believe in Free Trade. That's because I used to be a steward when the seas were used by British ships. Well, I think I'll be getting along. It's nice to have had a talk."

He nodded and left the table. I wondered whether I dare talk to the man on my left opposite. He was wearing a nice brown suit, better cut than mine. He had ginger-coloured hair and hazel eyes and a fresh complexion.

"You come from one of the Dominions, don't you?" I hazarded.

He mentioned one of the Crown Colonies.

"I've read some of your books," he told me. "*The Street of Adventure* and *The Middle of the Road*. Do you often come here?"

"Not often. Why are *you* here?"

He hesitated for a moment and then answered frankly.

"I got into trouble with my mess bills. That began it. My own fault, of course."

We talked about the war. He must have been very young when he was a second lieutenant in a division which was very proud of itself, and justly. He remembered my going up to see them somewhere in the neighbourhood of Thiepval. Halfway through the Passchendaele show his crowd had been sent to Italy under old Plumer and Harington. The Italian soldiers were odd fellows, very whimsical. No idea at all of sanitation! Their idea of war wasn't the same as ours. Well, sometimes he looked back to the war days with regret. Not too bad. All the same, the idea of a new war was horrible. Did I think it was coming, by any chance?

I told him that I thought we should push it off, and he was glad to hear that.

"This isn't much of a place," he said, looking round the long room where four hundred men or so were eating their cheap food. "I find the atmosphere pretty ghastly. It takes some time to get used to it."

"Can't you get your old division to help you?" I asked. "They might like to be helpful."

He shook his head.

"I daren't go near them. I've still a bit of pride. They were having the regimental dinner the other night. I gave it a miss. The fact is I shirk meeting any of the old crowd. Sometimes I meet a man I know in the street. 'Things all right?' he asks. 'Oh, rather!' I say. Of course, he guesses. They all guess. I haven't the face to go cadging. The other day I took the bus to one of the suburbs where I happened to know some nice people. Of course, I had the idea of touching them for a bit. Anyhow, it would be good to sit in a decently furnished room again and drink a cup of tea at a table with a cloth on it. But when I got near the house I turned back. There are some things one can't do. That's one of them, as far as I'm concerned."

"It must be—wearisome," I said, hesitating for a moment at the last word. One doesn't like to rub a man's wounds.

"Extremely boring," he answered. "That's almost the worst of all. One gets up in the morning with a blank day ahead. What the hell is one going to do? How can one put in time? Then there's the food trouble. Where to eat? These places take my appetite away. They're all right, of course. The food is perfectly good. But I suppose I'm a bit of a snob! Funny, isn't it? I find it hard to sit down among the casual labourers and the down-and-outs, and yet some of them are very decent fellows. Extraordinarily decent if one gets to know them. But I don't much. They think I'm a 'toff.' That makes them dry up. I don't get any real comradeship. My fault again, of course!"

"It's not easy," I agreed.

"The loneliness is really awful," he told me. "Sometimes I can hardly stick it. The worst of it is, everything goes bad at once. That's my case. The whole show collapsed under my feet. Everything went wrong. It's extremely difficult to get out of a situation like this."

"If there's anything I could do," I suggested. "If you would care to tell me your name——?"

He told me his name. For the moment he had no address.

We began to talk about books again. He had been very keen about my novel *The Middle of the Road*. Was I writing anything else? I helped him to forget for a little while that he was lunching at the poor men's table.

"I've enjoyed this conversation quite a lot," he said presently when I got up to go.

4. *Red Biddy*

"Yes," said the commandant of this Salvation Army shelter in Great Peter Street, "we get some very odd types! One man who lived here quite a time had eighty pounds a year of his own, and we looked after it for him. But he was always drawing on us to get drunk and was very annoyed if we refused to give him an advance. One night during the Jubilee week he came in with four men he had picked up in the streets and said very loftily, 'Put these gentlemen down to my account.' To tell the truth, we got fed up with him."

There was a brigadier of the Salvation Army in the room—a cheery man who kept his sense of humour in spite of a lifetime among human derelicts. He held up a bottle filled with some pink liquid.

"See this," he said. "It's Red Biddy, otherwise known as 'King Fergus.' "

Those names meant nothing to me until he explained.

"Methylated spirits. It's the last stage downhill to the bottomless pit. Men and women who take to this are beyond all hope —and quite a lot are taking to it. It's sold in the cheap drug stores. Six good drunks for sixpence. You can see the temptation!"

"It must be filthy stuff," I said, looking with a kind of horror at that bottle of pink liquid.

"Oh, they get over the taste of it. It's an acquired taste, like tomatoes or olives. It's the effect they like. So much quicker than weak beer! Very rapid as an agent of blind drunkenness and oblivion. There ought to be a check on its sale in the chain stores."

The commandant fumbled in a drawer of his desk and pulled out some envelopes.

"There's another temptation which drags these fellows down," he said. "It's very prevalent, and the tempters are very active in circularizing their victims. This is a favourite address of theirs. There's a heavy post bag every morning for our clients who give this as their address. I'm talking about dog racing. The old expression 'going to the dogs' has a new and modern meaning."

He opened one of the flimsy envelopes and handed me one of the circulars which I reproduce on this page.

LETTER COMMISSIONS
FOR
GREYHOUND RACING
ALL POSTAGE PAID

NO LIMIT
WIN OR PLACE FOR SINGLE EVENTS

Business is transacted on all Meetings under National Greyhound Racing Club Rules only. Commissions are accepted by Letter, Wire, or 'Phone. Telegrams up to £5 a Win or Each Way must be handed in at least thirty minutes before advertised time of Race. Over £5 and not exceeding £100, two hours before Race. Over this amount in accordance with Racing Rules. Letters up to £2 a Win or Each Way must be time-postmarked thirty minutes before Race. Over this, if sent by letter, must reach us on morning of Race. Cross Bets—Any to Come, Up and Down—accepted. The Limit paid over any Cross Bet will be 20–1 to the original stake, and 5–1 to the place stake. Systems, such as Trap Numbers, etc., are all accepted.

"That's the kind of thing which lures young fellows to ruin," said the brigadier. "They'll put their last bob on the dogs, hoping for a win. Needless to say the odds are against them. In the end they're brought low and join the army of the lost battalions."

He was still nursing the bottle of Red Biddy and held it up to the light as though it had a fascination for him as a ghastly exhibit. The devil's brew!

These two men who were closely in touch with the problem

of human degeneration talked about the need of discipline for youth. Like the policewoman in St. Martin's crypt, they had an admiration for Hitler's control of youth in Germany, and for their well-organized camps. They didn't think much of the Labour camps in England. They provided no real training in agriculture where experts are needed. The men just grubbed up the earth a bit and made a mess of things.

"The unemployed don't seem to take to camp life," said the brigadier. "They call it 'slave labour.' They want their liberty, even if it means mucking about without work or wages. This liberty is a much abused word. A man shouldn't have liberty to drink Red Biddy or let himself drift into loss of will power and loss of morale."

I heard some criticism of the Prince of Wales's Jubilee Trust for Youth.

"It's too much devoted to hikers and sports-grounds and established institutions for playing fields. There ought to be more done for training and taking these boys off the streets and away from the Labour Exchanges where they hang about for next week's dole, utterly without a purpose or a place."

"Look at all those poor fellows up north," said the brigadier. "Many of them came drifting down to London for the Jubilee, hoping to pick up odd jobs. Now they are drifting out again, but what are they going to do then? The problem is not being tackled. The nation and the newspapers are interested in nothing but sport. They don't turn a searchlight on the other side of things."

I had a long talk with these two experts in social conditions of casual labour. They talked in a hard-headed way, without emotion or sentiment, and with humorous anecdotes of the types they meet day by day.

Out in the yard groups of men were standing about listlessly. A blind man with a white stick tapped his way among them. Men were washing their feet in foot baths.

I walked into Whitehall and up to Piccadilly among the gay crowds again. They were all well dressed and looked prosperous. The battalions of women were out for the afternoon's shopping or lining up outside the picture palaces for a few hours' false romance in the dream world of the screen.

5. *Rowton House*

The Rowton Houses—long established now—are very useful to poor gentlemen and those who are temporarily out of work. I knew a gentleman of the old school who lived at one of the Rowton Houses for some years. He kept his dress clothes neatly brushed and pressed in a small chest of drawers and emerged now and then to dine with old friends.

At Rowton House in the Hammersmith Road the beds are occupied now and then by tea planters from Malaya, struck by a world blizzard, and also by artists from Chelsea who find no market for their works of art—it is not surprising when one looks at some of them—and other men of education and quality for whom the adventure of life in this jungle world has been too hard. But it is mainly frequented by casual labourers and men on seasonal jobs which afford no wages if the weather is fine, or if the weather is wet, or if it is summer, or if it is winter. Some of them were just arriving for the night when I went to Rowton House in the Hammersmith Road on a rainy day.

It looks a small place from the outside, but it has accommodation for fifteen hundred men and surprises one inside by the length of its corridors with hundreds of cubicles on each side, and by the spaciousness of its kitchens, dining rooms, reading rooms, and wash places.

The superintendent is a nice fellow with a passion for cleanliness. If he sees a speck of dirt or any untidiness he gets as peeved as a sergeant major when he finds a dirty rifle on parade. That is due to his army training—he was seventeen years in the Regular army—and a private conviction that cleanliness is next to godliness and not so hard to acquire. We had a talk about the old war, as men do when they remember it. He couldn't get wounded—that was his peculiarity in the Great War. He just couldn't get hit and had to stick it out all through the big shows. Afterwards he was like other demobilized heroes of the war who had heard the call, "Your King and Country Need You," and then returned to hear quiet voices saying in their ears and souls, "Your King and Country don't need you. There's no work for you. Why didn't you get killed, laddie?" The women had taken the men's jobs and did them very well. All the little girls from the London suburbs were earning pin money as typists and clerks.

This friend of mine looked one day through the plate-glass windows of the Royal Air Force headquarters. It had occurred to him, and to two hundred other men, that they might get jobs in the clerical department. Wasn't it in a way their right, having helped to save England in her hour of need? Well, anyhow, they wanted the jobs. But through the plate-glass windows they saw rows of young girls tapping typewriters or ceasing to tap to powder their pretty little noses. Two hundred ex-service men turned away.

"Come and see my kitchens," said my friend.

I saw his kitchens and was warm in my congratulations. They might have been the kitchens of the Ritz Hotel.

"Have a look at the food," said my friend.

I had a look. He didn't let me off a single potato on the boil or a single mess of pottage or a single pudding or pie. It all looked good and appetizing. The prices were cheap. Fine soup for tuppence. Most excellent-looking fruit pies for the same price. Kippers, rather expensive, I thought, for fourpence. For eightpence one could feed like a duke and be replete. For a shilling one could overfeed, handsomely, unless one had been without food for three days, as now and then happens to the paying guests in this establishment.

I went through the bathrooms, the lavatories, the wash places. They lived up to a high standard of sanitation.

"It's a bee in my bonnet," said the superintendent of Rowton House who couldn't get wounded in the World War. "I should have bad dreams if I thought these places weren't kept clean. It's my test of efficiency."

They passed the test with honours.

But I was more interested in the human side of things. That is the bee in my bonnet. I have a passion for the study of my fellow men. I wanted to talk to some of the fifteen hundred who were eating, reading, or sitting very silent, I noticed, without much talk among themselves, in the dining rooms and reading rooms.

THE SALVATION ARMY SHELTER

But first I went upstairs to see some of the bedrooms—like ships' cabins in the third class of an ocean liner, just as small and just as neat, with no room to swing a cat, if one happened to need that form of exercise. I imagine that expression refers to a cat-o'-nine-tails.

We were joined by one of the attendants who looked an ex-naval man and had been at Rowton House here for many years.

"Do you have many old residents?" I asked him.

He chuckled.

"Why, bless you, sir, some of our gentlemen have been here year in, year out. They find it economical and very convenient. No servant troubles. No landladies. No squalling kids or gramophones. It's like a service flat for them with the restaurant downstairs. Now here, for instance, is the room of a gentleman who has been here for seventeen years."

I went into the small bedroom. It was as neat as a new pin, with a bed, a small chest of drawers, a chair, and a bookshelf. My eyes were drawn like a magnet to the bookshelf. What sort of books did they read in a private room of Rowton House? On the shelf were Horace's Odes, a Greek grammar, a book on Egyptology, and other historical works. I had no need to ask where the inhabitant of this room spent his days. I could see him in my mind's eye. He would be in the reading room of the British Museum. His lunch would be a bun and a glass of milk. In winter he would wear mittens to keep his hands warm. He would walk back part of the way to Hammersmith to save a penny on the bus fare.

Downstairs in the reading room I fell into conversation with a sturdy-looking man going fifty, in black clothes without a collar. He was a coal heaver by avocation and a very intelligent, simple man, with brown eyes and a clean-shaven face, blue about the chin.

Before I talked to him, he was sitting there motionless, with his hands clasped between his knees. Next to him was a man in labourer's clothes. He had a kind of palsy, and his head and hands twitched unceasingly. There were about a hundred other men in the room. A few were reading papers, but most of them sat silent, without a word to each other. Some of them were boys.

"Mine is a seasonal job," said my coal heaver. "I've been turned off some months now because of the fine weather."

"Do you get the dole?" I asked.

He nodded.

"Seventeen bob a week. Just enough to keep living, but not much more. This place is expensive for the likes of me. I can't afford baccy more than once a week."

He thought conditions of labour were not improving. It was all on account of men coming down from the distressed areas.

These strangers took the bread out of the mouths of Hammersmith men. He was a bit disheartened. The fact was he was getting oldish and got tired walking about to look for a job which wasn't there. He had to get round to the yard at five o'clock in the morning and then be told he wasn't wanted. After that, maybe, he would take a train to Harrow. That cost him eightpence, and he heard the same tale of nothing doing.

"After that goes on for weeks one hasn't the heart to look for work. Then one gets fed up with nothing to do but just sit about like this. It's demoralizing. It's not good for man or beast. You see I've always been an active-minded man and very strong in the arms. Now they're getting flabby because I economize on food. Have to, you know!"

He talked about social conditions generally. In his opinion England had seen her best days. The world didn't want English coal or cotton or manufactured goods—not so much as they did. He was sorry for the young blokes. Some of them hadn't a chance. Hopeless. Well, that wasn't good. On the other hand, he was bound to admit the folk with wages had good wages. They were better dressed and had a better life than in the old days. Of course, he wasn't grousing about his own situation. He didn't believe in grousing. There were many worse off than himself, and some of them wanted another war, which they thought was better for them than this kind of peace. He didn't hold with that, having seen a bit of the last war. He couldn't quite see what good another war would do for Hammersmith.

We talked for some time about the state of the world and the causes of unemployment. He was a bit bewildered, he said, with things like the gold standard. He was no scholar. The newspapers wrote things which were beyond his education. But he was a thinker. He tried to think things out for himself and had plenty of time. One thing seemed pretty sure to him, and that was that another war wouldn't do no good to Hammersmith. I agreed with him. We shook hands on that agreement.

"Glad to have met you," said this nice coal heaver—a very good type of man and an honest soul.

In the passage outside I was introduced to a very distinguished-looking old gentleman. He looked remarkably like a duke, as one imagines dukes, though really, as a rule, they are not so distinguished looking.

He was very tall and heavily built, with a fine head for a portrait painter and powerful features with a heavy old-fashioned moustache. His clothes, loosely made of thick cloth, were such as one might see on a squire, having a look at the crops in a Sussex field, and he wore them with an air.

"My dear sir," said this old gentleman—aged nearly ninety, I was told—"I'm delighted to meet you. We have walked the same Street of Adventure together. I know your books. I followed your career as a newspaper correspondent. I myself graduated in Grub Street. I have heard the chimes of midnight from St. Bride's Church. You know my name, of course."

He was an old journalist of the old school. He had been in Fleet Street before I was born. He had served a great newspaper in many parts of the world. Now he was living in Rowton House.

"Times have changed," he remarked. "There's not so much wit as there used to be. Fleet Street has been mechanized. England does not produce the same character. Do you remember old Labouchère? Now he was a wit! A very caustic tongue! I remember his repartee to a man who kept using French expressions, badly pronounced. Of course, Labouchère spoke French like a Frenchman. '*Ce n'est que le premier pas qui coute*,' said the visitor. 'My dear fellow,' said Labouchère in his ironical way, 'if you would only speak English I should understand you so much better!' Amusing, don't you think? Witty!"

The Grand Duke of Rowton House laughed heartily at this reminiscence.

"Winston Churchill is the last of our wits," he told me. "I remember being in the gallery of the House of Commons when some member interrupted Churchill with the cry of 'Rot!'

Winston smiled and retorted instantly in his blandest way: 'The honourable gentleman expressed perfectly what is in his own mind.' Asquith was convulsed with laughter. A very brilliant fellow, Winston. He ought to have been Prime Minister. He is our only man of genius."

A number of men passed us on their way to the dining room. They were mostly casual labourers by their appearance, and one or two turned their heads to look at this old gentleman who stood talking to me in a rich full voice and the accent of the Guards Club.

There were certain aspects of Rowton House which he found objectionable to a man of his upbringing, he told me. The communal wash places were unpleasing to him. He also disliked swearing, which he heard too often. Only the other night the man in the cubicle next to his had objected to a sleeper who kept on snoring. Presently he started banging on the partition and swearing at the snorer.

"Most unreasonable," said the old gentleman. "Snoring, after all, is a harmless habit and not very disturbing. I knocked on my own partition and said: 'Sir, you are nothing but a foul-mouthed ruffian!' At my age these things are annoying."

Before leaving Rowton House I went into the cobbler's shop and had an interesting talk with the cobbler—an aged man, almost stone deaf, who has been here for thirty years. He was delighted to hear a human voice—mine has a penetrating timbre so that when I say something very private to my wife it is heard at the end of a large hall—and we had an agreeable argument on conditions of social life. The old cobbler didn't think much of modern times or modern men.

"This dole is the ruin of England," he told me. "Young fellows don't want to work if they can get hold of the dole. It's all wrong. In my days a man had to work or he had to starve."

"Many starved," I answered. "Are you in favour of that? Could we leave all these boys to starve because there's not enough work to go round?"

The old cobbler stared at me with red-rimmed eyes in a very white, wizened face with a million wrinkles.

"I believe in work!" he said in a high-pitched voice. "I had to work, didn't I? I have to go on working, and I don't object, though I'm very old."

He looked a thousand years old.

"My dear sir," he said, "I brought up a family of nine when the eldest was eleven. Often there was only a tuppenny loaf on the table between the whole lot of us. We went hungry sometimes. I'll admit it was hard. But isn't hardness better than softness? I got through all right. My boys were tough and got through. In my young days we didn't see young fellows propping up the public houses and leaning against the walls of labour exchanges. They was good old days with more happiness in 'em for most people. England was England then. Ay, we had fine men. And our mothers were good mothers. And there was good work for cobblers. Nowadays people don't wear their boots so hard. When they get a bit old they throw them away. Cobbling isn't what it was sixty years ago."

I argued gently with the old man. He had his fixed ideas that the old times were the good times—the old times when there was frightful drunkenness and brutality and poverty, and an underworld of misery and squalor worse than anything which now exists, except in dark places here and there.

"Thank you kindly for talking to me," said the old cobbler. "You've a wonderful clear voice. It's like a speaking trumpet. I get closed up in myself, you know. I don't hear other people's opinions. I follow my own thoughts."

His millions of little wrinkles puckered up as he smiled good-night to me and then went on tapping the tiny tacks into a leather sole.

6. Down East

I went up to Shoreditch one afternoon to meet a young—a very young—clergyman whom I call the Little Minister. He has lately come from Liverpool, where he had his first curacy, but already he has made many friends in Shoreditch, because they like the look of his dark eyes and the sound of his shy laugh and the friendly interest he has in their lives. For him it is like being in the front-line trenches, where there are many casualties day by day, as he finds in the hospital and homes.

But Shoreditch is not like it used to be before the war, when I went that way sometimes. I was confirmed in this opinion by a man on a bus who had been born and bred in Shoreditch and was old enough to remember pre-war times.

"You'll find a lot of change!" he said laughingly. "You won't know dear old Shoreditch! New buildings, new factories, new everything—except Shoreditch Parish Church. Why, God bless my soul, I remember the times when policemen had to go in twos and threes and when there were fights to the death, stripped to the waist—with knives out—every Saturday night in back alleys. The women started screaming. People were carried off on stretchers from the pubs. There were shouts of 'Stop thief!' and whistles blew, and there was no end of fun for those who saw the humour of it. Now—why, we're high class. Shoreditch is as good as the West End—and more respectable. Sorry, I have to get down here. Took a penny fare, you know!"

I was too early for my visit to the Little Minister. I went into Shoreditch Parish Church, a very quiet island in a sea of traffic. It's a handsome church in the eighteenth-century style, which as a rule was hideous. A woman dusting the pews told me that the Little Minister would surely be over at the Vicarage in Hoxton Square. But I put in three quarters of an hour with some of the inhabitants of Shoreditch. I saw a crowd of them in a courtyard at the side of the Labour Exchange. There must have been about two hundred men and boys waiting their turn for the week's dole. They were friendly when I chatted with them, after the first suspicion that I was nosing around. A boy with a white scarf round his neck who stood with his back to the wall was glad to give me a match in return for a cigarette.

"What's your job?" I asked.

He answered civilly.

"A packer, when I've got one. There's lots of us out."

"Do you get the dole?"

"Seventeen bob a week. Keeps one alive!"

"I expect you live at home?" I suggested. "Pretty young, aren't you?"

"I pay a bit towards expenses. My brother gets twenty shillings a week, and that helps. My mother has a little business and makes ten bob a week. Between us we keep the home fires burning. But it's no fun."

"What's the worst?"

"Getting bored! Hanging around. Not knowing what to do next. It gives one the pip."

We fell into a long talk. I propped my back up against the wall alongside this boy, who spoke pleasantly and thoughtfully.

The labour exchanges, he complained, didn't do much in finding work for men. They weren't closely enough in touch with the employers. And there was no encouragement for men to get other kinds of work than those for which they were registered. In fact, they were not allowed to try, at the risk of losing the dole. Some of the younger lot—fellows of his own age—got out of the habit of work. They wouldn't do a hand's turn. One could at least keep oneself in cigarettes by looking out for a chance job like carrying parcels or loading up a cart or holding a horse.

"There's one trouble at the bottom of all this," said the boy, glancing over at some of his fellow out-of-works. "You see, when a lad leaves school he gets a job as an errand boy, or light work in a factory. That lasts him a few years. When he's old enough to get a man's wage he's turned off and another boy takes his place. For them as get turned off it's not easy to find employ-ment. The girls have a better time. Less wages, of course, and cheaper for employers. That's a handicap for their brothers. It's a funny state of things when girls can find work easier than men and don't need it so much."

"Can't you look forward to anything?" I asked.

The boy shrugged his shoulders.

"Not a hope! A job now and then, and on the dole again. Later on no job. There's nothing doing for fellows over forty, if they're clerks and out of work. I don't see much sense in it. There's something wrong about it. But of course it's no use grousing. There are a lot much worse off than I am. The down-and-outs! I haven't reached that yet."

He grinned when I hoped he never would.

7. *The Umbrella Maker*

I walked about Shoreditch and Hoxton with the Little Minister, who introduced me to some of his friends. One of them was the caretaker of a school who had been in the umbrella trade, which, he said, had gone to pieces.

I was surprised at that, knowing that the English climate still maintains its reputation.

"Undercut prices," he explained with a smile. "Cheap stuff comes in from abroad and, anyhow, there's a good deal of sweated labour in this district."

He thought the factory inspectors ought to keep a sharper eye on the bad spots. They passed factory conditions too easily, in his opinion. Of course, there's no bribery in England—oh dear no!—but there's always a way of doing things. Call at lunch hour. Have a nice little lunch with the boss. Everything friendly!

We spoke of the old days, and, being a Hoxton man and proud of it, he thought the place had been given a bad name without reason. Imaginative writers had fastened on Hoxton as the home of crime, whereas he had always found the people most respectable and law-abiding. Well, of course, there had been some bad streets where it was unsafe for the police to walk alone. And of course there were cases of murder and wife beating and little things like that. But Hoxton wasn't any worse than other districts, nor Shoreditch, next door.

"Things are better now," I protested. "Hasn't a lot of the old squalor lifted? Don't people have better lives?"

He admitted all that. He didn't want to deny it. Barring unemployment, the whole standard of life had been raised. The old brutalities had gone. The children had a better chance. They looked after them in school and saw that they were clean and properly dressed and well fed. They were given milk in the morning. They came to school well shod—although parents were still careless. Only yesterday some of the children had arrived wet through in flimsy frocks.

This man had had a rough time himself, without employment for a long time and an invalid wife to keep. He had been undernourished and bore the marks of it. He knew the seamy side of life in Shoreditch and Hoxton—overcrowding—sixty families in a thousand were living more than three to a room—the sharp tooth of poverty in many homes. But he was cheerful and saw real progress and was glad of other people's better luck.

It was from a Jesuit priest in Poplar that I heard a story of two lads who, like so many others, had drifted into a life of crime, having no other work to do. They made it a point of etiquette to have a meal in any house they burgled and one night were sitting at table over some food pinched in a pantry when the master of the house surprised them. He was a benevolent old clergyman.

"That's all right, my dear boys!" he said in the kindest way. "Go on eating. Afterwards we will say a little prayer together."

It put them off their food a bit. They were not quite sure that, after the prayer, there would not be a call for the police.

"While the old gentleman was praying with his eyes closed," said my Jesuit friend, "one of the boys biffed him on the head. They explained in the police court that, according to the Scriptures, he ought to have watched as well as prayed."

"Oh, human nature! Human nature!" cried the Jesuit priest laughing heartily after telling me this story, and others from his own experience in a working boys' club.

But England ought to do something about the human nature of these young derelicts, who, according to those who know them best—like the Australian I spoke to in Trafalgar Square— are not without quality before they get down too far.

Or is it, as the policewoman said in St. Martin's crypt, that "England doesn't care" as long as tennis is going well at Wimbledon?

III

The Monstrous City

1. The Ant Heap

SOMETIMES I SAY I hate London. That, of course, is utterly untrue, and is due to momentary ill-humour because I have had to wait five minutes at one of the Belisha crossings while the traffic surges by, or because the sun beats down on the pavements, and the stink of petrol is in one's nostrils, and one has a sudden nostalgia for the countryside, where the air is scented with wild flowers or new-cut hay, and where there is a lacework of light and shadow in the leafy lanes, and a lovely quietude. If one hates London one hates life, and I haven't come to that.

It is, of course, more than a city. It's a world. It's a collection of worlds. It's a monstrous ant heap with millions of little ants, all with little individual instincts, desires, characters, dreams, busy with their particular adventure. Most of them are unknown to each other. Their lives don't touch much, though they pass now and then in a crowd. What does Belgravia know of Bermondsey? or Walthamstow of Walham Green? What does Mayfair know of Shoreditch, or the East India Docks of Berkeley Square? There are many Londoners born and brought up in South Kensington or Hampstead, or any other district, to whom some quarters of the town are as wildly unknown as Darkest Africa. There are strange names on the buses at Hyde Park Corner—these very buses go to those places. For a fourpenny fare—or maybe eightpence—one could go there oneself, if one had a spare afternoon and a spirit of adventure. One doesn't go. There is no spare afternoon from one's own lawful occasions. Anyhow, most people don't go beyond their own beaten track in this vast wilderness, and the limit of their exploration is bounded probably by a maiden aunt in the north, a bachelor uncle in the west, a second cousin in the south, and a poor relation in the near east.

I think I may claim to know something about London life, having been a journalist reporting its history, pageantry, and comedy, day by day, in Edwardian England. But I still get lost if I venture beyond the Harrow Road or lose the clue to Maida Vale. I am as a wanderer in No-Man's Land if I go to such places as Ilford, where few of my acquaintances have ever set foot.

Yet here in these teeming worlds—some of them so new that the bricks and mortar have not yet dried—there are people who call themselves Londoners, with perfect right, just as though they dwelt within the sound of Bow Bells or the boom of Big Ben. What manner of folk are they, these Londoners? Are there seven million of them now, or nine? What is going on in their minds? What kind of life is theirs? What do they think, if they think, of this post-war world and all its problems? What books do they read, if they read? Have they any ideas on art or beauty? Have they any kind of faith reconciling them to the baffling mysteries in which they move? Or are they all cut to a pattern by mass production, not only of the clothes they wear and the furniture they use, but of their minds and thoughts? They read the same papers in the buses and the tube trains. The same leading article, written by a professional propagandist in the pay of a newspaper peer, instils its subtle poison into three million brains before lunch time. The same news of murder or sudden death, divorce or suicide, war or revolution, has reached the consciousness of seven—or is it nine?—million people before tea time. They line up in queues outside picture palaces exhibiting the same screen drama, "released" at the same moment in a thousand cinemas. They turn a switch in a little box on a side table in their own rooms and hear the same speech or the same music at the same hour.

There is a danger—a terrible danger—that humanity may

lose its individuality and become mass produced. But it hasn't happened yet in London. There is a terrific resistance in the English character to standardization. By long tradition we are intense individualists and, unlike the Germans, hate being drilled, marched about, and coördinated. Perhaps that is breaking down a little. I think the war invaded the exclusiveness of English life and dragged people out of mansions, and small houses in mean streets, and cottages in country villages where they had built themselves barricades against their neighbours. The internal combustion engine, which I regard as the most destructive agent of ancient peace, present beauty, and future safety, has also broken down these invisible barricades which were built round an Englishman's home even if it were in a slum tenement. Londoners meet each other now on a by-pass road. They kill each other every Saturday afternoon. They get to know each other more, alive or dead, outside their own home circle and business place.

But these modern accidentals have not yet touched the innermost core of English character which is still shy of combination, except in small groups, not easily inclined to make friends with the next-door neighbours, and firmly defensive of individual rights. There are still wildly eccentric characters in London, still many people whose homes are hiding places for their souls, still men and women who think their own thoughts, and sometimes give tongue to them, without taking the line of that day's *Mail* or *Express*.

I go about among them now and then, getting them to talk. London is a place of many conversations, and I have been a good listener with dock labourers and taxi drivers, and city clerks and club men, and policemen and Cabinet Ministers, and artists and actors and all manner of folk. Give them a chance and they will reveal themselves, I find. The human soul is really very lonely. It desires sympathy but is sometimes shy. Here in London, within ten minutes' walk or a penny bus ride, one may meet every type of English character and every phase of emotion and every quality of mind. The light of genius still burns here and there, in bed-sitting rooms or quiet studios. Young men and women are reading, thinking, talking about this immense mystery of a world in which they find themselves

bewildered. In laboratories young friends of mine are peering
through microscopes or weighing delicate balances when London seems asleep. In drawing rooms and dining rooms of old
houses or new flats one meets now and then people whose
names will live in history because they have helped to make it.
One meets, even now, in this monstrous city, men and women
of romantic life, touched by the grace of beauty, and others
who walk through its streets as though they were in the Wood
of Arden, unspoilt by vulgarity or any ugliness. One opens
little doors into other people's lives.

2. An Actor of the Old School

There is one house in London—among others here and there
—to which I go once a month or so at tea time as one of the little
sanctuaries in the turmoil of life. It is a house in Bedford Square
built in the eighteenth century, when there were elegance and
dignity in these town houses of the gentry, and one steps into
this atmosphere out of the roar of traffic in the Tottenham Court
Road, if one comes that way by tube.

How pleasant to sit at this table, which is spread always with
good cakes, with a pretty girl at one's right hand, merry and
kind even to dull fellows like myself, and a laughing lady behind the tea tray, and interesting people of all ages who drop
in at this hour, and always at the table end a man whose voice
still haunts the memory of many playgoers, and whose face,
stamped now with the imprint of old age, still has the mould
which held an audience spellbound when they saw him long
years ago as the noblest Hamlet of the stage.

He is frail now. He is glad of an arm when he walks above
the long staircase to his drawing room hung with pictures
painted by himself when that form of art was his first love. But
his mind is still young, and his memory—except for names—
wonderfully fresh, especially for famous and lovely people
whom he knew fifty, sixty, seventy years ago. He knew Rossetti,
and the Pre-Raphaelites, who came to his father's house up in
the north of London to see this boy and his brothers act some
of Shakespeare's plays. Swinburne came, and was sometimes a

little the worse for drink until he had slept it off by the advice and quiet guidance of this boy's mother—whom he obeyed like a child.

As a young man he knew the painters and sculptors, and men of letters, and actors and actresses of that golden period in English history, the Victorian Age, which people think dull and unromantic but which was bursting with genius; and of all these people he tells the most amusing anecdotes, the most revealing stories.

He remembers his first meeting with Ellen Terry and speaks of it as when Dante—sometimes he looks like Dante—wrote of that meeting with Beatrice on the bridge. For he was always worshipful of women's beauty, and even now, when a lovely creature comes into his room—his own daughters or their friends—he pays them a very tender homage, like an old knight remembering his dreams of fair women.

He smokes innumerable cigarettes while he tells these stories or talks of contemporary affairs, in which he is still interested, or of books—new books which he is now reading. He is keen on history. He has great enthusiasm for the noble and romantic characters of history, even for those not so noble but very human, like Charles II and Nell Gwyn, and Napoleon, and Mary Queen of Scots.

He was a play actor and has the dignity of a great gentleman, and exquisite manners and an utter lack of affectation. His brothers were actors. His wife was a famous actress. One of his daughters carries on the family tradition. And the younger school of today and yesterday, the new claimants to fame and talent, are glad to pay homage to him with admiration and respect. Very rarely now can he go to a new play. But because of friendship to me he went to the matinée of a play in which my son was part author. He was a little bewildered when a young female on the stage fainted at family prayers.

"What's the matter with the girl?" he asked in that resonant voice which could be heard all through the theatre.

"She's going to have a baby," said his pretty daughter, in a fresh young voice which was also heard.

Several people in the stalls had to stifle their laughter at a serious moment in the first act.

Behind the scenes there was the knowledge that a great man was in front. It was Forbes Robertson. The company played up for all they knew, and he was pleased with them.

In London, behind the front doors of quiet squares and streets, one may still meet great characters, noble and charming minds, fine and spiritual souls, witty, wise, and gracious personalities, eccentricities of genius, odd romantic types, men and women lit by some inner flame at which they warm their souls, making for themselves little sanctuaries of peace in this noisy world.

Mass production, mass propaganda, mass standardization have not yet ironed out our individualism nor brought us all to the same dead level of mediocrity.

3. Club Men

There are two clubs in Pall Mall in which I wash my hands sometimes, and glance at a few papers, and meet people worth talking to. They are extraordinarily different in character, and together provide an interesting study of English life from two different angles. One of them is a hundred years old in history and was once the stronghold of the Whigs when they ruled England. It still maintains a tradition of Reform (though it has not reformed anything since 1832), and some of its members, though not many, still hold to the principles of Free Trade. Its interior architecture is noble, with a pillared hall which would check the levity of any light-hearted soul who might be tempted to raise his voice in light or ribald talk. Those strong columns seem to symbolize the strength and stability of English tradition, though once—it was on the day when England went off the gold standard—I thought I saw them tremble. Upstairs there is a gallery overlooking this spacious well, and here, after luncheon, when there is generally a full club, some of the members take their coffee as near as possible, in winter time, to a blazing fire in the centre. Leading off the gallery is a library stocked with all worthy books published during this hundred years past. No word must be spoken there, though it must be confessed the silence is as much for those who go to sleep as for those who read a little before sleeping.

There is good conversation in the gallery, and in the coffee room beyond, where there is a daily group of talkers—they form a clique—of high intellectual quality; so high indeed that, being a timid man, conscious of my own intellectual deficiencies, I venture rarely to join them but sit humbly on the outskirts, trying to catch a few words now and then of the wisdom and wit which fall from the lips of these dignitaries of law and letters and public life. It is only when H. G. Wells comes among them with a puckish humour which affects them with unaccustomed levity that I enter into this highbrow circle.

Among the members of this club are famous men who have served their king and country with dignity and honour. Some of them are still doing so, though not a few are beyond the age limit and look back upon life's adventure. The Lord Chief Justice honours this club with his presence now and then. Sir John Simon beams upon his fellow members from time to time snatched from the service of the State. I have even seen the white locks of Mr. Lloyd George gleaming across the gallery, though for a time his name was spoken here as one speaks of a lost soul or the bad boy of the family.

They look back very far, some of our members, when they think of how they heard the chimes of midnight and drained the cup of youth and love.

"Sir," said an old gentleman to whom I offered an arm up the stairway, "I remember seeing six men hanged—or was it five?—outside the Old Bailey in 1858—or was it 1860?"

For some reason my face recalled this sinister remembrance, and when he had settled himself upstairs in a deep chair and had got his breath back he kept me for an hour spellbound by his reminiscences of ancient history. He had been in Paris during the Franco-German War. He had seen the horrors of the Commune. He had driven in stagecoaches through Europe. He had gone to the Court of Napoleon III.

The other club in Pall Mall to which I have the right of entry belongs to a different world. It is partly a question of age. The members here are young, or youngish, for the most part. They are the men who are making the wheels go round—the wheels of English life. They are business men, engineers, manufacturers, merchants, agents for motorcars and aëroplanes, travelling

"B.B.C."
London

B.B.C., LONDON

salesmen in munitions, warships, and poison gas, exporters of leather goods, electrical fittings, and ladies' underwear, importers of rubber, cotton, tobacco, and everything else in the storehouses of Britain. Among them are cinema directors, gramophone producers, and publicity agents. This club is their headquarters when they come down from the north or the Midlands, bringing their local accent, broader than the mincing affectation—as it seems—of London English. The club is as crowded as a railway station two minutes after one o'clock. I find it very attractive after the grave dignity and quietude of that other club. Here is life. Here are the men who are doing things, making things, selling things. England depends on them for its prosperity. And I like their type—the predominating type —keen, practical, alert, active.

There is a quick-lunch counter where one grabs one's own food—an infinite variety of sandwiches and *hors-d'œuvres*—or, if there is time, orders fish-and-fried or sausages-and-mashed, ready in a minute from the hands of the white-capped server and his assistants, who are marvellous jugglers behind the counter and will pour out a small Guinness with lightning speed and not a drop spilt.

This quick luncheon place is underground, and very Roman in appearance because of its white pillars and flight of steps leading down to a great swimming bath where the water is green. It is amusing to lunch at a little table beside the bath and hear the splash of the divers from the high board or to watch the gleam of bodies cleaving through those green waters. Afterwards the swimmers weigh themselves, walking around in a state of nature between the weighing machine and the dressing rooms. Good-looking fellows, some of them, and conscious of their physical fitness, with fine torsos and wasp waists, like Greek athletes. They have probably been playing squash rackets in a court beyond the bath to which the Prince of Wales comes now and then.

Here, in these two clubs, I have had many remarkable conversations. If one wants to know what England thought twenty years ago—or sixty—one has only to go to the first club I have mentioned and wake up one of the old gentlemen in the reading room or wait till he wakes. Here also one may talk with men whose wisdom has ripened after long experience and whose views of this present world are without passion and finely balanced and wonderfully judicial.

In the other club, where there is an excellent back yard which catches the sun, and where in summer time there are flowers along the terrace to rejoice the eye with beauty, one meets the fighters in the arena and the men in the front-line trenches of the industrial battle. They talk of their gains and losses. They are very knowledgeable in all the problems of our times: financial and economical, imperial and international. Some of them can tell one what is happening in German factories and, sometimes but not often, in German minds. They know—some of them—what their competitors are doing in Czechoslovakia or out East in Japan. I have learnt a lot in the back yard of this club over cups of coffee.

4. A Prophet of Woe

It was in the other club, less dynamic but very dignified, that I had an interesting and alarming conversation which is worth recording. It was in the month of June last, when the spirit of Jubilee was still in the streets and parks. I came out of the sunshine with a conviction that England was a happy country. All these surging crowds were contented, prosperous, and even gay. They were enjoying themselves. They were well dressed. No look of care or any nagging of anxiety appeared on their faces. We are a lucky folk, I thought. For some reason or other we are getting back to prosperity though other nations are in a bad state. One sees no wretchedness here unless one goes to look for it in distressed areas. London looks good. Its people look pleased with life.

It was cool and quiet in the club. The hall porter nodded and entered my name in his book in case I might be asked for. The usual groups were up in the gallery over their coffee cups. There was my old friend, aged eighty, who walks every day from Kensington. There was the youngest man in England, seventy years young, who laughs—even in this place of hushed voices—with the gaiety of a schoolboy about some comic story in a book he has just read among his own ten thousand books. Downstairs, no doubt, was the bicycle on which he still rides to the club, and through England every year for a tour of cathedrals and old churches and old inns, where he sits and quaffs light beer with a good companion who is also a member of this club.

In the coffee room was a handsome man with silvered hair whom I knew as a famous economist. For twenty years he has been a prophet of all those economic crises which have shaken the world. He foretold their coming and why they were bound to come. He has a perfect right to say "I told you so," but that is an unpleasing phrase. He has been a prophet of woe which has come true, and because people don't like that kind of prophecy which is depressing to the spirit, they are inclined to shrug their shoulders at his words and say with a laugh, "He's the world's worst pessimist!"

I approached him cheerfully. At last he would be able to acknowledge that England was doing rather well, in spite of the black belt of unemployment. Trade was improving: all the reports showed that. We had a million more men at work than when the national government had taken office after the crisis of the gold standard. Even shipping was looking up a little. Imports and exports were rising. England was making Jubilee, conscious that the dark clouds had rolled by.

"What do you think of things?" I asked, allowing my cheerfulness its full tone. "Not too bad, I should say!"

The famous economist made room for me on the leather seat and offered me a cigarette, which I took. I was abashed by his answer.

"We're heading for catastrophe. Things are worse than they have ever been. I'm getting gravely alarmed."

The sun was shining outside. The gay crowds were looking at the flowers in the parks. I felt a sudden chill.

"But surely," I said, "there are signs of renewed prosperity in England? Aren't we getting out of the wood at last?"

He shook his head and smiled sadly. I understood from him that we were misled by a temporary gleam of light in the dark jungle of international affairs. We were advancing further into its gloomy wilderness.

England, I understood him to say, was having a little illusory prosperity which was partly due to the devaluation of the pound and cheap money which had stimulated internal industry, such as the building trade, and partly to the new demand for armaments—which would ultimately destroy civilization—and its stimulus to the steel industry. How could Great Britain prosper or establish any kind of commercial and industrial security when the rest of the world was going steadily downhill to the great abyss?

I admitted that a recent journey I had made in Europe had not filled me with renewed confidence in the economic state of Continental nations. Italy and France were having a bad time.

At the mention of Italy the famous economist raised his hands slightly with a gesture of despair.

"Italy is borrowing from its banks and giving worthless bills in payment. Mussolini's Abyssinian adventure is to distract public attention from internal conditions which are simply frightful from an economic standpoint. . . . Then there is Germany," he added.

"Certainly there is Germany," I agreed.

"Germany," said my friend, "must find an outlet for her exports. How, otherwise, is she going to feed her people? It is a question of food for teeming populations. Owing to tariff barriers and all kinds of restrictions Germany can't get rid of her manufactured goods in the world's markets. What then? She must seek new granaries. Poland is in the same condition. That is why Germany and Poland are looking towards the Ukraine. . . . Then there is Japan."

I agreed with him that Japan could not be ignored in world events.

"Japan also wants to ensure her food supplies. Manchuria is not enough. The Manchurians need their own food. China is vastly populated. . . . There is Siberia."

"Oh, Lord!" I groaned.

"I don't believe in another war on the Western front," said my friend, and I felt a slight sense of relief. "Germany wants to make peace with France and Great Britain. She is willing to make many concessions. But there is a real danger that Germany may join Japan in an attack on Russia. Events are moving in that direction."

He gave a survey of world economics. They didn't look bright when he had done with them. One sentence was depressing in its effect upon my new optimism.

"World trade has decreased by half in gold values since 1929."

He came back to England and asked me what I thought would happen if and when there is an end of ribbon development and the building societies find their demand for small houses dwindling because the supply is enough.

I wasn't prepared to answer that question without notice, as ministers say in the House of Commons.

"What is happening now," said the economist, "is the application of temporary palliatives to the breakdown of world trade and credit. They are merely plastering the cracks. They are bringing their reserves into operation to prevent the breakdown becoming complete. In some countries, like the United States, vast amounts of government credits are being created in order to maintain the unemployed and to support trade by subsidies. That, of course, is the road to ruin. . . . In other countries, like France, they are using their gold reserves, which are being rapidly exhausted. What then?"

I stared across the coffee room, trying to envisage the answer to that question. I failed to see it and felt uncomfortable.

"Our policy of national self-sufficiency," said my silver-haired friend in his quiet, pleasing voice, "is utterly disastrous not only to ourselves but to world trade generally. It is accompanied by a policy of currency depreciation to undercut other people's markets and by restriction of production to reduce supply below the level of demand. We have definitely gone in for high protection to support this policy. They were supposed to be temporary measures to meet a passing crisis, but they have hardened into the permanent policy of our Conservatives. Mr. Neville Chamberlain has said that 'if the whole world went back to free trade, Great Britain would remain protectionist.' That is a negation of everything by which we built up prosperity before the war. It is a sentence of death to our people."

The people didn't seem to be anxious about it. They didn't know, out there in St. James's Park, where they were crowding round the flower beds and looking at the view—that dream city of towers and pinnacles and spires—which is seen from the bridge across the water. "Regardless of their doom the little victims play."

"Think of it!" exclaimed the economist bitterly. "Our empire and all our world trade was built up by freedom of trade and freedom of the market for capital and credit, based on a sound currency. Now we deliberately adopt a plan of watering our money and putting up high barriers to slow down the exchange of goods and services. This policy of ours—restricting trade—is causing other nations to increase their restrictions, with the inevitable result that world trade keeps shrinking. That is not only an economic tragedy, creating poverty everywhere, but it is a political danger. It is the root cause of war, because peoples like Germany and like Japan must either trade or fight for the sources of food and raw material. Weren't we warned by the World Economic Conference? All the great experts who pre-pared the agenda were agreed that if this policy were continued international finance would be disrupted and the standard of life would be so greatly reduced that the present social order could not be maintained."

"Good Lord!" I answered in a low, small voice. "That is a bleak outlook. I hoped things were getting better."

The economist smiled at me sadly.

"They're getting worse," he told me in his pleasing voice.

He frightened me. He was telling me things which I had written in a book after much mental agony to find the plain truth of a world crisis as it affected the ordinary man in the street like myself, and as it might be understood without expert jargon. But since writing the book I had abandoned the pursuit of economic truth—too difficult for a brain like mine—and had hoped that things were getting better in spite of politicians, experts, and statesmen. It was very horrible to hear that we were still advancing towards inevitable ruin and that the death sentence had been delivered.

"Well, I've enjoyed our little talk," said Sir George Paish, the economist. "I'm making it my business to let the people know before calamity knocks at the door."

"It seems advisable," I agreed gloomily.

5. *The Inner Light*

In the pillared hall, built when the Liberal party was power-ful and when its leaders were among the noblest minds in Eng-land—their portraits hang on the walls—I met a friend of mine whom I call the Baltic Baron, although he is quite English. But his first language was Russian and his second German, and he was brought up somewhere, I believe, in the neighbourhood of Riga, where his people had great estates. He lost all those in the Russian Revolution, and other blows of fate befell him. He had begun to look tired and sad, I noticed, and was inclined towards the "elderly spread" which overcomes men when they have retired from active service. Now, as he turned and greeted me I saw that he was a changed man. He was thinner and looked very fit. He also looked very happy. After my conver-sation with the economist I was glad to meet a man who radi-ated happiness. It was in his eyes. It oozed out of him. It was in the pressure of his hand.

"We have had a marvellous time," he said. "Our meetings in Denmark were absolutely crowded—three a day and a thou-sand people at each meeting. I gave a broadcast over Denmark, and I am told that the whole country listened."

He laughed, and that happiness was shining in his eyes.

"Splendid!" I said.

He had been "changed," as they call it, in the Oxford Group Movement. He was devoting his whole life to the service of this mission, and it had given him a new purpose and a kind of spiritual rejuvenation. One day he had taken me round to the headquarters of the movement at Brown's Hotel, and I had been invited to tea with one of the younger leaders who had talked very persuasively about this call to faith as the one means of bringing peace to a stricken world.

"Astonishing things happened," said my friend. "First of all I was able to sell some shares—which I had quite forgotten and thought were worthless—to pay my expenses in Copenhagen. Then we had some trouble in getting an interpreter, owing to lack of funds. However, Frank—Buchman, you know—said,

'God will certainly provide us with one.' As a matter of fact, it was a Jew who volunteered his services, and he was so impressed by what he heard that he became 'changed.' Then something happened to the Bishop of Copenhagen. At first he was hostile to us, but presently he became one of our most fervent supporters. Our house parties in Denmark had an extraordinary influence, and thousands of young Danes have renewed their faith. Of course, as I have often told you, there is nothing denominational or sectarian in our message. Whatever religion a man has, he can belong to the Oxford Group Movement. It is a reawakening of the spirit and a new faith in God's guidance. I am convinced that it is the only solution of these world problems which are due to the spirit of evil and the greed and cruelty of men."

"How are you getting on in Germany?" I asked.

He hesitated for a moment and then sighed.

"The time is not yet ready for our work in Germany, and unfortunately the English intelligentsia are still indifferent, although we are making headway in many circles."

"You are looking wonderfully well and—young," I told him.

He smiled with that look of happiness which I found almost embarrassing.

"I'm a changed man," he admitted. "I feel ten years younger. I'm ready for any adventure in this cause."

My Baltic baron had that faith which removes mountains—at least, mountains of mental worry. I envied him.

Outside in Pall Mall, when I walked towards St. James's Park station, I thought of those two conversations I had had with the economist and the Buchmanite. They were at opposite poles of thought. One was convinced that we were striding along the road to ruin. All his thoughts were of raw material, manufactured goods, tariffs, quotas, restrictions of capital. The other man had pushed all that out of his mind and was thinking only of spiritual force and emotional faith. He was, I must admit, the happy one.

We are an odd people, I thought, as I walked down Pall Mall. We produce many strange types. One can't generalize about the English character.

A pretty lady accosted me, and I lifted my hat. It was a Flag

Day for some charity, and she smiled so alluringly that I knew I had lost sixpence.

"Tiring work?" I asked, putting that coin into her money box. She answered with a laugh.

"It makes one's arms ache, and it makes one's legs ache; and sometimes it makes one's heart ache!"

She pinned a little flag to the lapel of my coat, and I did not regret the sixpence.

London was still gay. These crowds of contented-looking people were quite oblivious of the dark forebodings of Sir George Paish, the economist.

6. Dinner at Dorchester House

I went to a private dinner party at Dorchester House, which was once the town mansion of a noble family, so recently, indeed, that I know a girl who used to go there to great receptions. Now it is like an American hotel—one of those super-hotels which used to excite the imagination of Arnold Bennett, who always wanted to see the kitchens and the service rooms and the working of the machine.

A number of handsome motorcars were parked outside, representing a good deal of wealth. Inside the central lounge, on the way to the cloakrooms, various parties were assembling for an evening's pleasure ending with a cabaret show. The young women were bare to their waists at the back—a fashion which I find amusing but unreasonable. Some of them had used too much lipstick, and their fingernails were scarlet—another fashion which may be amusing but has no direct appeal to my sense of beauty. But they were strapping young wenches, easy on the eye, as our American friends say. The boys with them did not strike me so favourably. They looked less vital. They looked anæmic and nervy and, perhaps, slightly effeminate.

There had been a considerable redistribution of wealth in England since the war. Here, in the Dorchester, one was aware of it, remembering the ancient ghosts of that site—the noble family and their friends who held most of the wealth of the land and seemed very secure in their pride and privilege until a

world war happened, costing eight millions a day, which somehow had to be paid for afterwards by super tax and death duties,
which they accepted without a struggle, nobly, as one must
admit, though it was the death sentence of all they had been
and stood for as a caste. These people at the Dorchester tonight
were mostly middle-class folk, the families and friends of manufacturers and merchants who had made good profit out of the
war or were doing well in trade in spite of dwindling exports
and the downfall of basic industries. It was all rather mysterious.

The party to which I had been invited dined in a private
room. We were a middle-aged crowd. The chief guest was a
Yorkshire manufacturer who was persuaded by his host to make
a speech. It was a good speech, in a strong Yorkshire accent,
with a lot of Yorkshire humour. "Millstone grits," he said, in
apology for his lack of elegance and affectation, "temper steel,
in our Yorkshire mill, but take no polish themselves." He told
a funny story about a corpse, and we all laughed heartily.

I remember snatches of the conversation. They were typical
of talk one hears at any dinner table in London where men and
women past the goodly flush of youth and with some standing
in social life sit down to eat as an excuse for talking.

Next to me was a lady whose name belongs to the history of
Scotland. She had appreciated the humour of the Yorkshireman. But she began to talk about social conditions and the
difficulties of young men in finding jobs. Her own son had not
found his place in life.

"The modern young men don't like secretarial work," she
told me, "and, in any case, the girls do it all now. They take all
the clerkships and push out the boys. I don't think it's good for
themselves."

"The boys?" I asked, keeping one ear open for the Yorkshireman, who was describing local conditions.

"The girls," she said. "Look at all these little shopgirls: they
look so tired. And women of today look so worn, don't you
think?"

Next to this lady was a doctor who does noble work in a
London hospital. He joined in the conversation and disagreed
good-humouredly with the lady.

"As a doctor I take another view! The health of the modern

girl is splendid. They all look to me like young goddesses, when I see them in battalions on their way to work. There's nothing wrong with the girls, really. It's the boys who don't quite keep pace with them."

Presently we began talking about Germany. I find that in this year of grace conversation at London dinner tables drifts inevitably to Germany and Germans.

"Personally I like the Germans," said the lady at my left elbow. "I believe Hitler means peace when he says peace. Why don't we take him at his word? After all, the Germans are the best organized people in Europe."

The doctor, that noble and charming man, had been educated in Germany. He knew the German people rather well.

"They are very industrious and efficient," he said, "but they have no originality of mind. We make most of the discoveries which they exploit. The English will find the cure for cancer."

"The Germans are great scientists," said the lady in a tired voice.

The doctor who knew Germany was of opinion that they liked to be controlled by their leaders. They liked discipline. They had the mentality of mass obedience.

"The great danger is Russia," said the lady.

The doctor was not afraid of Russia. He knew the Russians. They had gone mad about machinery but knew nothing about it. When they used an agricultural machine they couldn't repair it when anything went wrong. They left it to rot in the fields. It would take a hundred years to mechanize the masses.

The Yorkshireman was telling a story which caused laughter round the table. He was a good-humoured, hard-headed, generous-hearted man, and a great benefactor to the youth of England, and the dentists, because of the product of his factories. I was startled when, as the ladies left the table, I overheard his words to one of the guests.

"It looks as though Europe were boiling up for another war. I don't see how we can keep out of it, unless by some supreme act of faith and sacrifice we refuse to fight in any cause whatever."

"Is that possible, old man?" asked the other guest.

The Yorkshire knight touched one of the wineglasses and

looked at it earnestly, as though it concentrated his thoughts.

"I believe any country would be safe and would abolish war in Europe if it took its stand on the highest ideal of Christianity and allowed itself to be invaded, if need be, without resistance. No one could fight a nonresisting country. But of course no nation, least of all ours, has reached such spiritual height."

Strange words to hear at a dinner party in the Dorchester Hotel from the lips of a hard-headed Yorkshireman!

We adjourned to the cabaret show and changed partners. I sat next to another knight—of Fleet Street—who kept his eyes on the little dancing ladies—they wore a few feathers—but told me of his achievements in the book world. He had sold over two million of his own books—edited by himself—in the last twelve months: a statement which staggered me so much that I was inattentive to the dancing girls and their acrobatic feats. One of them presently was being flung from one strong man to another and then turned upside down and tossed about like a rag doll, so that I felt sorry for her.

"I find myself enormously bored with all this," said a tired young man at the table next to mine.

"I find it extremely amusing," said a bright-eyed wench with a backless frock. "Don't you get bored rather easily, old dear?"

"I'm waiting to see the three sailors," said the tired young man grudgingly. "I'm told they're amusing."

I also had been told they were amusing, but my appreciation of their comedy was disturbed by the conversation I was having with this knight of Fleet Street, who was describing a film he had helped to make. It had gone to every cinema in the country. It was a great moral lesson. It might do the hell of a lot of good, he thought.

The three sailors were spineless. They hit each other on the jaw, and each man thus hit fell like a rag doll until hauled up again by the slack of his breeches. One man drank some water and spewed it out again. The crowd in the Dorchester found them very funny. They were very funny, and I liked them better than a girl who sang American crooner songs, and another who shrieked out the jargon of the Bowery to the thump of drums and the squeal of saxophones.

We were on the site of Dorchester House. I wondered what

its gracious ghosts would have thought if such an entertainment had happened when they were the great hostesses in Victorian England. We have perhaps lost a little dignity.

But among the people sitting in this room in the party to which I belonged there were some whose lives were dedicated to the service of their fellow beings and were doing fine work in medicine and surgery without great reward. It was their evening off. They were enjoying themselves.

7. The County Court

"One of the growing evils of this country," said a friend of mine who is a County Court judge, "is the hire purchase system. These small middle-class people are tempted to buy things which they can't afford, and then get into trouble—if they lose their job, for instance—because they can't keep up their weekly payment. They furnish on the hire system, get a small car on the hire system, buy a wireless on the hire system, and own their houses on the hire system. These building societies are undermining the security of national life. Supposing we had another economic crisis? All this system of payment on instalment would collapse like a house of cards."

The judge was being robed by his usher. It reminded me of a priest being dressed for the altar before saying Mass. The usher, a little old man with a clean-shaven face and bald head, looked exactly like a monk. The judge in his blue gown was a friend of mine, belonging to the same club, where occasionally I take a glass of wine with him and discuss the latest book worth reading. But this morning, in his room at the back of his court, he began to disappear from me as a club companion. He was becoming invested with the majesty of the Law. When he put on his wig I felt a great respect for him and a sense of uneasiness. The Law is a very alarming business, however innocent one may be.

Outside the court, as I could see through the window, there was a small crowd of middle-class folk. They looked like clerks and shopkeepers, and lodging-house landladies, and factory hands. That is exactly what they were. The judge was going to deal with them in a few minutes. He would commit some of them to prison for nonpayment of debt. He would administer justice upon them according to the law and his own sense of equity. With this wig on his head he would look a very stern and frightening figure to any poor woman in arrears on her weekly payments. She wouldn't know that he had a sense of humour and a kindly soul—at least, when she raised a little book to her lips, swearing to tell the truth and the whole truth—though truth is so very difficult to remember or explain in a few timid words before a man in a wig.

"Have a cigarette," said the judge.

"Surely the building societies are doing great work for the country?" I suggested. "Every man under his own roof. Own your own home! I had an idea this was one of our steps forward in social progress."

As a matter of fact it was only a week or so since I had attended a banquet to celebrate the Jubilee of a great building society. There had been emotional speeches by a former lord chief justice and by other illustrious and eloquent men. They had been filled with admiration for the beneficent, noble, and even glorious achievement of providing houses for the people, who had a new sense of security and a new sense of pride and were thereby loyal citizens and free men. It had not only been a great commercial adventure but was inspired by a high moral purpose. And so forth, with pleasant songs by beautiful young women between the speeches.

Another gentleman in a wig came into the room. He was the registrar and a man of great experience in law and life.

"These building societies," he said, "are the very devil! Masses of people in these districts are paying more rent than they can afford. Some of them have to do midnight flittings. Then they lose all they have paid. And they are constantly being tempted to increase their responsibilities. Glib-tongued fellows come round to their back doors as representatives of the easy payment system. Another little instalment week by week! Very awkward if they get the push from their job or fall sick and get behindhand. It's the cause of quite a lot of wretchedness in these straggling newly built districts of Greater London. It's causing the demoralization of the lower middle class."

"As bad as that?" I asked doubtfully.

The registrar smiled.

"Well, we see the seamy side."

The judge stubbed out his cigarette. The usher spoke a word to him.

"We must get into court," said the judge. "I hope you won't be bored. Slip away when you've had enough."

All the people who had been outside the court were now inside. They rose when the judge entered. I sat by his side, trying to look as though I had some business there. On the desk in front of me was a small supply of liquorice lozenges, but I hadn't the courage to suck one of them.

I wasn't bored. Here was a typical collection of the people who dwell in those new districts which have advanced with mushroom growth on the outer ring of London's monstrous city. Here, as one after another appeared before the judge as plaintiff or defendant in some small action, it was possible to get a glimpse into their lives, their distresses, their anxieties. It was like sitting in the front row of the stalls watching a play by J. B. Priestley, or the raw material for his plays. These people revealed themselves in a few sentences of protest or passion or resignation or grumbling. They revealed themselves by the way they took the oath, carelessly, with false bravado, or with grave simplicity, or with religious fervour. Charles Dickens would have known them and ticked them off in his notebooks.

There was the widow woman with one sitting room and one bedroom, in which her boy slept with her—that boy for whom she was working her fingers to the bone. The old man, her landlord, wanted to turn her out. He wanted the room for other purposes. One could see a look of hatred between them.

"Speak to his honour," said the usher.

The old man mumbled. He was hard of hearing, or pretended to be when the judge questioned him.

"I'm rheumatic," he said. "I'm very bad in the legs, and when my doctor comes to examine me he can't get about the room because of a chest of drawers next to the bed. I want the sitting room back. This woman won't turn out."

The judge was distressed that the widow should sleep in the same room as her son of fifteen.

"It isn't proper," he said.

"I do my best for my boy," said the widow. "I give up my life to him."

A tall sad-eyed Jew came into the box and took the oath with one hand laid flat on the top of his head. He was summoned for nonpayment of instalments on a suite of furniture. He had lately lost his job as a salesman. His wife had a little business but was hardly paying her way.

"Pay half-a-crown a week," said the judge.

Down below the bench was a row of young barristers in their wigs and gowns. They kept bobbing up to represent the plaintiffs or to put a point to the judge, which he answered with admirable brevity and decision.

"As your honour pleases," said counsel every time the judge uttered a remark.

"I shall commit the man."

"As your honour pleases."

"It's not in my power to make such a ruling."

"As your honour pleases."

A young clerk appeared in the box. He had failed to pay his instalments on a gramophone. He earned three pounds ten a week and lived with his family, to whom he paid thirty-six shillings a week. He had his fares to town and his midday meal to pay. There wasn't much of a margin. Then there were his clothes. He had to look decent. Haircuts and cigarettes cost a bit.

"Half-a-crown a week," said the judge. "Give up cigarettes."

A square-faced, well-dressed man of middle age stated his case and the reason why he could not pay any more just yet for a car with seventeen instalments to go. He was a traveller in ladies' mantles, out of a job for seven months, and with a house bought from a building society with fourteen hundred pounds still due.

"How are you living?" asked the judge.

The middle-aged man smiled as though this question struck him as being humorous.

"I'd like to know that myself, your honour."

His honour drew further facts from him. His wife still employed a maid, because she was unwell and needed help. It was essential for him to have a motorcar for travelling purposes if

THE LITTLE HOUSE NEAR SLOANE SQUARE

he could get another job. He was unable at the moment to pay the instalments, but given a little time . . .

A man working in a factory—haggard-looking, I thought—complained that a summons had been served on him in the presence of his boss. It put him in a bad light. It didn't seem fair to him. Why couldn't they serve the summons at his house in the usual way?

It seemed unfair to the judge. He didn't like that kind of thing. It looked rather like intimidation.

"Your honour," said the man who had served the summons, "this man leaves home at eight-thirty and doesn't return until nine-thirty, when it's too late to serve a summons on him." . . .

A tailor appeared—like all tailors, argumentative and explanatory. He earned three pounds a week. His rent was twenty-five shillings a week. He had a wife and child. It was perfectly true that he had failed to pay instalments on a wireless set, but owing to expenses incurred in the funeral of his mother-in-law . . .

A master hairdresser was in trouble with his landlady.

A hawker of fruit with very blue eyes and very blue chin—he would have looked well in a play by Albert Chevalier—was in heavy arrears with his rent.

"Your honour," he said humbly, "I've had very bad luck lately with my barrow. I haven't earned enough to keep going. The fruit business ain't so good as it used for to be. It has its ups and downs, and it's perishable goods." . . .

So they came, one after another, clerks, young married women, small shopkeepers, commercial travellers, French polishers—it seems to be an unfortunate trade—widows who had seen better days, factory workers with good wages but high rents, and the owners of houses with a long vista of payments ahead and a sudden loss of work, or domestic expenses too heavy for their income.

The judge was lenient. He always seemed to find a good excuse to mark down the weekly payments—even as low as sixpence in one case—and to find some way of avoiding committal —that is to say, prison for debt—unless there was deliberate refusal to pay on sufficient earnings.

After three hours I knew more about the lives of those teeming populations in the outer world of London, where streets of new houses stretch out towards the by-pass roads and the ribbon development which has blighted the beauty of green fields. Many of them live on a narrow margin of security. Many of them take a chance with luck when they sign on the dotted line for a wireless set or a small car or a suite of furniture. Their rents or their payments to the building society bear a heavy proportion to the other items of their weekly budget. They are tempted to live up to a standard which is beyond their means if they get a setback by loss of trade or loss of employment. They have no peace of mind because of this financial worry. They were not a joyous crowd, or mirthful. The women among them had anxious eyes and pinched faces. The men looked rather beaten—these clerks holding a job rather precariously, with thousands of little flappers ready to invade their offices after a course in Clark's College; these salesmen on commission with uncertain incomes; these small traders challenged by the chain stores. For them this modern life is filled with nagging anxieties and drab, unlovely cares, which make for sleepless nights in small rooms where the bed is still unpaid for, beneath a roof with twenty years' payment still to go. They are the slaves of the hire purchase system.

What courage some of them need! What courage some of them have!

I know a man who needed it more than most. He lived in one of these outer worlds of London. He had bought one of those little houses and let out half of it. He was an excellent accountant, but his firm failed. Another firm failed after he found employment with them. Bad luck—but he was a good accountant and a hard worker. He applied to many offices. They answered politely, sometimes. He was well over forty—a bad age. He looked shabby, which is not a good introduction to glossy gentlemen in City offices. He began to get anxious. His little savings were vanishing. His boots needed repair. He economized in food. He addressed envelopes at sweated rates, but found even that job was given to girls at worse rates. He put the last of his savings into a small business—which failed. He was worn-looking and anxious when he had lunch with me one day. But I felt abashed by his spiritual outlook on life and the courage

with which he tried to bluff me. I knew I was in the presence
of a saint—a shabby saint from the wilder suburbs. One day he
came to lunch with me again. He walked into the club with the
air of a man who is master of life. He looked ten years younger.
He criticized the fish.

"Have you found a decent job?" I asked.

"I've something to tell you," he answered mysteriously. "A
miracle has happened. I'm a changed man."

He had come into a fortune from an old friend just as he was
joining the down-and-outs.

Such a miracle does not often happen in those outer suburbs
where the pavement ends, somewhere near Epping Forest.

He criticized the fish. I was amused by that when I had re-
covered from the shock.

8. The Barber's Shop

Barbers are men who know a lot about life and are given to
conversation with their customers, according to ancient tradition. It is astonishing, or at least notable, how their customers
fall into the habit of revealing their private history to their
hairdressers and air their views on all kinds of subjects while the
scissors go snip, snip. The barber's shop is still the place to visit
if one wants to hear the philosophy of everyday life.

I remember a very charming fellow who used to shave me
when I was first in need of such service and couldn't afford to
keep my razors sharp. He was a good-looking fellow with a little
brown beard and moustache, who worked in an arcade close to
Ludgate Hill. His clientele numbered sporting journalists and
young men like myself in publishing and newspaper offices.
But he had one client of exalted rank who happened to be one
of the directors of a publishing house in La Belle Sauvage yard,
where I first worked. He was also Minister for War, and knowing
very little about war on sea or land, became afterwards, according to the tradition of our country and its politicians, Secretary
to the Navy. He liked the barber with the little brown beard
and suggested that he might care to go over the Royal Naval
Dockyard at Portsmouth on one of his days off.

"Take a friend or two with you," suggested the great man in his most genial way. He was, by the bye, a man who froze the very marrow bones of Superior People like generals and admirals and could be more coldly insolent with a frigid stare from his perfectly blue eyes than any man I have ever known, but he was charming and courteous to his subordinates, of whom I was one. His name was H. O. Arnold-Forster, and I remember him with affection.

Three cards arrived for the barber. Upon them in a neat hand was written, "Kindly show these visitors round the Dockyard."

Three barbers arrived at Portsmouth and presented their cards. They were received with great deference by the admiral superintendent, who invited them to lunch. They had a royal reception. Were they not the friends of the Secretary to the Admiralty? They saw everything. Naval officers saluted them. Chief petty officers stood rigid in their presence. They had a great story to tell when they returned to the barber's shop in the arcade by Ludgate Hill.

I shave myself now, but have to rely upon my fellow man to get my hair cut now and then, and go sometimes to a small place in Chelsea which is downstairs from a tobacco shop. The barber has been there for thirty years and knows more about human nature in Chelsea than most inhabitants of a district which still has a certain character of its own and a charm which has departed from other parts of London. What could be more delightful than the Queen Anne houses in St. Leonard's Terrace? Who would not wish to live in one of the fine old mansions along Cheyne Walk? In the tributaries of the King's Road there are many little houses where one may meet dreamers and thinkers and painters and odd mad people, touched by a little genius or earning a precarious livelihood because of an itch to write, or a little talent with a paint box, or some quality of intelligence which keeps them poor unless they hide it.

"I expect you've seen a lot of change in Chelsea," I said to the barber when he was doing some fancy work at the back of my head.

He laughed and held his scissors quiet for a moment.

"Nothing but change!" he answered. "There has been a levelling up and a levelling down. Lots of my old clients have gone. I get a different kind of class. Some of my gentlemen were great sahibs. That's a word I learnt from them. They used to come in here and fluff out their moustaches and talk as though they were addressing their battalion. They were officers of the Guards, or retired colonels from India. Then there was the artist crowd. My word!"

The remembrance of the old artist crowd in Chelsea caused him to laugh again as he held one of my ears down.

"Some of them were as poor as church mice—regular bohemians. I had great trouble with their hair, which they only had cut when they felt like it. I used to listen to their talk—they got very hot about impressionists and futurists and other such styles of art. They thought themselves wonderful fellows and didn't know that I was laughing at them behind their backs. But I will say they were amusing, and very passionate on the subject of beauty. They used to get drunk at the Six Bells— drunk as lords they used to get! Jacomb-Hood was a client of mine. I daresay you've heard of him. He was what I call a gentleman artist, not bohemian like the others. Well, all that's gone, or most of it."

"Art has died, perhaps," I suggested. "The artists have starved to death, no doubt."

"Very likely," said the barber. "A world crisis is no good for art. Monk's shop in the King's Road—artists' materials, you know—doesn't do much business nowadays. The modern artist can't afford to buy his oil paints, they tell me. No demand for nudes. Too much of that in real life, perhaps."

A customer came into the shop and took up the *Daily Mirror*. He was a chauffeur in a smart uniform.

"Shan't be five minutes," said the barber.

"That's all right," said the chauffeur.

The barber referred back to the changes in Chelsea.

"Someone said, 'A little knowledge is a dangerous thing.' In the Bible, isn't it? Well, it's not true. Education has done a lot. When I was a nipper I used to live south of the river, on the Battersea side. Why, I remember seeing men stripped to the waist on Saturday nights. Bloody fights. Yelling women. Horrible brutality. All that's gone too. Manners have improved. The social condition of the people has been lifted up beyond all thought. Everybody talks the King's English—with a little American slang learned in the picture houses. Why, the old Cockney language can't be heard nowadays. Albert Chevalier was the last of his tribe. There are no coster girls as I used to see in my young days dancing to the barrel organs with feathers in their hats and high laced boots. Great changes, but all for the best, no doubt. Have a shampoo, won't you?"

I had a dry shampoo, to the annoyance of the chauffeur, who was listening to this dialogue with obvious impatience. He lit a cigarette and threw the match on the floor.

"Horse racing and dog racing are the greatest evils of the working classes," said my barber. "And not only of the working classes. It's the same with the small shopkeepers. I know heaps of cases when they've been brought to ruin by putting a bob on the three-thirty and winning a bit, and getting bitten with the idea that it's an easy way of making money. They get drawn into it by the bookmakers, who use barbers' shops for their place of business. They try to bribe us to put them in touch with clients, but I've never allowed that kind of thing in my shop. Don't hold with it! I've known men with good little businesses go right under. There was one the other day, and the man had a good shop and a nice wife and some fine kiddies. I watch them degenerating, as you might say. They begin to swagger a bit and talk loud in the racing way. Presently they try to borrow money. Then they take to the drink because they're getting worried. Then they get shabby and furtive. Then they disappear. It was always a mug's game, but it still goes on, and you can't cure it. Some men *will* be fools. They won't learn from experience. Dog racing is worse than horse racing for some of the people about here. Thank you, sir. . . . Shave, young man?"

"Haircut," said the chauffeur.

9. Londonderry House

I had the honour of an invitation to a reception at Londonderry House, though I can't think why. It was a very great affair, and I was glad to see it, lest such houses and parties might disappear before I received another invitation. So many have gone because of death duties and income tax and changing social conditions. Sutherland House is now a museum. Duchess Millicent no longer stands at the head of her staircase. She told me once, I remember, that Haig was the stupidest man she had ever met because he was the only subaltern in India who did not fall in love with her. But that's another story.

There was an immense crowd below the grand stairway up which it flowed slowly. Powdered footmen were in attendance, some of them wearing the Stuart tartan. For we were in the house of a Stuart with the royal blood in his veins. He stood with Lady Londonderry, receiving his guests at the head of the stairway—a noble-looking pair, I thought. He wore his orders and the ribbon of the Garter. She was in white silk, looking very handsome, and her tiara gleamed beneath the candelabra. I noticed that she shook hands with a rhythmic action, as though having learnt some trick of avoiding neuritis by this fatiguing exercise.

The crowd here recalled old days of splendour, when England was mightily rich under Victoria's rule, when all the Empire poured its wealth into the City of London, and the old aristocracy had not yet committed suicide, as André Siegfried asserts, by submitting to extinction by taxation. There were no signs here of such a downfall. These duchesses and dames still wore glittering jewels, and I could not bring myself to believe that they had been bought at Woolworth's. In spite of a social revolution and a world crisis, there are still great reserves of wealth in England, though the new poor have changed places with the new rich, and the old mansions of the landed gentry are now owned by merchant princes and manufacturers of soft goods, who, I find, are a very agreeable and generous-hearted crowd, totally unlike the vulgarians pictured in *Punch*—that paper of the snobs.

I narrowly escaped treading on a lady's train and pulling the frock off her body. As she seemed to be wearing little underneath, according to modern fashion, that was an escape from embarrassment. One has to watch one's step when going up a grand stairway with ladies who wear long tails to their gowns.

It was fifteen minutes at least before I got to the head of the stairs and bowed over the hand of Lady Londonderry. All the notabilities were here, that is to say, people of distinction who had the approval of Lord and Lady Londonderry on the Tory side of politics. I stood to one side of the gallery, looking down upon their faces as they moved slowly up. They were faces typical of English character and tradition. The men all looked like major generals or retired colonels, with rather square-cut faces, strong jaws, straight noses, grey eyes, and the resolute look of men of action.

Some of them were administrators of India and the Crown colonies. Some had been governors and governor generals. Many of them had been officers of the Guards or the Cavalry. They had sat for Conservative seats and served Conservative governments. They were hunting men. Probably they played a good game of golf. They liked fishing and knew a good deal about birds and beasts and even butterflies. Some of them had probably ruled over native tribes, and others had been advisers of Indian princes and had guns fired off when they rode out on elephants. Others had inherited old houses and lands which had given them a high place in English life, because of their title deeds.

Here, up this stairway, came the English nobility and gentry who used to be the ruling classes. Perhaps I was foolish in feeling a little pity for them as a doomed caste. Perhaps they are not so nearly dead as all that. It rather looks as though there will be some survivors, even after death duties and income tax.

A handsome, level-headed, good-humoured crowd. They would never fail in courage. Its badge was on their breasts— many ribbons and stars won on the Somme, at Gallipoli, at Zeebrugge. They would have a dry humour and a kind of boyishness even in the fifties and sixties—even in the seventies and eighties. They would find great amusement in walking round after little white balls, or playing bears under the table with their grandchildren, as Wellington did when Waterloo was an old memory, and like Sir Harry Johnson, that great African explorer, who was discovered at this bear game with two black children, by emissaries from Germany who, when he emerged and said, "I am Sir Harry Johnson," stared at him incredulously and said, "We're waiting to see your papa, young man." So he told me.

But there was no face I saw at Londonderry House which arrested one's attention by any oddity or unusualness. Never once did I think within myself, "There is a man of fine spirituality or with a noble passion in his soul." Never once did I see an artist face, or some look in a man's eyes which told of some little white flame of genius burning within him. Good fox hunters, they looked, good soldiers, good administrators, safe politicians, and men of admirable common sense, loathing fanatics or false emotion or emotion openly expressed.

But there were great men among them—or at least one. I spoke a few minutes to General Smuts, who must surely be counted among the great ones. There was a Smuts year at Oxford, when he won everything. He is a philosopher as well as a soldier and administrator and politician.

"I read a book of yours," I told him. "*Holism.*"

"No, no," he said. "I don't believe that. Certainly you didn't read it."

"Every page of it," I assured him, truly, I believe, though I may have skipped here and there.

"Nobody has read that," he said.

"I read it," I repeated. "But I couldn't understand a word from the first page to the last."

He thought that mightily amusing and laughed quite heartily under the candelabra of Londonderry House.

I stood talking with a lady I knew as we leaned over the gallery side by side. She knew everybody and told me their names. We pressed against the rail of the gallery to let a tall young woman pass. She was in white silk, I think, and looked very handsome, with a fine glow of colour beneath her skin. It was the Princess Royal, whose photographs do not give her justice.

Presently I wandered through the reception rooms talking a moment here and there to someone I happened to know. One of them was a man I had met during the World War when he was a fighting officer.

"What do you think of things in Europe?" he asked.

I told him that I didn't like the look of them.

He disliked the look of them even more.

"I'm afraid it's all beginning again," he said. "Germany has

broken the bars of her cage. The tiger is loose again. What are
we going to do about it?"

"Tame the tiger," I suggested. "Besides, haven't we asked
for what is happening now? The Treaty of Versailles put an
unbearable burden and humiliation upon those people. France
has thought of nothing but keeping them down and putting
salt into their wounds. They've been through enormous agonies
since the war, and now they're suffering from an inferiority
complex."

"It's a great menace," said my friend. "Is Hitler mad, do you
think?"

I wasn't inclined to think so then. I thought he was a typical
fanatic, with the faith of a mystic and a peasant mentality.

"I'm coming round to the belief," said my friend, "that nothing can save Europe but some system of collective security, so
that if a nation goes on the warpath all others combine to bring
him before the law."

"What law?" I asked. "Where's the court?"

"The League."

I groaned slightly, not loud enough to be heard above the
buzz of general conversation in Londonderry House.

"Can you ever get combination among the great powers?"
I asked.

My friend spoke in a grave voice, while he gave a quick glance
at the brilliant assembly in which we stood.

"Unless we can prevent another war," he said, "this sort of
thing will become a matter of history. Another war among the
great powers would mean a return to anarchy. Or is that a bad
dream of mine?"

"I'm thinking of the kids," I said.

"Good God, yes," said a man who had seen what modern
war was like from the front-line trenches of the Somme.

He looked round among his fellow guests at Londonderry
House.

"There's a lot of intelligence and statesmanship in this room,"
he remarked. "Can't they do something about it?"

"England is in no need of conversion," I assured him. "But
then, of course, we have everything we want—more than our
fair share of the earth's surface."

"It's all very difficult," said my friend with a laugh.

He raised a hand to me and slipped into another circle of human beings.

It was difficult, I found, to establish contact with these human beings. They were not my crowd. I am a man without a crowd, as most writing men are. I became a little bored after getting this picture into my eyes and watching its scene.

I regained my hat and coat and stood on the steps of London-derry House for a few minutes.

More guests were arriving. Down below was a throng of ordinary folk, eager to get a glimpse of these great people with their orders and decorations. Their own faces were white in the light of electric lamps. A cheer rose from them, and they pressed forward to see someone. It was a young man in evening clothes, wearing the Garter ribbon.

"Sorry I'm a bit late," he said to Lord Londonderry, who greeted him at the top of the steps.

It was the Prince of Wales, and I wondered what had kept him late. Perhaps he had been down to a working men's club in the East End, or had been sitting in a room at Toc H joining in a chorus. One night, as I think I have told, he sat for an hour in the crypt of St. Martin's, talking to the down-and-outs.

But he may have been listening to a cabaret turn, or playing the "traps" at a private party, or delivering a speech at a public banquet, and having to listen to other people's speeches—infinitely boring.

10. On the Dole

It was the Little Minister who took me to the central school in Shoreditch and introduced me to the headmaster and the mistresses. Their classes were on, and I stood on one side looking and listening while the headmaster dealt with them and ar-ranged for a talk with me by giving the students a formidable problem to do. As I glanced at the blackboard with these algebraical figures I knew that the intelligence of Shoreditch was beyond my reach in the matter of calculations. These boys and girls, getting on for fourteen, were a nice-looking lot. They were as well dressed, I thought, as the pupils of any high school in London. The girls especially were neat and nice in simple frocks.

This central school serves Shoreditch and Hoxton, which in the old days had none too good a reputation, and were the homes of poverty. Something had happened here—something of magic—to change the scene. Looking at these young students —knowing they were watched, they looked more industrious than youth can be for any long stretch—I had a sudden feeling of gladness and optimism. We are getting on, whatever the pessimists say. We are raising the standard of intelligence in all our people. We have lifted some of the squalor and un-happiness from life.

"Do these boys and girls get jobs?" I asked the headmaster when he could attend to me. "Or is all your education wasted by futility?"

"Not at all," he answered. "That is to say, they do get jobs, a very great percentage of them. You see, this is a vocational centre. We teach them the things they need to know for em-ployment in this district, and in London generally: woodwork, metal work, bookkeeping, and other specialized subjects. Be-sides, their general education when we've done with them is pretty good. They can fit into any vacancies for intelligent youth. They do!"

He showed me his books, with a record of the positions found for his ex-students. A high percentage had, as he said, found places.

"Of course we have our failures," he admitted. "Some of the boys are unlucky. Or they get dead-end jobs which they lose when they reach man's estate. That's a difficult problem. Still, on the whole, we are very successful and have no cause for despondency."

It was one of the mistresses who confided to me that girls from this central school have an easier chance of getting work than the boys.

"There are many offices and works where they prefer to take on girls," she explained. "They're cheaper, for one thing. Also, perhaps, they're more industrious at certain kinds of work which boys find tedious."

She complained that some parents were not keen to take

advantage of a central school for their girls because it meant losing any wages they might earn until the age of sixteen.

"It breaks my heart sometimes," she told me. "We had a girl recently who was brilliant. She would have done so well if she had had her chance! But her parents wanted her to bring in a few shillings, and so they put her to work, poor child. A shame, isn't it?"

She embarrassed me by announcing to her class that I was a novelist and writer. She said kind things about my books which she had read, and I stood there looking like a fool before these bright-eyed young people, who smiled and thought nothing much about a writer of novels. There was some pretty poor trash in the tuppenny libraries! They could do better for themselves. Still, one youth who heard about this was sufficiently impressed —to the great amusement of the Little Minister—to run after me in the street and ask for an autograph.

We went round to another institution in Shoreditch of a very different kind, but interesting as a glimpse of life in this city of seven—or is it nine?—million lives. It is what is called a community club for the unemployed. I can't say it was crowded, but it had not been long started.

I found myself, as the novelists used to say, in a long shed, furnished with a piano and three or four kitchen chairs. A physical instructor was there, and I was introduced to him: a dapper little man in a gymnasium kit, very alert, and quick on his toes.

"I'm trying to teach these lads a bit of boxing," he told me. "It pulls up their physique, and it's better than hanging round street corners. If you care to wait you will see some rather pretty fighting."

I was delighted to wait. The Little Minister looked rather out of place here, I thought, being of a gentle nature, hostile, I am sure, to pugilism, though willing to let it pass if it amused these unemployed youths. It amused them a good deal, especially when a young Jew, looking like one of Raphael's fallen angels, advanced upon his opponent on the balls of his feet, as delicately as Agag, and gave him a jab on the jaw. He had curly black hair and a long nose, and very dark, lustrous eyes, and was a lithe young man. If I had been a painter, I should have tried to get him as a model. His adversary was what our German cousins would call a Nordic, with straw-coloured hair and a blond skin. He had more muscle but less science than the romantic-looking Jew.

While this boxing was in progress I had a chat with one or two lads on the kitchen chairs. One of them accepted a cigarette and was willing to talk.

"Out of a job?" I asked.

He nodded. "French polisher. Lots of us out. I used to be in the army and liked it. A very good life."

"Why did you leave?"

"I had a civil conviction against me. Someone must have split. Now I've been out of work six months."

"Any dole?"

"Fourteen bob a week. It doesn't go far. And it's all very boring."

He told me something about that boredom. It was horrible getting up in the morning with a blank day ahead and nothing on earth to do. Some fellows took to crime simply to save themselves from boredom. It gave them something to do anyhow. It saved them from going balmy. With all this unemployment about, a young fellow didn't get a chance to make good. That's why he had come round to this community centre. It broke the spell of the day. It kept a fellow fit if he didn't overdo it.

The physical instructor joined the conversation.

"Of course I go easy with the undernourished," he told me. "A little at a time is my method. But you'd be surprised how they pick up. The fact is that men can do with very little food if they keep themselves fit. It's general physique which counts, and if that's all right there's no need to put a lot of food in the stomach. I don't believe in all this talk about degenerate youth. Give me any young crowd, and I'll pull them up to form very quickly."

I stayed there for the inside of an hour and then went to tea with the Little Minister in his vicarage, where, over some very good cake, he talked about his experiences, after a curacy in the north of England.

"I miss the homeliness of the north," he said. "One has to approach Londoners by indirect ways—obliquely. There's not so much warmth down here. But they're all right when you get behind their masks. Sympathy goes a long way. I always think a priest must establish friendship in his parish. He can't do anything without that."

"Are you ever able to talk religion with the younger men?" I asked.

He confessed it was difficult but not impossible. Many of them were hungry for some kind of guidance. Some of them were very intelligent, though deeply skeptical.

"I have an interesting life," said the Little Minister. "Now and again, of course, I have my feelings harrowed by hard cases. One comes face to face with human tragedy."

He looked a little tired, I thought. It was in the dog days, when the sun beats down on the pavement in Shoreditch, and the air is stale in the streets.

11. *The Waitress*

I was glad that she was glad to see me again, the head waitress of Groom's Café in Fleet Street. She was still calling down the speaking tube when she caught sight of me and raised her eyebrows with a smile.

"Two kidneys and tomato—and what's all the trouble about? And for the third time of asking, sausages—twice."

She turned to me with the smile still in her eyes.

"Quite a stranger! Years and years! Well, we're all growing older, aren't we?"

She didn't look older to me and hadn't lost her good-humour, even during the battle she fights at lunch hour when all her gentlemen come in at once—mostly from the Temple—and want their food quick in order to get rid of it in the right place for a game of chess.

They play chess upstairs in Groom's Café. It's very good chess. They played it all through the war—the elder customers beyond the age limit and carrying on the law as far as possible in a world which had put law on one side for a time in order to slaughter each other without let or hindrance. Younger men disappeared, having been called up to serve their King and

country in the trenches. But one of them, who was an officer in
the Black Watch, used to return now and then on seven days'
leave and play a few games with his old cronies, whom he
annoyed or kept amused by a running commentary on his game
and theirs, or by humming soldiers' songs while he thought out
his next move.

I too used to look in at Groom's on seven days' leave. It gave
me a sense of returning to normal life. Back at the front the
massacre of youth went on. The guns never ceased. The world
was busy in destroying its wealth. Thrones were trembling and
crowns tottering, but at Groom's Café in Fleet Street men went
on playing chess with their minds at peace while they played.

"You're looking fine," I told the head waitress when I went
there again a few weeks ago. "I suppose some of the old customers have gone?"

"Oh, Lord, yes! Old Man Death has copped some of them.
Couldn't escape it. Old Silverhair has gone." And she mentioned others who had been copped.

"Some of them have become too grand for us," she remarked.
"Little P—— for instance has become a judge. Funny, isn't it?
I used to serve him with kidneys and tomatoes and didn't think
much of him. A little weedy fellow and as timid as a kitten. Now
he's a judge. Queer, isn't it?"

"Does my old Shakespearean friend ever come?" I inquired,
mentioning the name of a dramatic critic who used to beat me
nine times out of ten when we played the game together.

"Lawks, no!" cried the head waitress. "Got far too high up,
he has. Speaks over the B.B.C. and all that. Excuse me, won't
you?"

She called down the tube again.

"Is everybody dead down there? Haven't I asked for poached
eggs on toast? My customer will starve to death if you don't
hurry up."

I went upstairs to the old room. Most of the faces were new to
me, but there were three or four of the old players who gave
me greeting. One of them was the officer of the Black Watch.

"Heil Hitler!" he cried, raising his right arm to me.

He was just a little stouter than he used to be when I played

BUCKINGHAM PALACE

chess with him after the war in a villa on the Mediterranean and tennis with him where a precipice of white rock on one side stopped the balls. Otherwise he hadn't changed. He was still singing little songs to himself as he hesitated over his next move. He was still insulting his opponent by suggesting that the gentleman's last move was due to the approach of insanity or a temporary aberration of reason. He picked up his queen and kissed its head.

"The old lady is going to strike the death blow in three moves," he informed his silent opponent.

In exactly five moves he was himself defeated.

We English produce many oddities of character. One meets some of them in Groom's.

12. The Leader of a Nation

At a small luncheon party (there were only four of us) I met a man whose autobiography, if he ever wrote it with complete candour and unsparing self-analysis, would be a very remarkable document, and would, I am certain, go onto the shelf of those books which will be read as long as history and the revelation of the human soul are read.

But I doubt whether he will ever write it. His eyes are not too good, and he looked tired when I met him at that luncheon table, with the sheer fatigue of a man who has been put to the rack mentally and emotionally.

"I'm tired, my dear Philip," he told me. "I want a rest. I need a rest."

Before we lunched he sat in one of the deep chairs provided by our hostess for her guests in a flat on the top of one of those immense blocks which have altered the skyline of London since the war, and he had the attitude of one whose physical strength was exhausted because of too long nerve strain. I didn't wonder at it. I knew what this man had been through before the war, and during the war, and since the war—especially in recent days. He had been the leader of a political party which had refused to follow his lead and had turned from hero worship to

hate. He had had to go through a tremendous struggle of conflicting loyalties. Often he had lain awake at night, tortured by
secret doubts and mental agonies. It's not easy or comfortable
to break the threads of old friendships and go into another camp,
to be acknowledged as chieftain by people of a different tradition, different ways of thought, different codes, who were once
the Enemy. Many of his old friends had accused him of treachery, though he had left them for what he believed to be a nobler
loyalty. Had he not saved his country? Some of his new followers
only accepted his leadership as a temporary arrangement for
their own interests. They were waiting to depose him. They
whispered against him in corners. They intrigued against him.
Such things wouldn't hurt a hard man. But this man was not
hard. He was at the core a sentimentalist. He needed affection,
friendship, emotional ties. That was why he was here today,
with two women who called him by his Christian name and
were gentle with him, knowing how tired he was.

I studied his face and listened to his talk at lunch. He was not
an English type, this handsome, romantic-looking man, haggard
and with a weariness which made one sorry for him, until
presently he fought it down and talked cheerfully and with a
flash of humour now and then. He might have been French or
Irish from the south, or even have had a touch of Spanish blood,
I thought. In the old days he would have been the leader of
some desperate cause such as brought many heads to the block
on Tower Hill. I could imagine him in armour. I could imagine
him in a ruff, sitting for his portrait to Vandyke, or as a Jacobite
in exile with the elder Pretender.

We talked about Germany. He was gravely apprehensive of
German rearmament, especially as he detested the Nazi mentality with its bullying and intolerance. He knew more than I
could tell him, though I had not been long back from Germany.
I understood from him that he was doubtful about European
peace.

"Europe is in a dreadful state," he said. "Take Italy, for
instance: Mussolini is out for adventure which is not likely to
keep the peace. Then there is France. They have many internal
troubles. Laval has a difficult course to steer. The economic
situation in France is very serious."

I suggested that France was being poisoned by excess of gold, and we talked for a while about the gold standard and the meaning of money.

"Since the war," he said with a laugh—it was good to hear him laugh—"I have come to only one conclusion about money. It's an illusion! It has no fixed laws. It means one thing today and another thing tomorrow."

We drifted into a conversation about agriculture. Our hostess has a model farm somewhere in the south of England. She has considerable knowledge of pedigree pigs. She was having trouble with her bailiff.

"I must be going," said a man who looked less tired after lunch. He lingered a little while, turning over the pages of a book which he couldn't read very well because his eyes were not too good.

"There are lots of books I ought to read," he said regretfully.

He offered to give me a lift to my club in his car. It was a big car. I noticed that we were accompanied by a man who seemed a kind of bodyguard to its owner. He was waiting for us when we went out. I had noticed him waiting when I went in. He had given me a searching glance as though doubtful of my respectability, until reassured by my look of innocence. He was certainly a detective. One can always tell by a look at a man's boots.

Outside my club the car waited for a few minutes. I was listening to a man who was telling me about the trouble with his eyes and other difficulties of a difficult job. I felt deeply sympathetic. We were talking as one human soul to another, without camouflage.

Though not an Englishman, he had the destiny of England in his charge. European peace depended not a little on his judgment and acts. He had striven for peace. Once he had risked his liberty for it, and all his ambition. He had begun his political career on the side of labour, though always he had had a touch of intellectual aristocracy. He had broken with his party in a moment of national crisis, to avert disaster. For ambition's sake only? No, I couldn't believe that. That was slander on a man who is finely sensitive of honour, I am certain—who could not depart from it without self-torture. He had saved us all from economic collapse, or at least from its menace. Is there no honour in that? . . . Now he was tired. He needed a rest.

On the curbstone I touched my hat to him. His car went on towards the House of Commons. He was the Prime Minister of England.

13. The Tower of Babel

There is a big white house in Portland Place which I thought an outrage when I first saw it. It is built rather like a ship in stone and is thrust into the genteel Victorian atmosphere of this quiet square like the portent of a new civilization, as indeed it is.

It is the headquarters of the B.B.C., that amazing organization which is the most powerful engine of propaganda and has the greatest potentialities for good and evil in our modern life. Its vibrations reach out to the other side of the world, carrying music, words, and strange noises to the human eardrum and the human brain in far places and to millions of homes. Somehow, for better or worse, the noises made in this house of sound must be changing, and are changing, the thoughts and actions of the English-speaking people. Their character must be affected and altered by what they hear by those vibrations coming from this house in Portland Place.

It is all a little confused as yet. It is like life itself with infinite variety of sounds, words, opinions; but never before in human history has all this been audible to one pair of ears by the touch of a switch in some little box. The music of great masters comes magnificently into a cottage parlour or the back room in a slum street. Also there comes the cackling of saxophones, the crooning of American Negroes, the inharmonious wailing of modern tone-songs, the incessant jig of jazz, the thrilling stroke of a Kreisler's bow, the magic of a Tauber's voice, the song of nightingales, the shriek of engines, the hoot of sirens, the whirr of aëroplanes, the laughter of a low comedian with jokes as old as Æsop's Fables, the affected accent of the gentlemanly ass, the march music of military orchestras, the glory of a London symphony. "You pays your money and you takes your choice," as they used to say at the country fair.

The B.B.C. is strictly impartial. All the party leaders have their turn. Having been persuaded by Mr. Churchill, the listeners are unsettled again by Mr. Baldwin, convinced, perhaps, by Sir Samuel Hoare, unconvinced by this minister or that, contradicting the last speaker's point of view. It is the hustings from which the politicians address a concourse of listeners unable to throw rotten eggs at them or otherwise to notify their disagreement. It is the nation's playhouse, university, debating society, concert hall, and knock-about show, directed through sound alone. By turning on a switch at the right moment, duly notified, one may hear all the experts on their own subjects in science, art, philosophy, and all aspects of human knowledge. They simplify a little for the sake of their vast audience. It almost seems as though one understands them; as when Sir Oliver Lodge talks about atoms, or Sir James Jeans about stars, or Ramsay MacDonald about our foreign policy.

They are wonderfully ingenious and successful in bringing to the microphone all the men and women who have made themselves famous yesterday or five minutes ago. From the other side of the world come voices of flying men or women who have just made a new record. From the other side of the world come the voices of statesmen or journalists interpreting the history of today before tomorrow comes. In this House of Sound the world vibrations, the very noise of a crowd still celebrating some national festivity, are collected and sent out again. We heard them singing in the Saar. "Deutsch ist die Saar" they sang in the streets of Saarbrücken. We heard the last siren of the *Mauretania* going to her death. We heard Hitler speaking to his folk. And here, to the big white house in Portland Place, come people from the crowd, in town tonight: costers, fellows of odd trades, actors and actresses, dog fanciers, down-and-outs, any type who can tell his tale without too much stumbling. It is a very wonderful institution, taking advantage of a miracle and doing it very well, with many good brains behind it and a guiding intelligence which keeps it on some kind of course and seeks to provide an entertainment of infinite variety for all kinds of tastes and minds, on a level which never goes to the lowest and sometimes reaches the highest of our average intellect—but not often.

One cannot deny that it has done a lot to kill the demon of

loneliness which afflicted many minds in many places. It has brought joy to blind men and sick men. It is surely breaking down the frontiers of thought a little here and there, those frontiers of hatred and prejudice and intolerance dividing one human brain from another. It has given a new interest to millions of people whose interests were much limited, in remote villages and ships at sea, and bed-sitting rooms and log huts, and tenement houses, and drawing rooms in Eaton Square and sitting rooms in Suburbia. But whether these new interests and this new distraction from people's own thoughts and meditations and quietude will make for wisdom and finer vision it is not yet possible to tell. It may be merely another anodyne for the prevention of thought, another attack upon individual souls by machine-made entertainment. In the end it may drive us all mad. One can't tell yet.

I had a voice test at the B.B.C. The Director of Talks—what a man of responsibility!—was anxious for me to speak over the microphone once a week or so, about the progress in slum clearance and other social work on behalf of the distressed areas. The Prince of Wales was going to lead off, and I was keen to do it. I passed the portals of that shiplike building for the first time. In the central hall was a small group of interesting people, and others kept arriving. Some of them carried violins and 'cellos. Others, intellectual-looking young men with the brand of Balliol on their brows, advanced very rapidly to a golden lift by which they were transported to the higher regions. There was a man in a Trilby hat who looked like an actor of the old school, and a young woman with pink fingernails and scarlet lips who looked like an actress of the new school but might have been a duchess or a flying woman or a novelist. One can't be sure nowadays.

I was tested for my voice by a pleasant and friendly young man who sat me down at a table in a quiet room and said: "Read something when you see a red light." It was the red light which alarmed me, and the quietude of the room, and that microphone a foot away from my mouth. I read a page of my own stuff with my heart in my boots. It was queer, really. I once spoke to eleven thousand Mormons in Salt Lake City and felt less nervous.

When I emerged the pleasant and friendly young man looked uncertain about my effort.

"I'm afraid you haven't a microphone voice," he said. "You will hear it for yourself. We've made a Blattner record. You will be able to judge what it sounds like."

It sounded terrible. It sounded really awful, and seemed to emerge from the very bowels of the earth and to be infinitely dreary.

"You have a melancholy voice," said my judge. "It sounds very sad, somehow. I'm afraid our listeners would burst into tears."

"I have a melancholy soul," I admitted. "It seems to break through."

There were other men in the room. The sound of my voice seemed to give them considerable pain, and I wasn't surprised.

14. Before the Microphone

I was turned down for that series of talks. But I came up again through a side door, as it were. The director of another department desired my assistance in a certain scrap book he was doing. It was going to revive the drama of the last year of war. I was to be the interpreter of some of the war scenes of which I had been an eyewitness.

My voice was hopeless, I told him. I had been turned down by the Director of the Talks department.

He was a helpful man with kindly eyes. Afterwards I knew that he had been one of the young officers who in time of war had gone out into No-Man's Land on the first Christmas and exchanged souvenirs with the Germans. I liked him for that and was anxious to serve him.

"Speak quite quietly and rather fast," he said. "It's only when you go slow that you sound a bit miserable. Keep the speed up and raise your tone."

I raised my tone by an octave. I gabbled down the microphone in a quiet small voice.

"I can't see anything wrong with it," he said. "It's rather bell-like. I call it good."

I took part in the rehearsals and am bound to confess that the B.B.C. makes its entertainers work for their money. There were four rehearsals lasting several hours each. Over and over again I had to describe the great retreat of March 1918 and the way back in the last three months of the war, the entry of Tournai, the first day of Armistice, and other scenes. I was a voice speaking between the sound of guns and the marching of troops and the skirl of Scottish pipes and other sounds of those dead days. But it was disconcerting not to hear the sounds. I had to speak to the signal of a little red light and keep very quiet until it showed.

There were others in the room—a strange company. One of them was a naval officer who had been in the train with Foch and the representatives of the Allies when the German delegation came to ask for an armistice. Now he was in this room of the B.B.C. to dramatize that scene. There were several men belonging to a variety troupe who had been in one of the divisional concert parties in the war. It was twenty years since they had sung to the sound of shell fire. They had grown older looking. One of them was a good comedian, but they hadn't forgotten the slang and the humour of the war days. Then there was a professional comedian who had a husky voice and was fine in the parts of sergeants and soldiers talking in their billets. Two speakers told the thread of the story with careful elocution and solemn dramatic tones. A famous actress, wanted for a woman's part, knitted incessantly while she exchanged repartee with a fresh-complexioned actor with silver hair, who pretended to make love to her when the microphone was not listening. Another little lady was with us. She was restless between the words she had to speak and always retired to a soundproof room on the other side of a glass window, where she sat on the floor and smoked cigarettes and sucked acid drops, which she was good enough to offer me when now and then I joined her and sat beside her on the floor.

The producer was in another room, invisible to us but audible. His voice called to us from afar.

"I would take that line again. Take it more cheerfully. . . . Miss Holmes Gore, would you mind doing the end of your narrative? Slow down when you come to the last words."

He spoke to invisible mortals in other rooms.

"It's all wrong, old boy. That gunfire came in at the wrong place. . . . That music ought to come in stronger. . . . I say, Concert Party, watch the red light, can't you! And start right in with a good swing—'Here we are, here we are, here we are again!'—That's better . . . get the effect of a lot of men snoring. Take it from that line—'Shut up, I want to go to sleep!' . . ."

There were two performances on following evenings, one on the National, the other on the Regional. I felt very nervous when I knew that it was my turn to stand in front of the microphone and read words which would be heard all over the country, and far away, perhaps, by millions of listeners. We had to creep about when the red light gleamed. We had to hold our book of words with artful and delicate fingers, because the turning of a leaf would sound like the tearing of calico. I sucked innumerable lozenges and felt rather sick.

The regulars were cool hands. They had done this kind of thing many times before. As soon as the red light disappeared they resumed conversations, and the comedian told the end of a funny story which he had left unfinished. There were two men who had been at Zeebrugge—heroic fellows. The younger man was on pins and needles. This broadcasting business was worse than Zeebrugge, he thought. The elder man was more easy in his mind, having more flesh on his bones.

There were terrible moments. One was when the funny man went to the wrong room. Two other men leapt to the microphone and spoke his words. I had a frightful moment myself—it seemed to last an hour—when I waited for the little red light, to speak one of my bits. The little red light failed to come at the time I had expected. I waited, as it seemed, interminably. They had forgotten me. What on earth should I do?

"Great heavens!" I whispered with an agonized glance at a man in charge of my section of the drama. He made a quick silent rush at me, looking unutterable things. That "Great heavens" was a whisper which might be heard round the world. The little red light appeared, and I spoke my words in a cold sweat.

I met the brains of the B.B.C. at a party given in Chelsea by an intellectual lady. There was the Director of Talks, who had turned me down. Sir John Reith came in, and I gazed up at him in awe, not only because of his height, almost as tall as Cleopatra's Needle, as he seems, but because it is his brain which has controlled the B.B.C. from its early days. He is the wizard who has let loose these vibrations which reach out to millions of human brains, giving them knowledge, laughter, music, the folly of clowns, the fairy tales of life, the miracles of this endless sound drama. He has to submit to incessant criticism. There is a never-ending conflict between the highbrows and the lowbrows, who try to tear him down, because the first accuse him of pandering to the lowest tastes and the others accuse him of intellectual snobbery. The Die-Hard mind charges him with using the air as an instrument of subversive propaganda. The Left Wing mind asserts that he is the paid agent of Toryism. Every owner of a wireless set paying ten shillings for his licence feels himself entitled to abusive criticism because when he switches on he hears something which is displeasing to his soul. A friend of mine gets hot under the collar if he hears an American crooner wailing his nitwit love for a nitwit lass; he curses the B.B.C. and writes to the *Daily Mail* about it. But others curse when they hear a sonata by Beethoven or the mathematical music of Bach. It is all very difficult for Sir John Reith.

But the B.B.C. has entered into the life of England with immense and irresistible influence. Yesterday, before I wrote these lines, I walked down a country road remote from the towns. The hedges, growing wild, were tangled with wild flowers. The little dog roses peeped like fairy faces between the leaves. Further on were quiet woods with clearings where young married couples have gone rustic and live somehow by selling "new-laid eggs" and "really new-laid eggs." In one of these clearings with the woods as back screen, a famous producer of plays comes to an old cottage with his wife for week-ends away from the smell of grease paint and the tragedy of plays to which the public refuses to go when they have been produced at great expense and by high endeavour.

The human habitations along the road are few and far between. There is a silence in the woods where nightingales sing and are not afraid. But as I walked that way I heard deep voices speaking. One voice was analyzing the policy of Japan in

China, another voice, in the middle of a glade, was describing a game on the centre court at Wimbledon. A mile further down I heard a singing voice. It was an Italian prima donna frightening the nightingales. These things, this miracle, can't leave us unchanged. The B.B.C. is the portent of a new civilization with new men and women, unless something happens—a new war, for instance—to end civilization itself and with it the house like a stone ship in Portland Place, with all its mechanism and its Balliol brains. Meanwhile the voice of England—innumerable voices—are calling across the ether—if there is such a thing.

This is the National Programme.
Before the news there is an SOS. Will anybody who saw the accident at the corner of Crouch End Lane on Friday last at eight p.m., when an old man was knocked down by a motorcar, receiving injuries which subsequently proved fatal, communicate with New Scotland Yard, telephone number Whitehall One two one two.

The news of life and death is announced by gentlemen with very cultured voices, and all things that happen in the world, tragedies, all the day's sport, go to make up the programme of the B.B.C. England speaks. There is no silence now, unless one turns off the switch to think a little. There are lots of people who never turn it off until the announcer says, "Good-night . . . *Good*-night. . . ."

15. Young Tories

I had dinner one evening at the House of Commons and was invited to meet a group of the younger men. My host was one of them, and when I arrived at the right entrance and went up the long lobby to the dining room I was introduced to the party and felt abashed. They were very tall young men who looked down upon me from high altitudes. They were very handsome young men. They were undoubtedly very noble young men, though their names were mostly unfamiliar to me, which is a proof that they hadn't made much stir in the House nor become familiar as household words in the country.

And yet when I dined with them I was impressed by their quality and intelligence. They were all, I think, Conservatives, but as talk went round the table I found that their minds were not at all limited by a party label. On the contrary, they had adventurous ideas in planning for a new world. They were not at all satisfied with present conditions and were urgently interested in the problem of the unemployed and the need of breaking that evil spell which holds back social progress. They were highly critical of the government inaction and of the gross injustice and inequalities which had accompanied the Means Test and the administration of unemployed relief. They were also impatient of our foreign policy and did not disguise their uneasy thought that we might be heading for new war.

I listened to this conversation of young back-benchers who had been brought into the House of Commons on the tidal wave which raised the national government into power. One of them knew something about Germany and Poland. He had been into the Polish corridor. Another had been to Russia. They knew Europe. They were thoughtful and far thinking. But of course, as they admitted, they had no influence whatever.

"Why not?" I asked, looking across the table at one of these good-looking young men.

He shrugged his shoulders and laughed.

"The Front Bench does all the talking. We just go like lambs into the lobbies."

"Why don't you make yourself heard?" I asked. "Why don't you make a row one day? We want the younger minds to speak out. We're tired of the old men. They've had too long an innings. We want new leaders."

There was a quiet laugh round the table, and one of the young men glanced over his shoulder uneasily.

"No good trying to make a row! We should get into trouble with the Whips. They're very severe. Besides, we have to play the game and behave like little gentlemen."

"A great mistake," I protested, for the sake of argument. "England will just go on drifting if the younger crowd is inhibited by the old tradition of playing the game like little gentlemen. We want them to play the game like intelligent men with the courage of their own opinions."

I knew I was uttering blasphemy, but it only seemed to amuse them.

"The machine's all powerful," said one of them. "We can't do a thing against it."

"Why not cultivate a spirit of revolt?" I suggested. "Form a new group. Defy the Whips."

They were much amused, and I could see that the Whips would have it all their own way and that the Front Bench of Elder Statesmen would continue to enunciate their platitudes. It seemed a pity to me that a House of Commons which brought in so many brilliant young men after the election for the national government should still be dominated by old minds of pre-war mentality. This younger group impressed me by their seriousness, their knowledge, their free-moving intelligence. But they might have been out in the street for all the effect they had upon government policy or the reshaping of political ideas.

"After all," said one of them apologetically, "experience only comes by age. We should probably make a mess of things if we had our own way. It's easy to talk!"

Perhaps he was right. Youth has not shown any spectacular wisdom in the handling of world affairs or national problems. It has put on different coloured shirts and taken short cuts to efficiency by brutality and intolerance. Perhaps our old-fashioned ways of muddling through are better than the short cuts of impatient youth and the rash adventures of immature minds, inventing new plans for new worlds and using the rubber truncheon as a method of conversion. But now and again one would like to see the younger mind raising its voice against the Elder Statesmen who are unable to adapt their traditional thought to new conditions and new problems and new dangers, fumbling with pre-war rules and thinking in terms of yesterday when all the world is in a state of flux. An outburst of passionate protest from the back benches, a revolt of generous minds, a call to comradeship across the frontiers, a flaming indiscretion in the cause of international friendship, the vision of a new kind of law in Europe and the world, would be good to hear now and then above the bland commonplaces of the Elder Statesmen who talk of peace but increase armaments, and prate of prosperity while the world sinks deeper into ruin.

I left the House of Commons by way of Westminster Hall and stood for a moment on the steps above the spot where Charles I was tried for his life, and looked down the dim vastness where, at night, there are many ghosts of English history, as far back as William Rufus. Beneath this timbered roof one hears the footsteps of many men who made our English tradition by their swords, by their will power, by their faith, and by their genius. Some of them died for the dream of liberty. Some of them died because they defended or denied liberty. Saints and heroes and blackguards walked across these stones. Among them were men of glib words and empty hearts. Among them were men of mighty eloquence and great learning and great qualities of character. They were passionate with purpose for justice or injustice, upholding laws of frightful cruelty in the name of justice, or reforming them as new ideas of mercy and tolerance and human reason struggled out of ignorance and brutality. Outside these walls for a thousand years there had been unending conflict, change, and struggle for life, in war, in disease, in poverty, in victory. Somehow, by the spirit of our people and by the genius of men who walked where I now stood in this silence and gloom, England had survived all perils, and her sons had gone out into all the world, taking with them our law and our speech and our strain of blood. There was no standing still, no respite from this eternal change. A million of our men had died in the last war, believing that it was for justice' sake. Now I had dined with a group of young men who believed that the dangers of another war as bad as the last, or worse than the last, were creeping close. But they could do nothing about it, they said.

"We must play the game like little gentlemen," they said.

In the silence of Westminster Hall, broken only by the sound of my own footsteps, I heard England speak from the past.

"Be ye strong. Quit you like men."

"Good-night, sir," said the policeman at the gate.

Big Ben was striking. There were fleecy clouds racing above its tower. A line of buses with lighted windows streamed in an endless tide over Westminster Bridge.

"Could you by any chance spare a shilling?" asked the voice of a professional beggar.

THE DESERTED SHIPYARD

chance of promotion in the County Police if he does well at Headquarters after traffic duty and the usual routine.

"How do you get on with the other men?" I asked.

He told me it needed a little tact. They were inclined to resent a man with a snob accent. The sergeants were inclined to give them the dirty work as a tryout. Still, he had managed to break down prejudice and got on very well.

"A rum experience," he informed me, with that shy look in his eyes. "The first thing that surprised me was the fact that men can starve in London. I had had an idea that it was against the law, so to speak. But when a man comes up to me and says, 'I haven't had a bite to eat for three days, governor,' all I can suggest is that he should smash a window so that I can arrest him. As a matter of fact, I don't suggest it. I say, 'You can get a free meal in Crispin Street by Houndsditch.' But that's a hell of a long way to go for a man with an empty stomach. It's a bit embarrassing, too, when a lady, slightly in drink, of course, holds on to my belt and says she loves me. Oh, it's a very rum experience. One has peculiar adventures."

"I'll look out for you in the Edgware Road," I told him. "It might be useful to me one day, if I get into trouble."

The young policeman looked me in the eyes.

"Excuse me for telling you that I have heard that remark before," he said. "Everybody says that when they know I'm a policeman."

I apologized for this lack of originality, and after shaking hands with him in the lavatory of the Middle Temple, where the Law was washing its hands, I walked through the Temple Gardens again and wondered if this new element in the police was a good thing for the public. Under Lord Byng of Vimy, and Trenchard, his successor, the police force has been militarized to some extent. It has also been intellectualized and is now very gentlemanly. My wife has had charming encounters with policemen who have the manners of Belgravia and the accent of Oxford. There is something to be said for the pre-war type of policeman, who belonged to the people and spoke their language and was a civilian among them, dressed in a little brief authority. He grew old in the force and developed a comfortable girth inside his belt. That type has gone, almost, and I regret its passing, though I have nothing against these smart young men who have joined the ranks. They have a pleasant sense of humour, and their manners are exquisite—as long as the crowd behaves itself. God help it if it doesn't!

17. Sick Souls

The general practitioner knows more about human nature than most of us, and I know one in South London who has become a philosopher as well as a doctor since he put up his brass plate on the gate of a Queen Anne house. That's to say he thinks about the lives and minds of his patients in their re-action to this modern civilization and is trying to find some key to the riddle of it all.

Having an imagination beyond that of the ordinary doctor, he is conscious of the romance of his own life—this adventure which leads him to other people's houses and into other people's rooms. At any time of the day or night a call for him comes over the telephone. Who now? Some artist who has been moping in his studio with unsold canvases? Some little shopgirl who has caught pneumonia by getting wet in a flimsy frock which she had bought at the cost of her lunches? Some rich lady in Cado-gan Square suffering from too many cocktail parties and too many cabaret shows, or the wear and tear of the London season? A young man who tried to gas himself in a bed-sitting room be-cause he couldn't fit into any scheme of life? A young husband and wife in an emotional crisis? A new baby about to appear in a world where elderly gentlemen seem to be arranging an-other war with an intensification of the machinery of slaughter? Every time the telephone rings there is a new adventure or the sequel to an old one.

Little doors are opened in three-story houses off the King's Road, or in blocks of flats round about Sloane Street.

"Come in, doctor," says an unknown voice.

He goes in. Sometimes he comes out again at dawn, when there is a glimmer of light over London, when there is a rustling of leaves along the Embankment, when the street lights are fading.

Very queer all this business of modern life. What does it mean? Are we making any advance? What's the purpose of it all?

Many doors are opened to him in this vast, mysterious city where people lead secret lives—secret from their wives or husbands—secret from themselves, mostly. Many of these patients hide themselves from their doctors. They lie, very often. One has to go roundabout ways to find the truth: the cause of a breakdown, the reason behind a brain storm, psychological factors which make people lack resistance to the influenza bug or any other. Now and again there is candour.

I had a talk about these things with my doctor friend. We sat in his garden on a summer day, with a friendly shadow across his crazy pavement and some pleasant-looking liquid on a table between us, with a box of cigarettes handy.

"Tell me," I said, "do you think our modern crowd—people in your own practice, for instance—find this modern life wears down rather hard on them, or do they face it fairly well?"

The doctor smiled and was thoughtful.

"I shall have to think that out," he answered.

He thought it out while he blew a wreath of cigarette smoke in the direction of the blue sky above us.

"It's a fairly severe strain on many people," he said. "There is a tendency nowadays for lean fellows—like you and me—to call on their adrenal reserves too often. They ought to keep them as reserves and not tap them for the energy required for everyday life. When they get a knock of some kind, or when worry reaches an acute stage, they've nothing left to call up. They've been living up to the limit, so to speak."

"How about women?" I asked. "Many people think they are able to get along with life better than men nowadays, and have more stamina. Do you agree with that?"

He agreed partially.

"Perhaps so, if they are all right in their emotional conditions. That is to say, if they are happy on the emotional side of things. Men worry less if they get turned down by Jill in favour of some other Jack. Women pay more attention to this love business, and because it means so much to them, they take it hard if things don't work out well in that respect."

We were silent for some minutes. It was very pleasant in this back yard of London. There was a twitter of birds in the trees. The noise of traffic was shut off.

"How about sex?" I asked. "Is that becoming a desperate problem because of its intensification by so many novels, and all the films, and the emphasis of modern thought?"

This doctor was inclined to think that this particular problem of life was not quite so much a cause of trouble—secret agonies and worries—now that young people talk more frankly about it.

"Schoolmasters tell me that boys consult them about this sort of thing. In my time at a public school it would have been unheard of. A master would have thought such a boy had gone mad or was utterly depraved."

"It seems to me all to the good," I said.

The doctor nodded.

"Heavens alive, yes! Personally, I am all in favour of co-education—although it has certain disadvantages. But it establishes normal relations between boys and girls, who are relieved from timidities towards each other. The English public school, cut off from girls' society, is very unnatural really."

We came back to the question of the strains and stresses of modern life for the average middle class, life especially in the great world of London.

"It's the insecurity of life which is behind so much trouble and distress," said my doctor friend. "So many of them are skating on thin ice—from an economic point of view. This world crisis, for instance, has hit many of my patients. I know an artist who used to make a good living, but for the last year or two has only picked up seventy pounds or thereabouts. Needless to say, he worries, and that saps his vitality. Then there are lots of people who live on the hire purchase system. They pay monthly instalments for their houses and furniture and cars. Perhaps there is some talk of a change at the office. What is going to happen if they get the push?"

"What about your fees in such cases?" I asked.

My doctor friend rubbed his lean jaw and smiled.

"That's an unpleasant subject. I always have to make a mental estimate of what fee I can decently charge for my services. I call that degrading to the medical profession, but under the present system one has to do it. Quite often, of course, one doesn't get paid. How can one expect to get paid by a married clerk earning three or four pounds a week, even if one attends him for a serious illness? A pound or two, perhaps, from the poor fellow. Still, some of them have the foresight to belong to one of the benevolent societies, which helps them out a bit in time of illness. That is a very good form of insurance, and in a way it's a step towards a state form of medical service which ought to come. The present system is utterly hugger-mugger. All this begging for funds, and advertising, and sloppy propaganda for charity seems to me disgusting and below the dignity of medicine. Those who uphold the voluntary system and private practice, say that the medical service would deteriorate if it were put under state control. But that's a low view to take of doctors and doctoring. It worked well in the war. Government officials in the Treasury or other departments can't be accused of slacking, as far as I know them. There is far more temptation now for a doctor to exploit his patients than there would be if there were a state medical service. Take Harley Street, for instance."

"Certainly," I said. "Let's take Harley Street."

I expected sinister revelations, but this General Practitioner said that many Harley Street specialists were having a hard and lean time because so many patients, unable to afford high fees, went to the hospitals for diagnosis and treatment. Here and there Harley Street men—specially renowned in some line—prospered exceedingly, and others, just a few—well known to the profession—were not too scrupulous in regard to the pockets of rich patients. There was certainly a good deal of temptation to be unscrupulous, resisted nearly always by the medical profession in England. One might mention some countries where they were not so honest.

He mentioned one country to which a patient of his had gone, dissatisfied with my doctor friend's assurance, after an examination by stethoscope, that there was not a trace of tuberculosis in him. The foreign doctor, to his great satisfaction, had him X-rayed, took blood and other tests, announced that there was a doubtful spot in one of his lungs, relieved him of a fair sum of money, and recommended him to a sanatorium directed by the foreign doctor himself. It was all pure bunkum, for money-making results. Most English doctors would have said, "There's nothing the matter with you, my dear sir, and now you can go away." The result would have been the same and less expensive.

We talked for about an hour, and in that hour I was given glimpses of the lives with which a London doctor comes in contact when the telephone bell summons him at all times of the day and night.

"I get pessimistic sometimes," this doctor confessed to me. "Often, when I walk back at night and think of some case I have attended, my mind runs on to general ideas. Are we making any advance towards a higher phase of civilization? I can't see it. Now and again I come across fine actions, a touch of nobility. But not more than in previous days, I imagine. People are certainly more intelligent—the ordinary crowd—but are they more happy? I hardly think so. They find life futile. Rich or poor, they find it rather empty and meaningless. That is partly because religion is losing its hold on many lives and they've nothing to take its place—not even money."

He laughed at some secret thought as he lit another cigarette.

"I'm thinking of my grandfather—a hard old business man. I believe he was happy. He belonged to an age which made money its god. They thought they were serving God if they worked hard in their business and prospered. It kept them cheerful and gave a meaning to life. God was with them beyond a doubt, they thought, if they were thrifty and saved up a pile and gave a bit of it in charity. But now people don't even believe in wealth. It's very insecure. It's constantly changing its values. It's constantly being taken away by the tax collectors. It's not worth while accumulating wealth in this England of ours—speaking broadly. That god has fallen from the altars owing to the breakdown of the economic system.

"Religion had a great effect upon the human mind. It made sacrifice and moral resistance to evil easier. If a man or boy was simply convinced that certain things were contrary to God's Will, the strength of that belief and the refusal to offend the Divine Law kept him on the straight path with a certain ease. If he obeyed these laws and had that faith he was happy. Now, without that faith, morality itself is more difficult, and the adjustment to life is less clear."

"Do you think there is anything in psychoanalysis?" I asked him. "What about mental hygiene and all that?"

He didn't think much of it. In his opinion psychoanalysis was in its infancy, and the evidence was lacking. People faked their evidence. A practitioner of mental hygiene cheers up his patients with a certain amount of Couéism. That was quite good. But it wasn't a new science. Any wise man with sympathy and understanding—a priest—a general practitioner—could do the same thing just as well. It was a very old form of treatment, and none the worse for that.

"Anyhow, you find the average inhabitant of this amazing city advancing towards the higher intelligence?" I suggested, thinking over some of his words. "Can you give me any idea why this increase of average intelligence seems perfectly ineffective in its results upon civilization as we read about them in the newspapers?"

That was getting beyond his range as a general practitioner, but not beyond his habit of thought.

"I can't see how intelligence can be made effective so long as we have this insecurity in private life and all this nagging care of how to keep a roof over one's head and how to feed and clothe oneself. That's a jungle life, and we must live according to jungle law, which is not that of reasonable operation. People's motives and ideas and actions all come down to primitive essentials under this system. A rich patient of mine proclaims his faith, his almost religious faith, in tariffs and quotas. That is because he is afraid of free competition in his own line of business. Another rich patient of mine proclaims his faith, his religious faith, in free trade. He is in the shipping line of business. They are not aware that their pockets are the place from which their convictions come."

I had some of the pleasant-looking liquid on the small table in this doctor's back yard. As I rose to go he looked at me and laughed. There was something curious—a little sinister—in that laugh.

"You were a war correspondent," he said.

I could not deny it.

"You will soon be busy again, won't you?" he asked, looking me in the eyes. "Europe is boiling up again, isn't it? Aren't we going to have another fine war for the slaughter of youth?"

I hoped not. I should not be a war correspondent in that war, if it happened. I should be in prison, perhaps.

18. Dining Out

Now and again I emerge from my own simple lairs in town or country—I am a cottager in both places—to lunch or dine with my betters. They are good enough to invite me to their tables, and sometimes I can't find the right excuse for not going. Not that I have anything against them, such as green envy for their wealth—if they have it—or the inferiority complex which makes some folk resentful of distinguished names, or contempt for their intelligence. But as a writing man I have my job, and social life is a grievous interruption if one lets oneself slide into this whirlpool. Yet now and again it's worth while to a novelist or student of contemporary life to sit at a table with those who have made history or are making it, and to listen over coffee and cigarettes to the talk of men who are behind the scenes of this English stage and pull the wires or know how they are pulled, before joining the ladies, who sometimes also are the wire pullers.

I remember a dinner not long ago when I was betrayed into an indiscretion which might have been regarded as heinous if my hostess had been less unconventional or less interested in affairs of state. As it was, I broke the rules of an English dinner party, to the annoyance, I am sure, of the inhabitants below stairs, wondering why on earth no one left the table until half-past ten o'clock.

On my left was a French lady who had acted brilliantly as a kind of liaison officer between French thought and English minds. On my right was a lady of high intelligence, a good old name, and some claim to beauty. Opposite was a young man who had been to Eton and Christ Church and was now looking round for a job. At the end of the table on my right was one of our Elder Statesmen, a man who has pledged this country to certain pacts which, for good or evil, tie us to the chariot of Europe. I had met him at Geneva, when he was busy with that work. Several times I had had long talks with him under the striped umbrellas on the terrace of the Beau Rivage, opposite Lake Leman, when the League of Nations was still the hope of the world, though subject to sudden and frequent crises which caused international journalists great excitement and frequent prophesyings of the League's early and certain death.

Among the other guests at table was the Ambassador of one of the Scandinavian countries, always very frank and friendly, and a young woman who writes clever novels—nearly all these young women do—and, of course, my hostess, who is witty, charming, and always interested in the affairs of the world.

It was the French lady who led me into a man trap.

"Tell me," she said, "how is it that so many of my friends are becoming anti-French and pro-German?"

I answered cautiously.

"Are you sure of that? I find most people I meet are anti-German and pro-French—at least, people of traditional instincts."

"Let us talk frankly," said the French lady. "I want to know. It is very important. I find people who were perfectly good friends of mine and friends of France suddenly becoming critical and abusive of my country."

It was before Hitler had announced the rearming of Germany.

She put another question bluntly.

"Why do English people think France is egotistical and a stumbling block to peace?"

She was asking for it, so I gave her the reasons why some people were thinking that way. I told her with frank indiscretion that many English minds believed that the policy of France had been too rigid in its insistence upon the fulfilment of the Treaty of Versailles—its impossible conditions—and that they had not given a fair or generous deal to Germany. I reminded her of the Ruhr, which had caused the inflation of German money and great agonies. I spoke of the failure of the Disarmament Conference, due to the utter refusal of France, and our own reluctance, to grant Germany anything like equality. I said Poincaré was the father of Hitler.

A man at the end of the table was listening. It was the Elder Statesman whom I had met at Geneva.

"You seem to be having an interesting talk," he said, leaning a little forward. "Are you defending German right to rearmament?"

He smiled with charming courtesy.

"Not at all, sir," I answered him. "But I am suggesting that if France and ourselves had shown a more generous spirit towards Germany after the war, and had offered a pact of peace in the spirit of Briand, who was discredited, there would be less danger in Europe today and some measure of general disarmament."

The Elder Statesman mentioned the Pact of Locarno. He had had something to do with it. It was still the guarantee of peace between France and Germany.

I reminded him that after the Pact of Locarno France had spent millions on strengthening her defences. It didn't seem to give a sense of security to the French mind.

Then I uttered dangerous words in the form of a question:

"Do you think English youth will hold themselves bound by a pact which was not of their making but would send them to the shambles if there were another war between two nations who can't live on friendly terms with each other?"

Something of the kind I asked in the course of this conversation.

It was an instant challenge to the very faith of this English statesman of the old school.

"My dear sir," he exclaimed, "are you suggesting that our young men should repudiate a pact signed on behalf of England in the most solemn way?"

"I was only wondering," I said weakly. "The younger minds of today might revolt against a pledge which means their sacrifice of life for a cause in which they don't believe—a quarrel in which they have no share—a pledge upon which they weren't consulted, because they were playing with their toes in their cradles at the time."

I looked over at the young man opposite.

"What are your views about that?" I asked.

He declined to state his views, if any.

All the fat was in the fire. I had spoilt a perfectly good dinner party. It had become a debate.

It was the Elder Statesman who talked most. He talked well, because he revealed the history of episodes in which he had been the chief actor and knew all the secret threads of English diplomacy.

"Germany is rearming," he said, looking me in the eyes.

He was able to give details about the rate of German rearmament.

I could hear the French lady on my left give a heartfelt sigh which was almost a groan.

"Couldn't we have prevented that by upholding general disarmament?" I asked. "Haven't we missed the boat by needless delays and prevarications?"

I was not provoking him, but trying to draw him out.

He gave an analysis of German mentality, and of French fears, which he thought were justified.

For the sake of argument I took the German point of view. I became Devil's Advocate, as the people at this table may have thought. I believed, as I still believe, that Germany had been treated with injustice.

The Elder Statesman admitted certain points I made. He claimed that he had done much to effect reconciliation in Europe. But Germany could not be allowed to repudiate the Treaty of Versailles without the consent of other powers. If treaties were to be disregarded with impunity by those who disliked them, then it was the end of law in Europe and the beginning of anarchy.

I drew him out again. He talked things worth hearing. He leaned heavily in sympathy towards France, and yet was fair to German aspirations and qualities. Never once did he say a harsh or bitter thing. Never once did he lose his temper at any provocative remark of mine. He was explanatory, persuasive, courteous, and reasoned. And yet I dared to think him wrong. I dared still to believe that the German people would respond more readily and with enthusiasm to fair play and generous gestures than to the hostility of nations determined to keep her down. I would not yield my conviction that our post-war policy had been too tied to the fears and neurasthenia of French statesmen and politicians. I deplored the malignancy of the French press in regard to any German offer of friendship or any attempt of ours to uphold Germany's claim to equality of status. So we talked.

This Elder Statesman, responsible not a little for the post-war system and policy, would not admit that human nature could change. It seemed to me that he was thinking along old lines and trying to reconstruct a ruined world—was it not in a bankrupt state?—by building on foundations which had suffered earthquake. Was it not for younger brains to get busy and step right away from that jungle world of alliances and counter alliances, ancient feuds and racial hatreds, to some better way of relationship between the tribes?

I looked opposite again at the young man just down from Oxford.

"Come to my rescue," I appealed. "Let us hear the younger view."

He smiled and shrugged his shoulders.

"I'm only a listener. My view isn't worth anything."

"Are you willing," I asked, "to abide by the pacts made by your elders, even if they lead to the slaughter of your own generation?"

"There can be no law otherwise," he replied.

"You are answered," said the Elder Statesman quietly.

"And rebuked," I admitted.

We went on talking. The whole table was listening. No other word was spoken.

In the end the Elder Statesman laid down his cigar, which had almost burnt to his lips, and asked a quiet and sinister question.

"As a man who goes about Europe, what do you think of the duration of this peace?"

I hedged.

"I meet many people abroad who think that war will happen within ten years."

He raised his eyebrows.

"As long as that? They are optimistic!"

There was a silence which lasted for several moments.

"In your view it is as bad as that?" I said, with a kind of despair in my voice.

"I am beginning to lose hope," said the Elder Statesman.

The hostess rose at last and laughed.

"It is getting late. The servants will wonder what has happened. But I must say we have had an interesting time."

Everyone rose, laughing a little.

But we had heard a dark prophecy from a man who knew what forces were gathering behind the scenes and beneath the thin crust of this peace in Europe. It was before more recent events, such as the conscription of German youth, the British Naval Pact with Germany, and other episodes which have altered the problem somewhat but not yet given the world a sense of security.

Looking back on that dinner party I believe it could only have happened in England. These people were all on the Conservative side of politics. Many of them belonged to the old traditions of aristocracy. Their minds moved within the framework of their social status. And yet, as I must admit, they could listen to an argument in which the side I put forward was strongly against their own opinions, and they were willing to give it a fair hearing. There was no sign of passion, though they were deeply moved by some of the things they heard. They heard that prophecy of war within ten years—before ten years—as though someone had said, "It will rain next week." And yet their blood, and their treasure, and their social standing would be called to sacrifice, and England would not escape from ruin and anarchy. Perhaps their imagination did not reach as far as that.

19. The Old Aristocracy

I have the privilege of studying the minds and manners of those who used to sit in the seats of the mighty—which are now rather rickety—at the house of a lady who maintains the old traditions of Victorian dinners. She is the widow of a great public servant, and if she had been like other widows she would have retired from social life into the hiding places of boredom. But she is not like other widows, being a woman of insatiable interest in the affairs of men and women of her own set—and in secret rumours and unwritten stories of life behind the scenes of public affairs. There were many of her type in Victorian England: the great English hostesses who stood at the top of the stairs in the mansions of Mayfair, Belgrave Square, and Grosvenor Square. There are very few left now, owing to income tax, death duties, and a social revolution.

This lady, who invites me to her table several times a year, does not dwell in one of those great mansions, but in a house of modest size, situate, as the house agents say, in a select neighbourhood not far from my own slum. Her dinner parties seldom exceed sixteen guests, but they are of a rare vintage. There are few houses in London where such a company sits down at the same table. On the way up I pass a few private remarks in the hall with the butler, as man to man, and get a smile from a maid who reads my novels. One cannot help being impressed by a collection of human beings whose names are on the roll call of English history, whose achievements have altered the map of the world, at a time when we were still painting it red, and whose appearance is not reassuring at first sight.

"Can they be real?" I thought, when I first met some samples of this exalted crowd. "Are they going to eat this dinner, or are there some ghosts about? Is this England of 1935, or have I gone back to the days of Queen Victoria, when England still had a sense of security and these people still had great places and power? Not yet, in those Victorian days, had they sold their Old Masters to American dealers. Not yet had they sold their land to jerry builders. Not yet had their own houses been pulled down for blocks of flats. Not yet were their sons and daughters living in mews once inhabited by their ostlers, or working in shops and garages, or looking for jobs in the City.

Their dignity at a dinner party is still tremendous. It requires an effort to get into human touch with some of them. Some of their lady wives have a superficial arrogance which is disconcerting. But I should be unfair to them if I made out that they are, as a class, intolerant or stuffed with self-conceit. On the contrary, after the first touch of ice, which is due to English reserve, they thaw very quickly and are simple minded, I find, and very direct, in their way of speech.

One lady, of what is known in dressmakers' shops as "out size," bearing a great name, fingered the little card at the side of my plate and turned to me with a good-natured smile.

"I'm sorry I do not know your name. What do you do in the world? Something great, I'm sure."

"I write books, ma'am," I said with humility.

"Really? You don't say so. How very interesting. I can't say I've ever heard of them."

I assured her that there was no reason why she should have heard of them.

She explained that she had not much time for books. She had to look after her husband's estate and the servants and all that. She was devoted to her gardens. She also had to take an interest in village life. She was also breeding pigs.

But I hear good talk at this table. How could there fail to be good talk, very educational in its revelation of unwritten history, when there, at the end of the table, is a little man who was once Sirdar of Egypt and who met General Marchand face to face when he planted a French flag at Fashoda, and when that episode nearly caused war between England and France; when on the other side of the table is a field marshal whose memory of history in which he played an active part goes back far beyond the Boer War; when in another chair sits an old gentleman who once governed millions of His Majesty's black subjects and did his best for them in plagues and famines?

They are not all people of the past who appear as ghosts of a dead world at this table. My hostess extends her hospitality to those who are still in active service. There is a very active-minded bishop who talks about unemployment in the distressed areas with first-hand knowledge and first-class sympathy, though he has no solution to offer. The German Ambassador bows over the hand of his hostess, and when the port wine goes round talks about fishing, as a safer topic than the Nazi régime. The Chancellor of the Exchequer comes with his charming and beautiful wife and discusses England's economic state without pretence of dark secrecy. A handsome woman, with a name which belongs to the romance of Scotland, has spiritual ideals of life which are almost too high for average human nature but are interesting to hear. A French literary man, famous as an interpreter of England, is watching and listening with smiling eyes as he glances round this company. In his next book he will describe them with a disguised irony, a very bland condescension, conscious of his own subtle intelligence. These people, to him, are the wax models in Madame Tussaud's, who have come to life, who talk, who eat, who move about, and yet seem a little unreal in a democratic world which is surging past them.

I regard them now without alarm. I feel a little pity for them. The more elderly among them look back across a broken bridge to a pre-war world, where there were peace and dignity and security, and in their own lives, perhaps, a touch of splendour. The little man who was once Sirdar saw a thousand swords flash when he rode out on his camel, innumerable black faces gazed at him with awe and obedience when he reviewed an army in the Soudan. He was a captain general in Egypt, with command over the land of the Pharaohs and the Ptolemies. Now he has a little house near the Green Park and has some directorships in the City, and not even a taxi driver salutes him when he passes by.

These people belong, many of them, to the old aristocracy of England and are a little sad and a little anxious, not in a selfish way, because the World War and its consequences took heavy tribute from them—an almost crippling tribute in many cases—but because they see the beauty of England being spoilt by the needs and advances of our seething democracy, and because they dislike and distrust the inevitable approach of socialistic measures which are destroying their caste and their tradition and their code of manners and morals, which they identify with all that England means. And it did mean something, one must admit, in dignity and honour and a sense of duty and courage, and even beauty, among the best of them. Now they see England becoming a bourgeois state, with its ribbon development, its world of small houses on the hire system, its invasion of the countryside with picture palaces and the blare of broadcasting. They are uneasy about the future, not for their own sakes, for they will be gone, but for the sake of the life coming after them.

At the table of this hostess who gives good dinners to her friends I have heard many words of apprehension because forces are gathering, they think, beyond the control of the old statesmanship or the old diplomacy, which may lead to another explosion, which may drag down, not England only, but civilization itself. They are afraid that India is slipping towards anarchy. They have no faith in Indian self-government. They see the approach of the Yellow Peril and the rising tide of colour. The women at this table have lived in India, Japan, China. They talk beyond the range of newspaper articles. They know a lot of what's happened behind the scenes in Germany, France, Italy. Their husbands were ambassadors or visitors, friends of those who ruled Europe before it broke to pieces and crowns fell. They are afraid, I find, of another crash, in which the younger holders of their names and all youth will be involved. And most of them, though not all, believe that the League of Nations is an illusion, that collective security is a vain dream, and that the only safeguard of England is to keep strong at all costs by sea, land, and air. The pacifism in the universities, the Peace Ballot, the India bill, the Geneva mentality, the policy of the Labour party, the lack of national discipline, seem to these traditional minds a surrender to cowardice or a pandering to mob mentality. They express their fears, and I listen with many mental reservations, because I see no safety at all in their philosophy of pre-war thought. They can't put back the clock.

Is there any city in the world where one may meet such romantic men and women as in London, or go into houses which have so much character of their own, or sit at tables where there are so many guests who have done things worth doing, thought things worth thinking, and have in their souls a refusal to surrender to the mechanization of the mind or the standardization of manners? There is a house in Hyde Park Gardens which looks very commonplace from outside. Inside it is like the castle of a Scottish chieftain, which indeed it is. It has a great hall with a great fireplace where logs burn on winter days, and on the walls, here and upstairs, there are frescoes of ancient battles between pikemen and bowmen and Scottish gentlemen with sharp swords or lances. They were battles in which the ancestors of the man who lives in Hyde Park Gardens played their part stoutly, but not such battles as he saw himself when he was a general in the Great War and directed the attack at Gallipoli. He shows his guests an iron ball with spikes at the end of a club. One of his forebears used it to crack the skull of Englishmen and other enemies.

He is a charming host to any friends who come to his table for luncheon. When he comes into the room after they have assembled, he has the knightly look of Don Quixote. He has a word of gallantry for each pretty woman, a genial welcome and a flash of wit for each man among his guests. At his table sit writers, painters, diplomats, and intellectuals of all brands. He was a professional soldier. Now he is a great peacemaker. He believes in fair play to Germany. Though he had fought against them, he was one of the first to speak words of chivalry on their behalf, and in return they gave back the drums of the Gordons captured on the way from Mons. He put his hand on my shoulder one day and said, "Work for peace. Try to advance the spirit of peace in Europe."

His wife is charming, witty, and gracious.

"My husband alarms me," she told me one day. "Most wives' husbands get older and older as the years pass. But mine gets younger and younger."

Sir Ian Hamilton is eighty-two. He has the straight back of a young man. His eyes still flash with the generous passion of youthful indignation for injustice, or moral cowardice, or human meanness.

20. Writers and Readers

There are literary "at homes" in London where one meets people who write books and plays, though they seldom read what the other fellow writes, unless they have to as critics—and even then they don't, it is said. Mr. J. B. Priestley invites a few friends to his house at Hampstead where once Coleridge lived —a lovely old house with a very fragrant spirit, like that of pot-pourri. I went there one night through a snowstorm. Was it a hundred or two hundred others who went through the same snowstorm? Mr. Priestley has many friends, all of them famous folk. Mrs. Priestley seems to know them all, and they are en-chanted to know her, because she is beautiful and kind.

Mr. Drinkwater is here and puts his hand wearily through the lock of hair which falls over his noble brow. He asks one a question but does not listen to the answer, because he has some strain of music in his mind or the first lines of a lyric. Miss Rose Macaulay is surrounded by a group which is sure to be smiling, because she has a very pointed wit. Miss Clemence Dane is there, a very gracious soul.

Here also are many of the young men and women who are writing the novels reviewed by Mr. Gerald Gould and Mr. Ralph Strauss and Mr. Cecil Roberts, with such enthusiasm now and then that I want to read them all but do not find life long enough. Certainly they are very brilliant, though as an old-fashioned man I find some of them too cruel and too candid in their delineation of life, and especially of the aspects of life which are most unpleasing.

These literary parties bring together just now and then writers who tend to dwell apart from their fellow craftsmen, in country cottages or hiding places which are not to be found in the telephone directory. They emerge from their lairs now and then to consort with each other reluctantly at the bidding of a publisher or a literary agent because they like to be kind, or have a sudden curiosity to see what men and women are like. I meet them in these rendezvous.

Mr. Gollancz has a party at the Savoy. Here come all the famous people whose names appear in big black type on the pages of the *Observer* and *Sunday Times*. Judging from the reviews quoted under their latest titles, there must be enough genius in one room to make this the Golden Age of English letters, though one is apt to forget their names next week, because there are many new arrivals in the hall of fame.

The House of Heinemann gives a party now and then, and it is in a very fine old house, haunted by the ghost of Dr. Johnson, who came here often to dine with his friend Mr. Topham Beauclerk. The walls are still panelled. The ceilings are still plastered with the mouldings of the eighteenth century. The furniture is in keeping with this period, and here one meets a distinguished crowd who give themselves no airs because they happen to be famous or on their way to fame. For nowadays the literary gentleman gets his hair cut in the usual way, and the literary lady is not to be distinguished from other females except now and then by the length of her cigarette holder (to keep the smoke out of her eyes while she is writing) or by a certain intensity in her style of conversation.

These writers have been tempted lately to show themselves in public and to make little speeches to their readers on literary subjects or life in general. Little Miss Foyle, who has the appearance of a Jane Austen heroine and the organizing genius of the late Thomas Cook, lures them to the Foyle luncheons on behalf of her father's bookshop, and will not take No from them if they are reluctant or shy. For two hours one day I said No, and then Yes, because she looked so charmingly distressed at this refusal. When invited first to Foyle's luncheons, innocent authors expected to speak in an old bookshop to a few book lovers. They were astonished to find themselves in a big restaurant, facing eight hundred guests who had paid for their tickets to see them. All the celebrities have appeared there: Dean Inge, with wit and wisdom drawn from a store of classical knowledge; Mr. Hannen Swaffer, looking as though he had stepped from the pages of Charles Dickens; Mr. Hugh Walpole, like a canon of his own Cathedral; Mr. John Drinkwater, all that a poet should look; Mr. Philip Guedalla, still with the style which he brought to perfection as president of the Oxford Union, and literary ladies who speak so much better than the men because they have learnt it all by heart.

Harrod's, in the Brompton Road, invites its authors to address the customers of its bookshop and library, and once again the reading public has a chance of seeing the men and women whose novels it has read and, now and then, bought. I can understand the curiosity which brings the public to these bookshops. They want to know what manner of man it is who writes so understandingly of love and who has such a romantic imagination or such a noble passion. It is disappointing for them if he happens to be a withered little man who blinks at them over his pince-nez and looks less romantic than a linen draper. They have been kept awake at night by an author who is very ruthless in his analysis of human nature—but terribly true—or by one who has given them a new revelation of beauty, or some reconciliation with life, or led them to some place of enchantment, or helped them to forget the nagging worries of their own world. It's unfortunate if he is not so noble in aspect as one of his own heroes, or looks like a caricature by Frank Reynolds in the pages of *Punch*. But it is not merely for self-advertisement that an author faces his reading public. He wants to see what they look like, these people in whose minds some of his characters may be known and some of his words may be remembered. Perhaps he has changed their view of life a little. Perhaps the words he wrote in a country cottage have reached out to them and touched their imagination or their emotions. They may have wept when they read that page in Chapter Ten of his last novel. In any case, a book or two of his has been into their homes, and his mind has lived with theirs for a few hours.

He has been the bedside companion, in all innocence, of many women. What kind of people are they, he wonders, these unknown friends with whom he has established a secret understanding and an intellectual comradeship?

So the authors go through the silk department of Harrod's, where elegant young women are showing off the latest fashions, and are taken up by a golden lift to the library in this big shop, and stand on a little platform, trying to look unself-conscious, hiding their cowardice in front of a crowd, mostly of women who stare at them—can it be with amusement? They are the ladies of South Kensington, who are great novel readers, or the ladies of those pleasant suburbs like Wimbledon and Streatham, where there is great intellectual activity in little houses with little gardens, where women read a lot of books to save themselves from boredom while their husbands are working in the City. If only some of these authors could get to know more about the lives of their readers in these bookshop audiences, what new plots they would get, what studies of character, what secrets of hearts yearning for the fulfilment of dreams, for an answer to many riddles!

As a writer of books I have faced my own readers now and then, at Harrod's, at W. H. Smith's, in the Earl's Court Road, in Literary Circles at Hampstead Garden City, and at a bookshop in Bermondsey.

It was in Bermondsey that I found the keenest readers, for here the young men and women read books not for amusement or to while away an hour of boredom, but to find out, if they can—it is very difficult!—something about life. They search the pages of Galsworthy and Arnold Bennett and H. G. Wells for enlightenment on this subject. They roam as far afield as Dostoievsky and Tolstoy. They read on their way home in tubes and trains, after a hard day's work in factories, sometimes while they are clinging to a strap. They make notes on the margins of cheap editions. They write essays about the books they have read, and their analysis is penetrating. There are great readers and thinkers in Bermondsey.

But on the way back from an evening among them a friend of mine asked me a disconcerting question.

"Is it good, do you think, that these young men and women should read and think so much?"

"Extraordinarily good," I answered.

He shook his head and sighed.

"Perhaps it only makes them unhappy," he said. "How can one be happy if one thinks? Isn't it better to play billiards at the corner pub, or go to a cinema in which thought is unnecessary? These young men and women are alarming. They're torturing themselves to find the clue to this eternal mystery of life, and of course it leads them only to a sense of futility and intellectual despair, and dissatisfaction with their own conditions. Isn't the martyrdom of man due to the accident which one day made a monkey self-conscious?"

I laughed in the corner of his car—he had a very good motor-car.

He cheered up later on the journey and talked about the eternal romance of London life.

"One can never get to the end of London. One is always finding new worlds. One is always coming in touch with different minds. I wish I could live a thousand years to know more than I shall ever have time to learn. Life is too short really. Take England, for instance: What do I know about England three miles away from Shaftesbury Avenue? I would like to explore England. I would like to meet its oddities, all its queer characters, all its peasants and fishermen and working folk. I would like to have a talk with the Bishop of Durham, and an old duchess or two, and a village blacksmith, and a tramp sleeping under a hedge, and a gipsy woman smoking a cutty pipe on the steps of her caravan. I would like to get to know what is really in the soul of England, if it has a soul. We are a most mysterious people. We all hide from each other. We are inarticulate."

He went on talking with great rapidity and with many fantastic thoughts. As an inarticulate Englishman he did rather well.

21. Young Scientists

There is one world in London—that city of separate worlds— which is very important, though it does not find its way into novels or newspapers. It is the world of London University, with its separate colleges scattered over a wide area and without a close communal life, linking them all together. University College knows not much of King's College. The Royal College of Science doesn't pass the time of day with King's. The young women of Bedford College, in the neighbourhood of Regent's Park, do not enter into social relations with the medical students in Gower Street or the art students in the Strand. The London School of Economics is a republic of its own. It is strange that this great city has not yet established a corporate sense of university life which has been in Paris for a thousand years.

But here in these colleges thousands of young men and women graduate in the arts and sciences every year, and go out—some of them—to the far ends of the Empire, to pass on the torch of knowledge or to apply their studies to the practical jobs of life, as doctors, engineers, surveyors, mineralogists, and chemists. Indians, Chinese, Japanese, come to London to study the science or philosophy of the Western world and go to their own places to make use of it against the white races, or to disturb their own, or, let us hope, in the long run, after many other chapters of human anarchy, to unite mankind at last in an orderly system of coöperation for the common good on this little crowded earth ball.

I have been privileged now and then to see something of the life within these colleges, though I have never studied in them. It's a busy life, because here, in London, students mostly come to learn, and not only to have a good time. Some of them are very poor. They economize over meals. They buy their clothes

off the peg. Many of them live in poor lodgings, or in hostels
provided for their use. But like all students, they have the
treasure of youth, which is a great compensation for hard times.
Is there not laughter? Is there not comradeship? Is there not
even, now and then, a little love across the table of an A.B.C.,
or in the gallery of the Old Vic, or on a hiking adventure down
Surrey lanes 'twixt Saturday and Monday? Is there not the
endless adventure of knowledge which may lead to great dis-
covery, or at least to a mining job in Peru or a chemist's job
at the I.C.I.? They have their debating societies and their
operatic societies and their dances. I am, though heaven knows
why, vice-president of the Geological Opera Company of
King's, which is called the Geoids. These young geologists put
up a very good show of Gilbert and Sullivan. One of their lec-
turers is a born actor with a fine voice. One of the students has
a rare humour as a comedian. I attended the birthday party of
another geologist and played parlour games with the students
and found strange young women sitting on my knee for odd
moments in some innocent sport devised by an earnest lecturer
departing for an hour or two from the mysteries of crystallog-
raphy and petrology.

I was invited to dine one evening in the students' hostel of
the Royal College of Science in South Kensington and had some
interesting hours there, with a glimpse of this earnest life of
study and research. One leaves the roar of London traffic. It is
very quiet in the quadrangle, where on one side the buildings
are ivy-covered, like the walls of an Oxford college centuries
old. There were some good hard tennis courts, I noticed, and
I had a feeling of envy. How good to be young again, and a
student here, with the ambitions and dreams of youth!

My host was a young man who has a doctor's degree in
science after studying in a German university, where he learnt
the language and studied German character as well as science.
He introduced me to the warden, and we followed a hundred
men into one of the dining rooms, and sat at a long table, and
bowed our heads a moment when the warden spoke a Latin
grace.

I entered into conversation with a young man on my left and
found he was interested in foreign affairs. He wanted to know

if I thought there would be another war before long and doubted my assurances that nobody wanted war. He stated his own faith.

"I'm not a pacifist," he informed me, "but I'm against war."

"I'm glad to hear it," I told him. "You're not alone in that dislike."

On the other side of the table was a young Australian who talked to me in the general buzz of conversation. I found him interesting.

"Many Australian students come over here on wheat ships," he told me. "They work their passage and come to get experience as architects, chemists, engineers, and so on. They're better fitted for the jobs when they go back again."

"What do you think of the crowd here?" I asked indiscreetly.

He smiled over his mess of pottage.

"The English fellows seem so tied to England!" he answered, after some general and agreeable remarks. "They don't push about the world enough. It's because of the comfort here. They've no inclination to rough it for a time. The old pioneer spirit seems to have died out a good deal."

I turned my attention to the warden and asked him about the chance of getting good jobs when students had taken their degrees. I remembered several young men in King's College who, a year or two back, had waited for jobs until they were sick with hope deferred.

"It's not too difficult," said the warden cheerfully. "They all seem to find a place for themselves somehow. There's still a call for engineers and chemists and geologists and so forth. Now that world trade seems to be improving a little—anyhow within the Empire—young men are wanted again."

The young Australian opposite had a job waiting for him in Johannesburg. Another man was going out to South America. Another was bound for Kenya.

I was taken by my young doctor of science to his own rooms and quaffed wine with him. The young man who was not a pacifist but disliked war joined us and talked more freely. He had come from Huntingdon and was a good English type, physically and mentally, with charming manners, rather rare nowadays in the opinion of pessimists. On the subject of war

he came out into the open and expressed the views of his own
crowd, I think, as well as his personal convictions.

"What we're afraid of is that we may be juggled into another
European war by the folly of our politicians and Elder States-
men. In that case I wouldn't fight. Much as I should hate it,
I should join the conscientious objectors."

He spoke sympathetically about Germany, which he knew
a little. He thought the Germans were perfectly right in claiming
equality with the other powers, and he thought they hadn't
been given a fair deal.

We got on the subject of the Locarno treaty which pledged
him and all his contemporaries to fight on the side of France if
Germany provoked an aggressive war, or on the other side if
the boot were on the other foot.

"It was a pledge made without my knowledge and consent,"
he said with a laugh. "I should hate to be caught by it. In any
case, do you think we should go for France if they invaded
Germany on the pretext that it was a preventive war or that
Germany had been aggressive? It's unfair if it works only one
way."

He had, I found, a complete contempt for the Parliamentary
system. It seemed to him ineffective, old-fashioned, and time-
wasting on futile verbiage. But he listened very politely when
I defended it as a better system than Fascism or Hitlerism or
the intolerance of any young men in coloured shirts ruling with
the cudgel or the rubber truncheon. We launched into the
realm of the ideal government, that will-o'-the-wisp which has
been chased by many generations of students since Plato walked
his groves and talked thereon.

My doctor of science spoke some very wise words, being a
young man of balanced mind. Time slipped away as we drank
his wine and smoked his cigarettes. Outside this quiet sanctuary
London was beginning its night life. Thousands of people would
be inside the cinemas watching the false drama of the screen.
Thousands of others would be dog racing. They would be dancing to jazz bands. There would be dinner parties at the Dorchester and at Grosvenor House. In millions of little homes
London would be listening to its wireless sets. But here in the
Royal College of Science, long after working hours, there were

young men who would eschew delights and live laborious days, far into the night.

I was taken to see some of them. I was taken down long corridors with hardly a flicker of light. I went into laboratories where my friend's friends were busy with strange gadgets, and into his own laboratory, where he exhibited a complicated system of retorts and tubes and explained to me his exciting pursuit of Free Radicals. They behaved very strangely, as far as I could make out. They had no party loyalty but combined with other elements like the group system in the French Chamber. He was able to isolate them by artful means, and I had a suspicion that he was on the track of new knowledge which one day will make this world more unpleasant than it is at present, by increasing the powers of the human mind over natural laws, which they pervert to the destruction of their fellow human beings. But that was a reactionary idea which he assured me had no reality in fact. He is a student of pure science, for knowledge's sake alone, and has no use for its practical application or misuse.

He took me into one laboratory and showed me with enthusiasm a contraption fitted up by a friend of his for whom he has great admiration as a Brain. I studied this puzzle with interest but without understanding. Here again were many tubes and mechanical devices. They were tied up with string and wire and bits of rag and wedged round here and there by cotton wool.

"Marvellous!" said my friend, gazing at it with delight. "What ingenuity! What persistence of effort!"

He pointed to the bench, which was untidy and disorderly. It hadn't been dusted for some time. It looked as though mice might make their little homes there.

"There's a brain behind all that," said my friend. "It's fine to see the workings of a good brain. Infinite patience is there. The fellow is keen. That's what I like."

We went down other corridors, dark and dim. I felt like a metaphysician who, they say, is like a blind man searching for a black cat in a dark room. A door opened, and we entered another laboratory, where a very young, keen-eyed lad was watching some retorts boiling above Bunsen burners.

He greeted my friend with a cheerful salute. They talked

together in a jargon which was unfamiliar to me, and roared over jokes which had no meaning to me.

"This place is lousy with organics!" said the keen-eyed young man.

That was one of the remarks I remember without comprehending its inner significance.

This student to whom we paid a visit was testing the atomic weight of radioactive lead, and I regretted it. I think he would have been much better employed in doing a crossword puzzle, because as a complete reactionary, as regards scientific progress, at least as far as physics go—and they seem to go very far—I am convinced that we need at least a thousand years to control what knowledge we now have and to prevent it from destroying humanity itself. The machine has become a Frankenstein monster. Science has put powers into the hands of men who are still unable to control their own passions, though they may wield the thunderbolts of Jove. But I disguised this prejudice and did not allow it to stand in the way of admiration for intelligence and the adventure of knowledge. I stood in front of a balance which will weigh even to the millionth part of a gram. Think of the genius which has gone to the making of that machine! The mind from which it came, the fingers which modelled it, reached beyond material things and touched the abstract laws.

"It's a marvel in its way," said my friend.

I took leave of him and left the Royal College of Science and went into the streets of London. A taxi driver was good enough to drive me home, and we had a little conversation while I fumbled for the fare.

"There's a rum lot of folk in this city," he told me, "and we taxi drivers get to know them. Some of them are very absent-minded and will leave almost anything in the cab. There was one gentleman I drove who left his false teeth on the seat. Now would you believe that?"

I could believe anything about London and its inhabitants. I once met an old gentleman who wore over his chest the brass image of a goose wearing a top hat. I once met a Persian prophet in a London drawing room. I travelled on the top of a bus with a Hairy Ainu. One meets every kind of human eccentricity in London. I walked one day into the Holborn Restaurant—a most prosaic place—and encountered a coal-black Negro who led me into a room where many Mohammedans were on their knees, bowing their heads in the direction of Mecca. I was once asked the time by a drunken sailor who had five watches on the fingers of one hand—he had put his fingers through the rings—and an alarm clock in his hand; he had won them in a raffle and then had missed his boat. I was accosted in the Strand by a little man who wore pink plush breeches, a green velvet jacket, and a top hat. He was walking round the world, and for all I know is still walking. As for leaving things behind in taxis, I can say that I have left almost everything behind at one time or another, if it was not attached to my body by chains.

22. *The New Bohemia*

It is a new and strange phenomenon of London life that the mews has—or is it have?—become the dwelling place of advanced thought and often of the Bright Young Things who now, thank God! are not quite so bright as they used to be. Perhaps it would be more true to say that the mews has—or is it have?—become the new Bohemia of that modern intelligence which somehow avoids the old squalor of La Vie de Bohème, provides cocktail parties instead of wine without a label, and attends its revels in two-seater cars and evening dress, if the hour be late. Mimi no longer hangs her petticoat across the window. There are dimity curtains bought at Peter Jones'. In these rooms above a garage someone has been busy with a nice taste for interior decoration, and a little money to spend, although heaven alone knows where it comes from, as the owners of these places are generally unsuccessful novelists, or actors out of a job, or young married couples without visible means of subsistence. Almost every night in London in one mews or another there is a party of this kind, where very odd collections of people, mostly young or youngish, get together for conversational purposes and sit about on cushions which, during the course of the evening, they probably throw at each other.

"It's an odd thing," said my taxi driver, who took me to such a mews for such a party a few months ago, "but these places

which used to be slums are now becoming very fashionable.
I can't understand it myself. Of course, it's all right if you
have to live here, same as me, for instance, but I don't see any
catch in it for young women with bare backs—funny fashion,
ain't it?—and young gents who would look more natural in
Mayfair."

"It's a question of economy," I told him. "It's part of the
social revolution which happened after the war."

"To my mind it's nothing but a craze," he answered, dis-
believing that social revolution. "You can't make me believe
that these people couldn't afford better lodgings. Why, look
at those cars which have just arrived. Very smart, if I know
anything about cars."

Certainly I have met exalted people at some of these mews
affairs. One lady I know, who lived in Apple Street Yard off
Duke Street, St. James's, thought nothing of crowding her rooms
with Russian princesses, very poor, no doubt, English count-
esses, governors and ministers of British Dominions, and incredible numbers of beautiful young women whose position in
life I was never able to establish. But then she was a woman
journalist with many friends in high places and a social pull.

The mews to which I went in a taxi whose driver was contemptuous of this new craze was inhabited by a man whom
I first met in a front-line trench when he was writing a letter
home by permission of the German guns. He was a most un-
suitable size for trenches, being a very tall man, but by some
freak of luck he escaped having a bullet through his head and
lived to become an actor on screen and stage. After a successful
career at Hollywood he was pushed out of the United States,
being outside the quota for three New Zealanders allowed into
that great land of liberty at certain intervals. Lately the English
theatre has been in the doldrums, and my friend had been
resting, as they say, for longish spells, during which he has become an agent for tea—extraordinarily good tea—and—to keep
his hands and heart active—a sculptor, or at least a dabbler in
clay, as he prefers to say. Undoubtedly he has innumerable
friends. They all came to his party, which was more than a
sherry party. It started with a dinner for a select number of
sixteen or so. There were many courses to this dinner, all per-

fectly cooked and served by my host himself, with the assistance of a guest or two.

"Our friend must have come into a fortune," said a lady at table with me. "This dinner must have been cooked by the chef at the Carlton."

That dinner had been cooked by a New Zealander who was also an actor, a tea merchant, a sculptor, and, I forgot to mention, a poet.

We helped or hindered the clearing up after this sumptuous meal. There was a hooting of motor horns in the mews below. The bathroom became heaped up with ladies' cloaks. Most adorable women appeared, clothed in beauty and nice-looking frocks, not obviously home-made. Certain it is that some of them were very costly. Faces which I had seen from afar— sometimes so far as the pit in my younger days—appeared through a haze of cigarette smoke. Surely that was Irene Vanbrugh. Surely that was Maud Allan. A very merry lady sat near to me, and I engaged her in conversation. It was Marie Ney, whom most folk know because of her charm and talent.

She began by being merry, and I liked the laughter in her eyes, but presently she became desperately serious and fired with enthusiasm, and inspired to such eloquence as might have swayed a meeting at the Albert Hall, which takes a bit of doing. Her subject was Equity. I had heard of it but vaguely. Equity, she explained, was an Actors' Trade Union—more or less. It undertook to examine contracts, to deal with managers, and especially with fraudulent managers, to insist upon certain rights for the theatrical profession which would prevent it being swindled or blackmailed or sweated by unscrupulous managements.

"I'm in it up to the eyebrows," said Marie Ney, and she had, I noticed, very nice eyebrows. "I am ready to fight to the death for it."

Her eyes flashed. She was not play-acting. She believed in this Equity business as the safeguard of her profession, so much in need of vigilance against its own weakness on the business side of things.

Foreigners think that the English people are inarticulate. That may be true of some sections of English life. But it was not true of this party in a mews. They talked in groups with great earnestness. Maud Allan told me the story of her life, or part of it. Other people told me the stories of their lives—or what they believed was good to let me know. Everyone here had some claim to achievement, or at least some quest of art or fame or daily bread. They were, like all artists, emotional. They had suffered more, wept more, laughed more than ordinary folk. They are the people I like best in the world, because they have ideas, however foolish, and strive after beauty—though often failing to find it—and have a humorous outlook on life, except when they weep at its tragedy. They were artists in one way or another. One finds them still in this world of hiding places which is called London.

And some of them are very poor and go round to their uncle now and then for instant help in time of trouble, though my taxi driver thinks they are all very prosperous. You never can tell nowadays unless you happen to know.

The sherry party is not only to be found in a mews. It has been adopted in Eaton Place and the higher social reaches, and indeed in the outer suburbs. It's an economical form of entertainment, replacing the formal dinner party, which is costly, inconvenient, and pompous, and limited in scope. At a sherry party all the guests stand, and after it is well started the host can slip away if he likes and go for a walk, as a friend of mine does. Many young people of today, especially in the neighbourhood of Shepherd's Market, go from one sherry party to another, feeding until they are replete on little sandwiches and little sausages. It saves the expense of a meal at a restaurant, and they meet their contemporaries for conversation, which is never dull because, if there is the least chance of that, they can evade the boresome wench or the wearisome lad and flutter off to another group. Someone is sure to say, "Come along to my lair, won't you? I dare say I can rake up a drink or two and something to bite." Someone is sure to be talking somewhere until two o'clock next morning, with a box of cigarettes handy and a cushion for one's head against the wall, or a pouffe one can share with an intelligent young woman, not too repulsive to see if one looks at her. There is a young set and a young crowd who behave that way after working hours, if they work. I have

"The Village Shop".
E. Linder

THE VILLAGE SHOP

a glimpse of it now and then. It exists. But not in large numbers. Not to anything like the extent one would imagine after a course of reading modern novels written by young women in Bloomsbury. They grow out of it. They marry and live at Wimbledon. They are more virtuous than they like us to believe. But I confess that I am only a rare visitor to their haunts.

23. *The Garden Party*

There is an old garden in London surrounded by high walls on which there are chevaux-de-frise with long spikes. Ordinary folk never get a glimpse of its lawns but are aware sometimes, as they hurry along the line of its walls, that it has fine trees in which birds build their nests. If the traffic didn't make such a roar one might hear the song of these birds, and indeed, just after dawn, if ever one takes a walk that way, as some men do because it was a hard bench on which they tried to sleep, one can hear the twitter of birds.

Two or three times each summer the owners of the garden, who have kind hearts, give a party to their friends there, and crowds of Londoners who have not had the luck to get an invitation stand at the gates to see the guests pass into this private paradise in the heart of the town. During the year in which I write these words the garden party—it was given by the King and Queen—was slightly larger than usual, as it was the last social event of the Jubilee. There were twelve thousand guests, among whom I happened to be one, in a top hat, fancy waistcoat (which the Americans call a "bib vest"), and striped trousers.

It is necessary to go correctly garbed to the King's garden party. I remembered that, because a friend of mine, who is now a famous dramatic critic and was then a reporter on a London newspaper, was sent with his editor's ticket to one of these garden parties at Buckingham Palace, and having come to the office in a straw hat, arrived in that headgear on the green lawn just as their majesties were about to come into their garden. He was addressed very politely by one of the King's gentlemen-in-waiting, who whispered to him anxiously:

"I say, old man, would you mind standing behind a tree until the King and Queen have passed by? That hat, you know! It rather spoils the picture, don't you think?"

It was a pleasant picture of London life last time, and foreigners there among the guests must have envied England and marvelled at it. For within these garden walls, and on the lawns behind the King's house, English social life seemed to have been unchanged by world events, including a world war, which have upheaved so many countries and smashed their old traditions by revolution, dictatorships, and economic calamities.

Those people at the gates seemed to have no envy for those who went in. There was no class prejudice in their hearts against the gentlemen in grey toppers and the ladies in their summer frocks, whose motorcars were in solid blocks of shining metal down Eaton Square and half a mile away in all directions converging upon the Palace. The King and Queen were in no need of armed guards among their guests, unlike certain dictators in Europe, who never feel very safe in a crowd.

I went with a lady in a summer frock who was pleased to walk in this garden. One walks below a winding rampart of earth with high bushes as a screen to the great house beyond, and then across rustic bridges which span a lake with weeping willows on the banks and water lilies like stars on its silver mirror reflecting the sky through a tracery of leaves. There are many noble trees here which were young when a young queen ruled England and full grown when King Edward strolled under their shade, smoking an after-dinner cigar. Beyond them the lawns sweep away to the far-off terrace at the back of the Palace, and not a daisy is allowed to show its head on the smooth-shorn grass, which is very soft to the feet and very green to the eyes. The back of the Palace gets the afternoon sun, and all the sun blinds were drawn on the day of this garden party when, as usual, there was royal weather, and a shimmer of heat in the open spaces beyond the shade.

These twelve thousand people who had been honoured by their majesties' invitation belonged to a class which the proprietors of coconut stalls in country fairs advertise as the Nobility and Gentry, and whom vulgar people still call "the Nobs." I scanned their faces as they passed in groups, but saw types rather than individuals. There were immense numbers of middle-aged men wearing immense numbers of grey toppers. At first glance they all looked exactly the same. Most of them had grey moustaches closely clipped, and good, hard, lean English faces, more Norman than Saxon in the cut of their jibs. They all looked like brigadiers or retired colonels. There were immense numbers of elderly women, probably their wives, who talked with that particular intonation—very frank and direct— which one hears in country houses where there are still horses in the stables. There were immense numbers of young women, probably their daughters, who were very tall and very slim and long in the leg, with the stride of golf-playing girls, and— here and there—very beautiful, with the clean, fresh beauty of youth untouched by the paint-pot, as far as I could see. There was no distinctive fashion, I observed. Some of these young women wore little hats perched sideways. Others wore big, spreading hats which flung shadows across their faces, so that one had to peer to see their loveliness, if they were lovely. Some of them were clothed in fine linen, snow white, with bows stuck about them for no apparent purpose. Others were in draggle-tail dresses, flower-coloured, with fluttering sashes. Others again were in frocks like the sheaths of flowers, so tight to their bodies that one wondered—though one ought to check such wondering—how they got in or out.

I noticed that several of the guests arrived in Bath chairs wheeled about by footmen with cockades in their hats, who wilted as the afternoon wore on because of the heat and the burden.

I listened to odd snatcehs of conversation.

"Tell me," said a lady who had taken possession of a chair on the edge of the great lawn—"it is forty years since I've been here—do the King and Queen come this way to their pavilion?"

"You know, my dear," said another lady of elderly years, "this is one of my afternoons off. Endless committees. But I issued an ultimatum and said, 'Ladies, I've been invited to the Royal garden party and I'm going, even if you pass this ridiculous amendment behind my back.' "

"Poof! Isn't it hot?" cried a young and charming-looking

creature in one of those sheathlike frocks. "I'd like to take all my clothes off and dive into the lake."

"Well, for goodness' sake, don't, my dear!" replied her mother anxiously, as though not at all sure that this girl would not yield to her desire for immediate nudity.

"In my opinion," said one of the elderly men in grey toppers, "the Italians won't have a walk through Abyssinia. Mr. Mussolini will come up against a gas bracket—*un bec de gaz*—as the French say. I hear that the Italian troops are already going down with malaria and enteric. General Disease will fight on the side of the Ethiopians."

He was answered by an elderly man who might have been his twin:

"Personally I think we ought to keep neutral in that affair. Italy must expand or burst. And after all, we can't raise our hands in holy horror because they want to get a bit of Africa or carry the blessings of civilization to untutored savages. We did a good deal of that ourselves in the more or less distant past."

"I'm getting wet with perspiration," said a distinguished-looking woman, full blown like a July rose. "If I don't get something cool to drink I shall go off pop. I'm just sizzling, my dear."

One lady in my immediate neighbourhood uttered a remark which I found startling in such a company.

"Well, this kind of thing almost makes me a Socialist!"

"Hush, my darling, for goodness' sake!" said her anxious husband, looking round nervously.

I am still wondering why this garden party should have made that lady inclined towards Socialism. Perhaps it was due to the failure of her husband to get her any refreshment. It was difficult to get refreshment, although there was an immense pavilion with a long buffet laden with cool drinks and ices and raspberries-and-cream and other exquisite things. I noticed that the baser attributes of human nature are apt to be revealed even at a Royal garden party. I was painfully aware of this when I was commanded by my own lady to bring her some elixir. There were three rows of people pressed against the buffet. The first row remained firmly in possession of their advanta-

geous position. They did not retire when they had obtained iced
coffee, cress sandwiches, or raspberries-and-cream. They re-
freshed themselves *in situ*, thus preventing parched souls from
approaching the goblets and the fruits. As Mr. Tennyson once
remarked, "Kind hearts are more than coronets and simple
faith than Norman blood."

It was on the edge of the refreshment pavilion that I met a
melancholy man who, though he had just obtained possession
of a strawberry ice, regarded the splendid scene on the great
lawn—the Queen was moving along a line of guests where all
the ladies curtsied as though blown down by a breeze when she
passed—with gloomy and apprehensive vision.

"In ten years' time," he said, "there will be no more Royal
garden parties at Buckingham Palace."

The lady whom I was attending raised her finger and cried,
"Pessimist!"

"I am," he admitted. "We are, of course, living in a world of
illusion which one day—not far off—will be dispelled by unpleasant realities. All these people think they are safe! They
think this kind of thing is going on! They think England is
getting prosperous again!—while Europe is lurching towards
another war and ultimate ruin."

"I wonder if I could get anything to drink?" said the lady
upon whom I was in attendance. She refused to be frightened.

"Perhaps I ought not to speak like this in such a place,"
said the melancholy man. "Allow me to get you an ice."
He departed on that desperate mission. We did not see him
again.

The Diplomatic Corps were favoured. They had the right of
entry to a private lawn roped off from the others, and next to
the Royal summerhouse where the King and Queen would
take tea after these diplomatic gentlemen with their ladies had
been presented. Argentines, Chileans, Brazilians, Japanese,
Siamese, and Chinese, Finns, Danes, and Swedes, French,
Italians, and Germans, passed between two posts with fluttering
pennons and crossed the private lawn with some self-consciousness, because there were thousands of eyes watching them from
the other side of the ropes. The ladies with them had more
assurance and chatted gaily. A little distance away a lady whom

Romney ought to have lived to paint was giving her hand to ladies who dropped into curtseys before her. By her side was a little princess whose name is Elizabeth and who may bring a new Elizabethan era to this land of England later on.

It was a hot day, but several gentlemen who were among the King's guests were heavily wrapped in blankets and wore heavy cloth headdresses. They were Arab chiefs. Across the lawns moved Indian ladies in flame-coloured silks. And close to me for some time was a little man who interested me a good deal. I wondered why he had been invited to this party. Like the dramatic critic of whom I have told, he wore a straw hat. It was a very shabby old straw hat which looked as though he might have fished it out of the sea while searching for crabs at Margate. He wore a flannel shirt, rather grubby, and a blue serge suit, bagged at the knees.

Among all the top-hatted folk he looked entirely at his ease, without self-consciousness, and presently took out a cigarette from a threepenny packet of Wild Woodbines and smoked it while he waited for the King to enter his pavilion.

He may have been a duke. The late Duke of Norfolk, they say, was very careless of his clothes. But he looked like a down-and-out who would sleep in the Park that night or find a place in St. Martin's Crypt. He might have been a poet, with a soul contemptuous of tailors. I wanted to talk to him, but hadn't the courage without an introduction. I might have been snubbed.

We walked to an entrance by Hyde Park Corner, and I went into the outer world again and took a taxi home. And all the way home I tried to fit this picture of the Royal garden party into its proper framework and to get its essential meaning in English life. Those twelve thousand people looked happy and prosperous. No shadow of anxiety seemed to fall across this scene, although in Europe trouble was stirring and dangerous forces were moving. That night in my country cottage I heard the drone of aëroplanes. They were making a sham attack upon London, testing its power of aërial defence. They broke through, I believe. There is no defence of London from the air, I am told. But twelve thousand people in the gardens of Buckingham Palace were not worrying, it seemed. It is the English way not to worry in advance.

They were a good crowd. Among them were the men and women who serve on all the committees which carry on the machinery of our social and administrative life. In one way and another they were all public servants devoted to their ideal of duty and service, without any ulterior motive of gain or honour. One wouldn't suspect them of graft or dishonesty. In private life these elderly men who put on grey top hats for an affair like this would be simple-minded, upright men, with a rigid code of honour and an unconscious code of manners which would be a second nature to them. Most of them would like horses and dogs and birds and flowers. At luncheon time they would go to their clubs in St. James's Street and Pall Mall.

I know their type. I have listened to their talk. I know the right answers. I know what silences are necessary. They are the English gentry, and though a caricaturist could be cruel to them, and foreigners find them unintelligent, England is in their debt for many qualities of character and for ungrudging service within the limits of their imagination and sense of order. If their type is passing, if one day it disappears, if their grey top hats are put into the dustbin with their code, we shall no longer be England, for with them will pass an old tradition of integrity, and a code of good form which they learnt at Eton and Harrow, Winchester and Westminster. It will be another kind of England, perhaps better, but also, perhaps, worse.

24. *The Man Who Sells the News*

The man from whom I buy my evening papers stared towards the sun at the other end of the King's Road Chelsea. The traffic was surging round Sloane Square, and City workers were pouring out of the Underground. Hundreds of little shopgirls were boarding the buses after their day's toil and going home to Putney, Barnes, and other places where they would wash their pretty faces, powder their pretty noses, and prepare for an evening's pleasure at the local cinema or dance hall; unless, for once, they would stay with poor old Pa and listen to the wireless, or read the end of a novel from a tuppenny library. An elegant young creature in an evening cloak over a draggle-tail dress hailed a taxi and departed for the Berkeley restaurant where doubtless a nice young man was waiting for her.

"Life," said the man from whom I buy my papers, "is full of inequalities."

"Perhaps that's what makes it so amusing," I suggested.

He withdrew his gaze from the sun at the other end of the King's Road Chelsea and looked at me sternly with his very blue eyes, which once had scanned the far horizon from the deck of a ship.

"It's not amusing for a man on thirty bob a week with a wife and kids and a high rent to pay," he told me reprovingly.

"That's true," I agreed. "But most of them get more than thirty bob a week. Three pounds ten a week is more likely, if they have a decent job."

"Ah, but there's many what haven't! They're on the dole, or poor relief, and no fault of theirs. Now, what gets my goat is the fact that dishonesty pays in England."

"I can't believe it," I said.

"It's a fact."

He paused a moment or two to sell an *Evening Standard* to an attractive young woman who slowed down her car at the curb-stone and held out a penny to him and called out, "Paper, please!" A young policeman also bought a pennyworth of news in the *Star*.

"Now take these professional beggars," said the newspaper seller. "They play on people's emotions and make a good thing of it. There's a nasty bit of work calling himself an ex-officer and earning ten quid a week by selling matches with a whine. The other day he put half a quid on a horse. It's not right. You can't make me believe it's right."

"It seems too easy," I answered.

He called it by a harder name.

"Then there's the police," he announced.

"What's the matter with them?"

"Favoured," said my blue-eyed friend. "Pampered at the expense of other men who can't get jobs. They get pensions, don't they, after short service? Then why should they get first call as commissionaires, outside hotels and restaurants? Why not give a chance to the unemployed and ex-service men? It's not fair. But there's a worse evil. In my opinion it's a crying scandal."

"Tell me," I said, having a respect for this man's knowledge of life in London and for his sincerity.

He sold the *Evening News* to an elderly lady from the Christian Science church at the back of the telephone exchange. He also sold the *Star* to a young man who stopped to read it.

"Women in men's jobs," said my friend darkly. "It's not right, you know."

"Well——" I said cautiously.

"No, it's not right!" he argued. "I know a woman who earns three quid a week in a factory while her husband earns seven quid a week and owns six houses. Is that right? No! In my judgment, she ought to step off her job and leave it vacant for some unemployed man eating his heart out because he can't get work. Take all these girls scrambling for the buses. I've nothing against 'em. They're pretty little pussies. But what I hold is that they shouldn't keep men out of work while they earn pocket money for going to the pictures. Mind you, I'm not talking with any personal grudge. This job isn't too bad. But I think something ought to be done about the inequalities. Things ought to be sorted out. I'm not a Bolshevik. Far from it! But things seem disorderly. Some have too much, and some have nothing. It's the system. Or, as you might say, it's a lack of system. I was reading in the *Daily Herald* yesterday——"

He was interrupted by a heavy pressure of customers at his paper stall. I touched my hat to him and went further up the King's Road to buy some cigarette holders at Woolworth's. One doesn't mind losing them. They look as good as real amber and cost less. "I see you buy them there, too," said a distinguished admiral across a dinner table one evening as he pulled out one of these Woolworth holders in high company. He winked at me.

At Woolworth's I had a chat with the girl behind the counter. Business was slack just before closing time.

A gramophone was playing a Negro coon song.

"You'd be surprised at the people who come here," she told me. "Duchesses, some of them, I wouldn't be surprised. They buy cocktail glasses and every old thing. Of course, we get others! Most of our customers are mothers with squalling babes, and people who have to count their pennies. This is an all-sorts shop. Rich and poor and the in-betweens. Oh, one sees a lot of life in Woolworth's!"

A young man approached one of the counters. He wore an old jacket and grey flannel trousers and looked as if he had slept in them. His hair was somewhat in need of attention, but he had a look of intellectuality and was undoubtedly a highbrow. Probably he was a novelist.

He had some difficulty in producing a penny for which he searched in one of his trouser pockets.

"Holy smoke!" he exclaimed. "I believe I'm undone—with a hole in my pocket!"

That remark was addressed to a Woolworth girl, who found it amusing.

"Have another look," she advised. "You might find it inside your sock."

He groped despairingly in his pocket and produced the penny.

"A razor blade," he said haughtily.

I always pay threepence for a razor blade at Woolworth's, and buy four of them at a time. But then I'm lucky.

Perhaps this young man's novels—if he is a novelist—have not yet found a publisher to risk his money on them. There are lots of young men like that in bed-sitting rooms this side or that of the King's Road Chelsea. Now and again one of them puts a shilling in the slot machine and turns on the gas in a room where he has pasted up the cracks. At least, I know of one to whom a doctor friend of mine was summoned in the nick of time.

25. Charterhouse

I went to see an old colleague of mine who is now a Poor Brother of the Charterhouse. We used to be together on a paper called the *Tribune*, which was too good to live and died one day in Bouverie Street when the lights went out and the machines stopped printing and eight hundred men or so found themselves on the street which is a tributary of Fleet Street, where the road is very rough for out-of-work journalists.

Charterhouse is round the corner from Smithfield, where tourneys used to be held—it was called the Smoothfield then— by knights who rode down Giltspur Street. After that its green place was used for burning and killing martyrs of faith, witches and unfortunate wretches seized by the officers of law for all villainies. Now, as all the world knows, it is the central meat market of London.

It is not an attractive place. The smell of raw meat is not fragrant, especially to nostrils which like the scent of new-cut hay and honeysuckle. The meat salesmen and porters are big brawny men who look as though they ate a lot of their own beef. On the outskirts of the market are small shops with a dilapidated look. But the contrast is great when one steps through the archway of Charterhouse.

A few yards away there is the peace of old grey walls and pleasant lawns. Not a sound of the London traffic comes inside. It is a cloistered place where in the old days monks said their prayers and read their missals and studied the Fathers of learning, until one day they were sent to the rack and gibbet by a bearded, pot-bellied man who wanted to divorce his wife against the laws of Holy Mother Church, of whose laws he was impatient.

It was a man named Thomas Sutton—a great merchant— who made use of these buildings for founding a school where Elizabethan boys might learn their horn books and other knowledge fitting them to be good citizens of decent piety. Where monks had prayed youth scrimmaged, shouted, fought, and played. They drank beer for breakfast. They were flogged for false quantities in Latin or for misspellings in English. On their hard benches they sat and shivered during London winters, and blew on their frozen fingers, and kicked each other under the desks, and tortured the smaller boys. It was the beginning of Charterhouse School in which Steele and Addison were scholars, and other famous men who somehow survived the rigours of English school life in the eighteenth century. The racket they made must have been trying at times to many old gentlemen who had house room not far from their playground.

They were the Poor Brothers, who found a sanctuary here after the adventure of life when all passion is spent. They were professional men of the army, the law, and government service. It was, and is, an alms house for poor gentlemen. Most famous of them all is an imaginary character drawn with love and admiration and tenderness by a writer who was supposed to be a cynic because in Victorian days he told a little truth about well-to-do folk who did not like to have their frailties exposed. Thackeray's Colonel Newcome lives as the portrait of a Poor Brother of the Charterhouse for all time.

It was many years since I had been here. I was a boy then and went with my father, who loved to poke around the old places in London. Now I had a touch of grey at my temples and the lines of life which Time marks upon the human face with an ineffaceable imprint. It was in 1906 that I had been a colleague of the man I came to see. Good Lord! Had all those years slipped by?

We did not recognize each other for a second when I stood outside his room down one of the corridors of Charterhouse. He was dressed to go out to dinner, and his door was open when I spoke his name. I looked at this man inside the room and saw that he had changed. Those crows' feet had marked him as old. He had been a sturdy, upstanding, cheery man, with a ruddy face and the manner of a naval officer. Now he looked pale and worn and, I thought, a little frail.

"Hullo," I said. "Glad to see you again, old man."

He stared at me and then held out his hand with an exclamation of astonishment.

"Good heavens!" he said, and left it at that. Twenty-nine years was a long bridge to cross backwards to the days of our friendship before a world war and other episodes of history.

And yet in another moment we were talking as though we had met only yesterday. I sat in his armchair while he finished dressing. We talked of old friends. He threw some papers onto my knee and said, "Have a look at those."

They were chapters neatly typed about the history of dead newspapers. I turned to one which dealt with the *Tribune*. I had written a novel about that. It was called *The Street of Adventure*.

"I'm going out to dinner," he told me, "but I should like to show you round a bit. It's worth seeing. A place of old ghosts."

Yes, it was worth seeing, and I felt the presence of the ghosts. He showed me the Master's House, and the Preacher's House, and took me up an old staircase worn by the footsteps of past ages, and into the chapel where the Brothers say their prayers. He showed me the room where Thackeray visited his friend who sat for the portrait of Colonel Newcome. He nudged me as some of the Brothers passed.

"That man is a C.B. That fellow had a distinguished career. . . . There goes an old lawyer."

"Come up and talk to the Preacher," he said presently. "He's a genial man and has a charming wife."

We went upstairs and knocked at a door. The Preacher and his wife welcomed us, and we talked awhile of Charterhouse and its history. The present Brothers carry on the ancient game of bowls and had challenged the Royal Household. The Preacher laughed when I asked if he had a good team.

"Not brilliant. They're all crocks with one foot in the grave."

That seemed to me a trifle too candid, but it did not seem to hurt the feelings of my old colleague. It was the Preacher's sense of humour, bluff and hearty.

I looked out of the window to the playing field where the old Carthusians had kicked many a football to rags. They had all gone now and there is no shouting of boys to disturb the peace.

Before leaving I stood awhile in the courtyard. I was on historic ground. These old walls about me were immensely old. They had stood when the bells of London rang for Plantagenet victories and for Tudor enthronements. They had heard the tolling of bells for men who were to die on the scaffold. They were built long before the Great Plague, when there were cries of "Bring out your dead!" They had glowed to the bonfires in Smithfield when men were living torches. Queen Elizabeth had passed this way. The Stuart kings had come here. It is still a very quiet sanctuary in the turmoil of London's heart.

26. The Talk of the Town

In London I live in a little house in a little street which has one inestimable advantage. No one can find it easily even if he has the right address. No taxi driver, outside a very small group who know it as the secret hiding place of a lady for whom they have respect occasionally lapsing into roars of laughter—she is very humorous with them—is familiar with the name of that street, although it is within a minute of Sloane Square.

The little house itself was once, I am told, a farmhouse. It was on the Duke of Westminster's estate when there were market gardens in Eaton Square and Belgravia. Afterwards it became a greengrocer's shop. More than two hundred years old, it was once, I imagine, a haunt of villainous-looking highwaymen who held up coaches from Putney Heath before going their way to Tyburn, but that, I must admit, is pure fancy. Anyhow, it now has a painted sign over the front door with the name "Little House" on each side of the panel, and a picture of an English village with smiling meadows in the best style of my friend Stephen Reid, though there isn't a meadow for miles now that London has reached out far, and it's hard to say where the pavement ends. Inside there are low ceilings and long beams, just as it was when my imaginary highwayman sat there and unloaded his pockets of the rings which he had plucked most brutally from the taper fingers of an (imaginary) lady. But behind the beams are cunning lights, and from top to bottom there are ingenious devices of lighting and heating which make this cottage habitable by modernists.

During my possession of it many remarkable conversations have created new vibrations in its old beams. Certain friends of mine have the clue to its whereabouts and come to discuss life, art, and world politics until late hours. One man finds his way to my front door when most honest folk are abed. He paces stealthily across a grating which gives air and, on lucky days, a gleam of light to a basement room. If there is a light burning behind the window blinds of my sitting room he knows that, in all likelihood, there is still a chance of expressing the pent-up passions which surge in his soul after another day of intellectual adventure. I hear his quiet tap on the door. There is no servant awake. I open the door and find him standing back in the blackness of night but with his eyes shining like a cat's.

"You!" I exclaim, pretending to be surprised.

"God!" he said, "I'm in despair. I feel extremely unwell.

The fact is, I can't see any escape from the downfall of civilization. This country is on its way to ruin. And I haven't written a word for weeks. I haven't an idea in my head. I'm finished!"

"Come in," I say quietly, reminding him that it is less than a week since he confided that he had just finished sixty thousand words of a new novel.

He comes in, sinks into a leather chair which is so long in the seat that one could go to bed in it, and gazes in the utmost melancholy at a beam with a crossbar like a gallows.

"My dear lad," he says, "you and your fellow pacifists are the greatest danger to this country. You've led us into a position which makes us the laughing stock of men like Hitler and Mussolini. We can't enforce any decision. We have no strength in the air or on the sea. Our army is negligible. I'm seriously thinking of becoming a British Fascist. We need a leader."

He is a man of many moods. A successful novelist, he falls into extremities of despair between one book and another because he believes that he will never find another plot. A poet who writes good verse easily, he is very knowledgeable on subjects of finance and economics, and reveals to me with a thousand unanswerable facts that this country is on the edge of ruin or—next week—beating the whole world in its revival of prosperity. He works himself up into a passion of indignation against the politicians, the churches, literary critics, literary agents, and any other group of mortals who happen to have aroused his ire during the past twenty-four hours. He attacks my ideas on almost everything with a violence, an irony, and a humour which I find extremely entertaining. He finds out the weak places in my intellectual armour which, I confess, is as full of holes as a sieve, and drives his rapier through with unerring touch.

He has an astonishing gift of words and rare quality in debate, and sometimes I am almost convinced that there is something in his arguments, even though I know that a few nights later he will take the opposite side with an equal passion of sincerity.

Other men drift in for conversational exercise, so that sometimes the rafters fairly quiver with a clash of ideas and emotions, for some of these friends of mine dramatize themselves and life and are highly temperamental, so that they express themselves with great violence about art, philosophy, and morals. Any stranger coming into the room would imagine that this company was having a first-class row likely to end in bloodshed. But it is only a friendly and vivacious argument about public schools, or the sculpture of Epstein, or the causes of war, or the relations between the sexes.

Strangers come and send in their names, which I don't often know. Often they come to borrow money which I can't afford to lend. One young gentleman—he was black—sat down in an armchair and with a kindly smile said, "Sir Philip, I know how much you are interested in modern youth, and I am sure therefore that I shall make you very happy when I ask you to lend me two hundred pounds." I made him very unhappy by refusing to lend him two hundred pence. Russian refugees desire my help. German victims of Nazi oppression come to tell me of their sufferings. One young German from the Saar who was a Catholic and much distressed by the New Paganism, told me that the German mind was a dark labyrinth which led to a cotton-wool world of illogical thought and Wagnerian nonsense. That, from a German, seemed to me the hardest thing I have heard against German mentality.

Into my rooms sometimes come people of many nationalities, and men and women who have been great travellers about the world and discuss its problems—they are nearly all tragic nowadays—with first-hand knowledge. Americans come to tell me about the New Deal. A lady from Ceylon, dressed in native costume and looking beautiful, told me more than one can get out of books about that island and its people. But I am guarded, because of the strangers who come to borrow money or sell vacuum cleaners or waste my time—not of much value—by odd and sometimes mad requests. Occasionally awkward incidents happen at my front door, owing to the difficulty of detecting the difference between honest men and rogues or sane men and madmen.

One was when my wife happened to open the door and saw a shabby-looking man in a raincoat standing outside. He inquired for me rather nervously. He had all the appearance of being a professional beggar.

It was unfortunate that he turned out to be a man of very

BILDEN'S FARM, SURREY

great importance who wished for a little advice on a literary matter outside his range of experience.

"I'm afraid he's not at home," said my wife. "What name shall I give?"

When he gave his name it was rather startling. He was one of the great folk who live in the mansions within a stone's throw of my cottage.

Youth honours me now and then by a visit and talks freely. The samples of the younger generation who find their way to my sofa and chairs are, I find, extremely intelligent, charming in their manners, and very well informed. Some of them do not disguise their belief that our present system of civilization is rotten and likely to smash up in general conflict and ruin.

That is the impression I get from a young woman of considerable beauty with pink fingernails. She was brought up in Egypt. She has lived much on the Riviera. She has a father who is a student of international politics. She is vivacious, gay, and highly amusing. But when she talks about world politics and problems she alarms me because she is very ruthless and realistic in stripping our present conditions of life from all camouflage. To her life is still a jungle. She has no faith whatever in the League of Nations or any pacts and pledges. She is certain that there is going to be another world war. She has no illusions about the passions of nations or individuals. She makes pretty little gestures with her pink-nailed fingers and prophesies the doom of the white races. On moral questions she is equally realistic and ruthless. Once she advocated the sterilization of the unfit with a candour which alarmed Mr. Oliver Baldwin, who happened to be present—and he is not easily alarmed by free speech.

They are very remarkable, some of these young people of today. A brother and sister sat on my sofa one evening. The young man is at Oxford. He is one of the leaders of the Pacifist movement there. His sister speaks German and French and has wandered about Europe on tramping holidays. I thought I knew a few things about European conditions and the conflicting ideas of nations. But these two young people, very grave, very simple, perfectly unaffected, knew far more than I did and

said things worth hearing. They had talked with the ordinary
folk in Germany and Austria. They were in touch with the
younger intellectuals in England. They were talking the
thoughts that are moving in the minds of the younger people
in London and Oxford, and in youth hostels and Bloomsbury
debating clubs. I listened attentively to the voice of young
England, or at least that section of it which has become strongly
pacifist, and refuses to be juggled into another war, and looks
forward to a comradeship across the frontiers with an idealism
which has courage as well as faith. I did not try to disillusion
these Babes in the Wood or warn them about the Big Bad Wolf.

From the little house I go walking into the heart and soul of
London.

"You're a great rambler," says my road sweeper. "I never
knew a man who was more fond of a ramble."

I ramble at a quick pace, and friends of mine tell me that
I pass them like a flash of lightning or a haunted man. That is
because I walk for exercise, having no other chance in London.
But I like to drop into an A.B.C. or a Lyons café and smoke a
cigarette over a cup of coffee and watch life at the other tables.
I like to see the young men who play dominoes at lunch time.
I used to do that myself once. I like to listen to the chitchat of
the waitresses during a few moments' lull.

I like to study the faces in these places. These are the true
Londoners, types of the massed population of the monstrous city.
They are the wage earners on moderate means—just enough for
respectability with a little margin for the cinemas now and then,
for a fortnightly holiday at the seaside, and for shopping expeditions in Sales Week. Foreigners think we are a happy people,
and on the whole I think we are happier than we believe ourselves to be. But in London I notice there is an anxious look in
many eyes, a strained look on many faces, as though there were
a wear and tear at the nerves. There is not much serenity in
the expression of the people who pour into tube trains and
make an endless line on the moving stairs. The economic struggle is fairly hard in these people's homes. There is insecurity of
tenure in the work that many do. They take patent medicines
too much. They economize over their lunches. They are worried
by many trivial and nagging cares: the burden of a house on

the hire system, the difficulty of bringing up a family, the alarming prospect of another baby coming.

The rhythm of London life is restless. The traffic dodging is an unconscious strain. Noise is another strain on the nervous system. There is a battle to be fought during the rush hour, especially by shopgirls and City girls waiting for a bus in the rain with fifty people ahead of them round the lamppost where the bus stops.

And in these people's minds are unsatisfied desires, emotional suppressions, revolt against resignation, boredoms, and bewilderments. Some of them hate the drudgery of their lives from which there is no escape. Some of them drug themselves in the dream world of the picture palace and come out again to find life disgusting. The newspapers are drugs as well as stimulants. Their million readers get mentally excited about a brutal murder or a sensational trial. All the tragedies and crimes of the world are reported for their home-going reading. They get worked up about cricket and tennis games and feel depressed if England does badly, though it doesn't matter a row of beans to them—or to England.

In the mass, Londoners are worn-looking, and beauty is rare among them except where the shopgirls and City girls come streaming to their work. But now and then, in an A.B.C. or a tube train, one sees lovely faces, both young and old, and one's eyes are arrested by some face in which there is nobility, a spiritual light, or the look that comes to men and women who have suffered much and have not been beaten.

Often I am struck by the faces of labourers who come into the Underground trains after their day's work on some new building or road mending. They are dog-tired. The skin on their faces and hands is like the clay on their clothes. They lean up against each other, and now and then one of them drops off asleep against his mate's shoulder. They have splendid faces, many of these men. All the strains of English blood are in them: Celtic, Saxon, Norman, Roman. I have seen young men in corduroys who would serve as models for Arthur's knights. Some of the older men step out of Plantagenet England. It was men like these who fought at Agincourt. They are very civil to each other. "Here you are, mate," says a man to one of his friends fumbling for a match to light a fag. They are good, honest, kindly fellows, though sweaty in their clothes and smelling of London clay. I get into talk with them now and then by the way of a cigarette, and I have a great admiration for their courage, their simplicity, their decency.

It has been my luck to open many doors in London life since I was a boy in the Street of Adventure. There is always some new character worth meeting. In every room there is a different drama or a different dream. In the monstrous city which we call London, though it is a hundred cities, all the problems of modern life, all its hopes and despairs and fears and weaknesses and valours, have their dwelling place. There is enough tragedy here to make God weep if He sees it all with pity. There is enough comedy here to make God laugh, if He laughs. There is enough courage, patience, endeavour, and intelligence, to make a good world. It is London, but it is also England, and in mean houses or mansions, in slum streets or broad highways, the old traditional character of the English as Shakespeare saw it, and as Chaucer first recorded it, remains, I think, strangely unaltered by all this modern stuff of jazz, and motor traffic, and flashing lights, and cinema morality. It surges up irresistibly in times of crisis or of pageantry.

IV

Beyond the Town

1. Rural England

THERE is still a rural England where men and women live simple lives close to the earth in old houses and cottages unchanged, or hardly changed, since their forefathers built them in Tudor times, with thatched roofs, or tiles, and low beams and sunken floors. It is astonishing, really, how beyond the reach of the cities so much of this rural England remains untouched, outwardly, by the horrible paws of the beast who delights in the destruction of beauty and calls it Progress, gloating when a cinema in cement replaces a row of timbered houses, or when a new estate with raw red roofs invades a woodland where nightingales used to sing, or when a Woolworth's store is painted red in the middle of an ancient High Street.

Londoners are apt to exaggerate the extent and rapidity of the jerry builder's abominable advance and the despoiling of the English countryside. It has done dreadful work for thirty miles from Charing Cross. The ribbon development follows the new roads with an endless line of little houses, new shops, factories, petrol pumps, and picture palaces, where even ten years ago there were quiet fields and noble trees, and old farmsteads with great barns, and footpaths wandering through meadows and glades. The midland and the northern towns have done the same misdeeds in a disorderly and disgraceful way, which a little planning and a little reverence could have avoided.

One can't put beauty back when once it has been blotted out.

One can't—I admit—put back the clock or stop the motor traffic which surges along the by-passes and the country lanes. One can't abandon the industrialization of England or check the breaking up of old estates belonging to a system which is out of date. One can't deny a site for new factories, needed for the employment of men who otherwise would be wageless and workless. Life must go on and adapt itself to new conditions, whatever the cost in ancient grace. The modernization of English life and its mechanization go on apace, and the tempo of its change is increasing in speed. The railway train created a social revolution in England but left great tracts of country still remote from its lines. The motorcar—unrestricted in its journeyings even in the narrowest country lane—has done far more to break down the isolation and loneliness of rural England. It has invaded the minds of the rustics as well as their villages. Presently the air age will alter the time-table of daily life and annihilate distances and change the outward look of things even more than any previous change. It will give new angles of vision to the human mind, and create new styles of architecture, if it avoids a war in the air and leaves any buildings standing.

Not long ago I stood by the side of an old gentleman who belonged to one of the great families of England. He and his crowd had ruled the land for several centuries as great lords and landowners. Now he lived in a little old manor house, though still the owner of four castles which had fallen into ruin. He gazed over a stretch of country which had once been in the possession of his family, and turned to me suddenly and spoke in a distressed voice:

"I tremble to think what will happen to this countryside in three hundred years from now."

His wife was standing by his side, and I heard her laugh.

"My dear Henry," she cried. "Three hundred years? I tremble to think what will happen to it in three years! Already I see the sinister figure of the jerry builder advancing upon it. You and I, my dear, may live to see the week's washing over the garden fences of a new estate."

"Horrible!" cried the old gentleman with a shudder as he gazed over an open heath crossed by the Pilgrims' Way.

I once built a little paradise of my own. It was after the World War, when one needed such a place. It was very good. We had a garden of some acres, in which flowers grew. Beyond the garden gate were clumps of noble trees, and fields in which the grass grew tall. Near us was a wood of beeches whose tall columns rose like the pillars of a cathedral. Up the lane foxglove climbed the high banks and there were patches of loosestrife giving rich colour. It was very quiet there, though close to the ancient town of Dorking, which lay below us. At night there was no sound but the hooting of a white owl. I adopted the philosophy of Voltaire to the extent of cultivating my own garden. I had a log hut with a thatched roof. Rambler roses climbed up it, and outside there was a good show of snapdragons and stocks and other sweet-smelling blooms. Here was peace.

But one day I saw a city-looking man with an assistant who carried a winding tape. They measured out certain spaces beyond the garden, and I was afraid. They came on other days and made white rings round the tallest and noblest trees.

I spoke to the city-looking man and asked what he was doing. He was frank and cheerful about his plans. He was, in fact, planning a New Estate. There was room for many little houses. They would be built, he said, in the best style. A good many sites had already been bought. New roads would be made. The Estate would have all the conveniences of gas and electricity.

"What about these trees?" I asked desperately. "Must they come down?" I put my hand on the tall trunk of a noble beech.

"Well, we shall have to do a bit of clearing," said the cheerful estate agent. "But it will all be done in the best taste."

We heard the swing of axes and the crash of trees before we fled. The birds fled. Beauty fled. There is now a New Estate where I had built my private paradise. I had to go further afield to find another. Once again I'm getting afraid. There are boards up along the country lanes: "Finely wooded plots for sale."

But there are still green fields and open heaths, and some of them are being safeguarded by societies for the preservation of English beauty. England, as a whole—beyond the cities and the new estates and the new by-passes which cut great gashes through the countryside for the sake of racing motorists and

baby-killers—is amazingly old-fashioned. The cathedral towns
—Canterbury, Winchester, York, Durham, Lincoln, and others
—have not lost their ancient peace, or not much of it. Life goes
on there outwardly, and even in the minds of their inhabitants,
much as it did before a world war or the first aëroplane. The
canons and the minor canons live in the same old houses, and
old ghosts speak to them. Their peaches ripen on the same old
walls. In their libraries are the same old books—Horace's Odes,
the letters of Pliny, Homer, Shakespeare, Dryden, Fielding,
Smollett, Jane Austen, and other works which were read by their
eighteenth-century predecessors.

In their walled gardens are the flowers which Shakespeare
knew; and in these cathedral towns the lady wives of the clergy
have hardly altered their habits or their minds since Anthony
Trollope made use of them for his portrait gallery.

The English counties have retained much of their ancient
character, the villages their old remoteness from modernity,
when one gets beyond the track of industrialism and the trail
of the crowds. Not long ago I explored some parts of rural
England again, apprehensive of what I should find in Norfolk
and Suffolk and Lincolnshire, or in Oxfordshire, Wiltshire, and
the west. I found the manor houses, farmsteads, and thatched
cottages which the soul of England once inhabited. The farms
were still being tilled by men whose names went back far in
English history attached to these fields. They lived under the
same roofs which had kept out the rain and wind when their
forefathers were yeomen in Tudor England. The bells were still
ringing from churches with Norman towers and Early English
transepts. In thousands of English villages there is no house
more modern than the Georgian style, and those are rare among
the old post-and-plaster houses of Elizabeth's days, or among
grey stone fronts which faced them when the Merry Monarch
came back to his own. In Somerset and Dorset the tall towers
of Langport, Bridport, and Huish still rise above small towns
where life is not very fast or very noisy. The ploughs still follow
the old lines of the furrows down in Devon. From Land's End
to Berwick one touches stones which vibrate with the memories
of England when the pace of a horse was the limit of speed. In
Norfolk and other good counties there are market towns where

the farmers gather to sell their stock or their grain at prices which fill them with rage and despair, and they are the same kind of men as their forebears three centuries ago, who came to the same old inns, with the same old grudge against politicians and the price of oats.

How old, how very old, is still the structure of rural England! It does not change its garment of stone and timber and thatch and tile, except by patching here and there. The gabled fronts still lean over the streets of Exeter as when Drake and Raleigh walked beneath them, and in the High Streets of innumerable little towns, through which knights and gentlemen of England went riding from castles on their outskirts, now in ruin. In many of these towns the grammar school has the same walls as when the sixth Edward established it. One passes under gateways which were chiselled by men who came over with the Normans and could speak no English. One walks into cloisters where monks with bare feet paced silently along these stones and sat over manuscripts and missals against these pillars which one's living hand touches for a moment. It is an old shell, this England, if one gets beyond the reach of the jerry builder. We live in old clothes and hate to change them.

And, as it must be admitted by any traveller in England beyond the by-pass or the seaside resort, we live in a lovely and pleasant land. Nature builds more grandly in other countries. She has not given us her most spectacular splendour, nor any touch of terror in sublimity. But England is incomparable in sweetness and graciousness. It has a good variety of heathlands and woodlands and parklands and downlands. One can still find loneliness, and walk holding one's breath at the silence where prehistoric man searched for his flints. One can still wander through many woods where Titania might lie undisturbed. The English lane, deep cut, with overhanging trees showing their gnarled roots, is not to be found in other lands. Somewhere it leads to a village embowered in flowers, because every cottager loves his garden. One does not find such flowers outside the cottages in France or Germany or Italy. We love close-cut lawns like velvet carpets sloping down to a river bank. We can find them still. The English garden of the well-to-do is not so formal as the French nor so stately as the Italian. But the best garden in England is the best in the world, with its terraced lawns, noble trees, clipped hedges, and glory of colour in its flower beds.

England is still beautiful, and one's heart bleeds when the tape of the estate agent stretches out to spoil its loveliness for a factory or a New Estate.

2. A Country Cottage

In that part of the country where I have a cottage there are many old farmhouses with tiled roofs weathered for three centuries and more, and with tall chimney stacks, and old beams, and low ceilings, which belonged to yeoman farmers in Tudor times. Some of them were there before Elizabeth ruled England, and some of them were manor houses as well as farmsteads which belonged to the rustic gentry of their time. Now they have been "modernized" with all conveniences in the way of plumbing and lighting and heating, and they are inhabited not by rustics but mostly by retired business men, or men still active in the pursuit of wealth, who use these places for week-end sanctuaries. The farmers, if they still remain to plough the fields or pasture cattle, have sold their old houses and built new ones more to their taste with higher ceilings—they hate those old beams—and fewer draughts and less beauty.

My own cottage was once a little farmstead. There were manure heaps in the front yard where there are now flower beds, and cows were milked in the sheds which are now used for keeping gardener's tools and storing apples and writing books like this. I have made a very good study of the main cow shed by boarding over its floor and laying down a carpet and putting boards between its roof timbers. Its family name is "the cow study," and when I am in search of inspiration— which never comes—I lean over the lower half of a green door, sucking a metaphorical straw and looking like a cowherd. The walls of this sanctuary are hung with pictures and prints, some of my own handiwork when, like Mr. Winston Churchill and other writers, I suddenly was taken with a passion for oil colour and tried to put a little beauty onto canvas, with infinite satisfaction to myself and the smiling pity of my family, deepening to alarm when I began to neglect all other work for this passionate pursuit of light and shade.

Friends who seek me out in this rural retreat stand and laugh when they come into the front yard and have their first glimpse of my little house. It is like a coloured drawing by Kate Greenaway. Its beams are all crooked, and there is not a straight line to any window sill. Those timbers are as rough shaped as when they were first axed for the framework of this dwelling house before the Armada had been fought. Inside it is amusing and pleasant, except for tall people who crash their heads against the low beams, especially when they go up a narrow stairway with a death trap at the top.

There are some noble beams in the chief sitting room, which was once called a parlour, and from these in olden days bacon hung in the smoke of a chimney which went on smoking after my ownership until desperate measures were taken.

From the back of the house there is a view as far as the eye can reach across the wooded country to the Sussex downs. Dim in the distance, the clear eye may see Chanctonbury Ring, where fairies used to play until the trippers scared them right away and left litter under its gnarled old trees. There is now a rose garden where once the cattle fed, and flower beds where thistles grew. It is a countryside as good as any in England, though the menace of the jerry builder draws near. Not far away westward is a line of hills which are the happy hunting grounds of hikers, though on a weekday they are very lonely, with a quietude which is enchanting when one finds it, because it is a rare thing.

The woods below my fields are the home of the cuckoo when spring comes, and in the centre of them is an old house whose tall chimneys are hidden by the surrounding trees. The glades about it are wonderfully carpeted by bluebells and primroses when the cuckoo comes. I have never seen elsewhere, except perhaps in Devonshire, such clumps of primroses as along these woodland tracks. It is as though the pale sunlight of English spring had made these flower patterns even in the shade of the trees.

Over my hedge on summer evenings the sunset flames in

glory, sometimes with long rose-tipped feathers above pools of gold and emerald lakes. The hedge grows black, and an old apple tree, which would fill the heart of a Japanese artist with ecstasy because of its decorative shape, is etched sharply against the sky. The grass darkens. The first stars break through the pale curtain of the sky. A new moon rises like a sickle, and a friend who comes into this garden very often bows to it three times and turns his money. The colour fades out of the flowers, and they look like little ghosts of themselves. When the dew falls they give out their scent more richly, the scent of a thousand roses and of old-fashioned herbs.

My cottage is like a stage set for a rustic play. It looks good when the lights are lit inside while the curtains are still undrawn. A lady in the parlour is bending over a bit of tapestry. The brass gleams like precious metal. The mirrors are like the one in which the Lady of Shalott saw life pass by.

Several villagers seem to have been born or bred in this small house, which was the subsidiary building of a larger farmstead deeper sunk in the fields below my bit of English earth. Aged men approach me and say, "I was born at Bilden's," or, "I well remember as a lad sitting at table there eating bread and bacon after a hard day's work. It wasn't much of a place then. The front yard was ankle deep in muck. It was a boggy old place, as I remember, and the chimney smoked enough to make one's eyes smart."

In the Georgian days, as one of them told me, it was used by smugglers for storing casks brought up from the coast on the way to London, but that may be a fairy tale. What is true in history is that Romans passed this way before the Saxon gave a name to the village, and before the Normans built the village church which still stands with their handicraft. Below my fields there is the track of the road they made striking straight up to Winterfold on the hills above. It is marked on the ordinance map, so there can't be any doubt about it, and sometimes at dusk I fancy I see the figures of Roman soldiers moving along the edge of the wood, and the glint of light on the officer's helmet. But that is only make-believe for the sake of a small boy who is keen on history.

3. The Village Carpenter

There is an old friend of mine who talks to me about the rural life of England and the changes he has seen since his boyhood. He is a carpenter, and his woodshed is not far from my cottage. There is nothing that he doesn't know about wood, and I like to stand in his shavings and sawdust now and then, among his wheelbarrows and ladders and field gates, which he makes for the village folk, while he leans over his bench with his plane at rest for a little conversation about life and politics. He is getting on in years and has put on flesh—there are moments when he reminds me of that robust knight, Sir John Falstaff—and he complains sometimes that the strength has gone out of his arms, though one would never think so when he wields his ax to split a log—that sharp ax which took off one of his fingers in a careless moment.

"Youth is the best time!" he told me. "When I was a young fellow I was as strong as an ox and up to all kinds of fun. Now I'm an old crock and feel my age. Well, I can't complain. I've had a good life."

He is a great reader of newspapers and keeps little cuttings for me in his waistcoat pocket: odd snippets about this strange world. He has a great admiration for Mr. Hannan Swaffer and other clever gentlemen on the *Daily Herald*. Leaning over the gate of his cottage garden after working hours, he likes to watch the village life go by and pass the time of day with old cronies, field labourers and others whom he knew as boys, or see the girls ride past on their bicycles—he still has an eye for a pretty wench—for a dance at the village hall. He is fond of his garden, where he grows old-fashioned flowers, and he invites me in, now and then, to see how his plants are coming on, or to taste a glass of elderberry wine made by his wife, who is of the old-fashioned type: "my old lady," as he calls her with humorous affection. Once he was a great fellow with the cornet and played in a village band. He knew a lot about good music and went as far as St. James's Hall to hear a concert; but he gave up music when jazz came in. He can't abide it, he tells me. It turns his stomach up.

He was reminiscent the other day when I went into his woodshed and sat on his bench for a while.

"I remember the days of crinolines," he said. "You would hardly believe that, would you? Nowadays young women don't wear any petticoats under their frocks and walk around the roads in breeches. But I well remember my mother wore a crinoline until I was ten years of age. Some women found it hard to leave them off, and young fellows used to break their hoops to make them take to the new style. It wasn't too bad— the crinoline. It left their feet free, and looked pretty covered with muslin. But it was a bit awkward if they had to get into a cart. Of course, there were no buses in those days for country folk in a village like this."

He pulled out one of his newspaper cuttings, and we discussed world politics for a while. He didn't think much of Hitler or Mussolini. Fellows like that, he thought, were a danger to humanity.

"I was always a Liberal," he told me. "I thought no end of old Gladstone and the Liberal leaders who followed him. Nowadays young fellows don't take much interest in politics. They're more interested in listening to the wireless and taking their girls to the cinema. But when I was a youngster I thought a lot about Liberty and the Rights of Man and all that! It was dangerous in country districts for a working man. To be a radical was as bad as being Satan in a wig, I can tell you. The gentry didn't like it. Some of them was very arrogant, and I couldn't talk to them like as I'm talking to you, free and easy, and with no discomfort. They would put a man out of his job if he didn't vote for their way of thinking. And the parsons were the same. Some of them used to get men dismissed from their jobs if they attended radical meetings, or if their daughters got into trouble with the young fellows. Why, I remember a friend of mine losing his job because he talked to some friends outside the church porch on a Sunday morning after bell ringing. Not that I'm against the clergy as a whole. Some of them were very kindly and well-meaning. I can remember the High Church movement which made such a stir. My mother didn't like it, being of Low Church mind. When a young curate talked to her one day in a white surplice and a long gown, she asked him what was the meaning of it.

"'This surplice is a symbol of purity,' said the young parson, smiling at my mother with her pretty face. As quick as lightning she answered back, 'There's a lot of black underneath it!' I've never forgotten that. It still makes me laugh when I think of it."

He laughed then and apologized for these anecdotes of his early youth, though I was enjoying them.

"When one gets on in years one thinks back to one's boy-hood," he explained.

"How are things now?" I asked. "Do you think people are better off?"

He thought over that question and was not to be trapped into a hasty answer.

"Wages are better," he said presently. "Conditions of life are better in some ways. There's not the same poverty, I'll admit. And the gentry don't put it over the lower classes as they used to do sometimes. But if you ask me, I think there was more happiness in the old days. We got more out of life, as you may say. When I was a lad we had a lot of fun. We made it for our-selves. Nowadays the young people have it made for them. I remember old evenings in the White Hart. The young farmers used to come in at eight o'clock and sit round with their church-warden pipes. If a labourer came in they stood him a pint, which cost tuppence. Then there would be choruses, with a bit of harmony, very pleasant. 'Say a Kind Word if You Can,' that was one of the old songs that we sang. Or 'The Shining Goblet' went the round of the young farmers, very sweet and nice. Then we sang 'Drink to Me Only with Thine Eyes,' a rare old song that melts the heart. It used to remind me of Oliver Goldsmith's village. Now that kind of thing has gone, and more's the pity. I often think of the old faces. They're mostly gone too."

He sighed heavily and then laughed again.

"No use being sentimental. Still I regret the passing of good beer. This modern stuff is no good. Why, the old English beer we used to drink would stick to the roof of the palate. It was food and drink, very warm and friendly. It made a man of one.

As a boy I used to drink it for breakfast. It gave strength to one's arms. I was a good carpenter in those days. I felt the sap of youth in my veins like a young tree."

He told me more about those days of youth, those good days of laughter.

"It was when I played the cornet. We used to travel about and play for social evenings and benefit societies. They used to enjoy themselves no end, and our music put a dance into their feet. Lordy! I remember seeing them dance on the tables with their hobnailed boots; and at the village dances the young women were so pretty with their little feet that a young fellow felt his heart stir against his ribs. They still have dances in the village hall, and I daresay they enjoy themselves, but not so hearty as we did. It's all this jazz stuff, mewing and squealing. If that's music, then I don't hold with it. Give me the old English tunes, which have a sweetness in them and good harmony. 'I Know a Bank Whereon the Wild Thyme Blows.' Can you beat that? 'Drink to Me Only with Thine Eyes.' That's English. Now it's Negro music with the tom-toms. My old cornet was better than this saxophone with its howling and gobbling."

He came back with a jerk of the mind to the modern world around him, after these reminiscences of an old-time England.

"There are no great leaders," he complained. "Now take Stanley Baldwin. A nice gentleman, I dare say. He knows something about farming and country life. He's English all right, which is something. But he doesn't drive his point home. He doesn't get a move on about unemployment. This present government is made up of commonplace chaps. Where's the type of Gladstone, nowadays? Where are the old leaders with dash and spirit? There's Winston Churchill, you'll say. Well, he's a brilliant man, one can't deny. But he's unsteady. You can't rely on him. The Labour party is lacking in leaders. There's old Lansbury—a Christian. We could do with a lot like him, but one has to be something more than a Christian to make a politician and a leader. Sir Stafford Cripps? He doesn't understand the working classes. He's not one of them. He talks wild, and people don't trust him."

"What do you think of the younger men of today?" I asked the old carpenter.

ON THE BEACH, SUSSEX

He didn't think much of them. At least, he didn't think much of their manners.

"They're not polite to each other," he said. "They're offhand with everybody. There's a lot to be said for good manners, and I don't see them. In the old days we were taught to behave ourselves according to the place we were in. We were civil to the girls and respectful to all women and old folk. Now these young chaps with their motor bikes go rushing around regardless. Still, I've nothing else to say against them. The young men of England did well in the Great War. They'll do well again if anything happens. It's only a difference of style. Take the women, for instance. They would have shocked my mother. She wouldn't have understood them going about and showing their legs without shame. Why, the other day a young woman passed through this village in a bathing dress and thought nothing of it. In the old days we didn't see much more than a woman's ankle, and I remember Charles Dickens told my aunt Grace that he could always tell a lady by the shape of her ankles, and I find myself looking at them even now to see if it's true."

"And is it?" I asked.

He wouldn't give himself away on that point.

"Things are not so narrow nowadays," he admitted. "There's more tolerance. We've broader views about life. Why, when I went from here to Hertfordshire, as carpenter to Lord Aldenham—he was a Gibbs, too—they called me a foreigner, until one day I knocked a fellow out for saying so. After that they admitted I was an Englishman and worthy of respect."

We talked for a while about the Jubilee, and it reminded him of Queen Victoria's Jubilee, when he went to see the bonfires on the hills and got word that his wife was going to have a baby.

"Apart from all politics," he said, "the English people are still very loyal to their king and country. Now this here Jubilee proves that beyond a doubt. The same spirit comes out again. There's not a man would say a word against the King or the Royal Family. They're nice folk and mean kindly. Over the wireless the King speaks to the people with humanity and means what he says. He wants to see them happy. He's a good sort, as no one can deny."

I thought of my road sweeper in London who thought the Royal Family a very respectable lot. If Kings can establish that reputation with their people, they need not fear a revolution.

"I'm bringing round a bottle of my wife's elderberry wine," said this old carpenter.

He brought it round, and it was very warming to the cockles of the heart, and in its flavour was the spirit of English hedges and of old farmhouses, where once they quaffed this country wine and sang old songs on winter evenings.

4. The Radical

The leader of radical opinion in my village stands outside his shop near the postoffice—which used to be an inn—and surveys life as it passes. It passes quite a lot, in good-looking motorcars, on motorcycles, and on ordinary "push-bikes" ridden by young girls in a hurry.

Then there are the tradesmen in motor vans which hurtle through these lanes recklessly as they convey the product of shops in the neighbouring town—more than a village—to big houses hidden by trees at the end of long drives. There are also the Green Line buses which stop outside the Bull between their journeys, when the driver and conductor smoke a cigarette or two and read the latest tragedy of world news in the *Daily Mirror* or some paper which gives all the news in brief with plenty of pictures for those who have no time for reading.

Old ladies stop to buy a tube of toothpaste or some throat lozenges from the chemist's shop with a Georgian-looking front. Two or three nurses with babies in perambulators try to see something new in the other shop windows. Oh, there's a lot of life in my village, round about the cross where the names of the boys who died in the World War are inscribed in stone, though nobody reads them now.

The leader of radical opinion sells bicycles, lawn mowers, and wireless sets, and will repair the same for a consideration, or charge a battery when it runs down. He is a man past middle age, but active, lean, and straight, with searching eyes and a sense of humour. He knows all about bells, having been an enthusiastic bell ringer from youth on. He has rung the bells in four hundred English churches, and there are few men, if any, who can boast a record like that—a record that holds so many vibrations which have added to the music of English life and to his own happiness in old villages and towns to which he used to cycle tandemwise with his wife when cycling was first in fashion. He has a name which is forever associated with bells in English fairy tales, because they rang in the ears of a boy who rested on a milestone at Highgate.

> *Turn again, Whittington,*
> *Thou worthy citizen . . .*

"It's all a question of rhythm," said my radical friend one day on the question of bell ringing. "You must have a sense of rhythm or you can't be a bell ringer. I've known fellows who hadn't the least idea of it. They couldn't come in at the right time, either too soon or too late."

He explained the art of bell ringing as a poet will talk about metre and accent.

"There are many bells which aren't pure," he told me. "Nothing will ever put them right because they were turned out wrong in the casting. Others, of course, get cracked. Now Big Ben, for instance, is all wrong. Its vibrations are jangled."

I was sorry to hear it. I have a great respect for Big Ben. It always gives me a thrill when I hear its booming strokes over London, and I know men who when they have heard it over the wireless far away from England have felt like weeping, because it means all that London means and stirs their very soul.

On my way to the postoffice I have interesting chats with a man who is not only a bell ringer and a radical but a village philosopher. There are times when I disagree with his views, but they're honest and represent the opinion of a man in the street, where this one always stands when customers are few and work is slack.

"How are things going?" he asked one day.

I answered with a fair show of optimism.

"Not too bad, I should say."

He looked down the village street, with one eye on the Green bus, which he proposed to catch when it arrived in due course, and laughed ironically.

"The national government has appointed new ministers and MacDonald is no longer Prime Minister. Well, what does that mean? It's the same old government, isn't it? Just a reshuffle of the cards! What are they going to do about unemployment? Just nothing! They say there's going to be an election in the autumn. What's going to happen then?"

I couldn't tell him.

"They'll exploit the Jubilee," he said. "That's what they'll try to do. But the people are getting too intelligent. There are two million who read the *Daily Herald*. It's going to make a difference. They're thinking. You can fool some of the people some of the time, but you can't fool all the people all the time."

I agreed to those last words. I had heard them before. But I had secret reservations as to whether the *Daily Herald* is the fount of all wisdom and all truth.

"I see Geneva has turned down the forty-hour week," he remarked, with another glance towards the Green Line bus. The conductor was lighting another cigarette.

"Vested interests again," he explained, in answer to my nod.

"My contention is," he insisted, "that vested interests are at the bottom of most economic trouble. Now, take machine-made goods: It stands to reason that the machine must be controlled. The machine ought to produce goods at cheap prices for everybody. People talk as if the machine were an enemy of mankind, whereas it ought to be our servant, creating more leisure for humanity. But what happens? Men are turned off their jobs because employers want to earn big dividends instead of spreading the work round and absorbing more men."

I raised an argument for his consideration.

"That might put up the costs of production so high that we couldn't compete in world markets unless by general arrangement all round. We have to compete now with cheap oriental labour which undercuts our export trade."

"My contention is," said the village economist, "that we shall never get back our export trade as it existed before the war. We have too many competitors who have learnt to use our machines. Many other nations have become industrialized.

We shall have to adapt ourselves to altered conditions and become more self-supporting. Nobody wants Red Revolution in this country. It's against the spirit of the English people. We're too intelligent. But there'll have to be a social revolution, and the sooner it comes the better."

"It has happened already," I answered. "It has happened in this village."

"My contention is——" said the village radical.

The Green bus was moving towards him. He excused himself and made a run for it.

I have called him a radical, but he is all for charity and human kindness. He would never advocate the Russian method of persuasion by a bullet in the back of the head.

"I'm a George Lansbury Socialist," he told me one day, "and that's just the same thing as Christianity. A Conservative can be a Socialist. Many of them are. The Sermon on the Mount was pure Socialism, wasn't it? What we want is for the spirit of Jesus Christ to chase the moneylenders out of the Temple. My contention is that the financiers are at the root of all evil. Take the munitions business, for instance—this traffic in arms. Iniquitous!"

I felt self-conscious about this subject, as I happened to be serving on a Royal Commission to inquire into its iniquities, if any, and to remedy them if practicable and desirable. I hedged a little and explained the difficulties of stopping the export of arms. If we did so alone, it would merely hand over the market to other countries.

"Two blacks don't make a white," said my honest friend sturdily. "Let's put our own conscience right."

He jerked his thumb towards the tower of the Norman church up the steps a few yards away, where the village cross tells of young men who died in a world war.

"The Church ought to give a stronger lead to peace," he said. "Half our parsons are militarists. They bless the guns and the bombing aëroplanes. Now, I'm a believer in Dick Sheppard. He's a man and a Christian. The other day he preached a sermon in a Nonconformist church. There's nothing narrow about him. It's narrowness and intolerance that I'm up against."

"I'm glad to hear it," I said heartily. "That's our English way, isn't it?"

"Well, it ought to be," said my Christian radical. "There was a Blackshirt who came to talk to us the other day. Friends of mine wanted to chuck him out and give him a bit of rough stuff. I didn't hold with it. 'We stand for free speech,' I said. 'He has a right to his opinion,' I said. 'Kill him by ridicule,' I said. That's our English way. Laugh at a fellow when he talks rubbish. Keep on laughing."

We disagreed about the visit of the British Legion to Germany. He objected to it as long as Socialists were in German concentration camps.

"My contention is——" he announced.

Sometimes when I am going to buy stamps or cigarettes I hear the voice of the bell ringer inside his shop. "My contention is——"

In every village and hamlet in England there are men like that, lovers of liberty, haters of injustice, indignant because of life's inequalities, dreamers of Utopias when all men will be free and prosperous and happy, with lots of leisure for self-culture and the beautiful things of life. They are regarded as very desperate men by conservative old ladies who happen to hear their views. But they have the Christian tradition as their mental background and are not brutal or bloody-minded.

5. Madam, Will You Walk?

Walking along a country road one day, a mile or so from my cottage, I met a young goddess. At least, she had very fair hair and very blue eyes and strode along like a young Diana. On her back was an enormous pack, heavier, by the look of it, than the burden of Christian in *Pilgrim's Progress*. I spoke to her in a language which I guessed was hers.

"German, aren't you?" I asked.

"How did you know that?" she asked in amazement, still striding on.

"I looked at you," I said. "No English girl would shoulder a pack like that. Allow me to carry it for you."

She laughed with her blue eyes. She knew—and I knew she knew—that if I had carried her pack for a quarter of a mile I should have lain down and died.

But she was glad to talk, partly in German and partly in English, which she spoke almost perfectly. She had been walking all through England from the Lake District downwards, with occasional rides on buses and motor coaches. She put up for the night in one of the Youth Hostels provided now for hikers. She was on the way to one at Thursley, about twelve miles from where we stood, and it was very near lunch time.

We discussed German politics while we walked—I had to lengthen my stride to keep pace with her.

"What do you think of Hitler?" I asked.

"He is wonderful! He has done great things for Germany."

She told me some of the great things Hitler had done for Germany. He had restored its faith in the future, after great despair. He had given hope to youth. He had done away with a lot of unemployment. He had given unity to the German Reich—a miracle.

"What do you think of the murders on the thirtieth of June in 1934? The killing of Roehm and others?"

She was distressed by my way of putting this.

"Do you call them murders?" she asked incredulously.

"Yes. What do you call them?"

"Executions. He destroyed the traitors who had conspired against him—men who had been his friends, like the friends of Cæsar, who were traitors."

I found her interesting and, apart from her hero worship of Adolf Hitler, which I thought exaggerated, very intelligent and charming. I felt a little pity for her under that great pack, with twelve miles to walk before lunch time. I took a chance which I knew was hazardous.

"Won't you come and lunch with me?" I asked. "I live near here in a country cottage."

She saw that I was a simple and innocent man, and after a moment's hesitation accepted with pleasure. I advanced with my young goddess into my own garden, to the amazement of my wife, who was among her roses.

All went well after that moment of consternation. The goddess washed herself and sat down to our meal and talked—in almost perfect English—about England and the English people.

She found them kind. She regretted that young people in England didn't have the same opportunities for physical culture as those in Germany, and I refrained from telling her that the great stadiums and swimming baths and sports grounds in her country had been built by loans from England and America, afterwards repudiated and still unpaid. She herself was taking her degree in English literature and physical culture: a combination of studies which seemed to me admirable.

She kept us laughing with a narrative of her adventures in country omnibuses and country lanes. Everybody was astounded and shocked by the weight of her pack, which she carried so easily that she often forgot its burden.

"The English people everywhere," she said, "are wonderfully good-natured. I have made many friends in the Youth Hostels, and when I go back to Germany it will all seem like a fairy tale."

It was this young woman who wrote and told me that she had heard King George speaking over the wireless on Jubilee Day.

I meet other people like this German girl when I walk in Surrey and Sussex lanes. They are young people: generally a boy and girl, but sometimes in groups of ten or twelve. They are lightly dressed, the boys in white shirts and shorts with packs on their backs, the girls often in the same kit or in frocks with bare arms. They belong to the gallant company of hikers, a new order in English life, and one of the best.

The inspiration for this organized hiking came from Germany, where I used to meet the *Wandervögel*—the Wandering Birds, as they called themselves. They wandered up hill and down dale, camping in the forests and singing folk songs in the villages. They had a faith and code of their own. They believed in the simple life and in nature. They believed in peace and beauty. They thought that the health of the mind was helped by health of body. Anyhow, they were young and liked this adventure of comradeship as they went singing along mountain paths and through the woods. An elderly man who loved youth established a hostel for them, where they could stay the night for a few pence and cook their own food. It was the beginning of many hostels all through Germany, so that the Wandering Birds could go from one to another with a day's walk between them. The German hostels still stand, but the Wandering Birds and the Youth Movement to which they belonged have been taken over by the Hitler Youth, and the free spirit which they first professed has been brought under the discipline of the Nazi code.

In England this new enthusiasm for "hiking"—it's not a good word—has been encouraged in the same way by the Youth Hostels Association, which has built or bought many places where these young tramps may spend the night cheaply, with facilities in the way of washing and cooking, and with a common room where, after the evening meal, they may sit and talk or sing till bedtime. They too have a code and a faith. Their code is to preserve beauty and not to spoil it. They pledge themselves to respect the property and privacy of country folk, not to disturb game or stock, not to leave gates open, not to light fires where damage may be done, never to leave litter about, nor disturb the quiet and peace of rural life by noisy vulgarity in a hooligan spirit. Their faith as hikers is that humanity must get away from the industrialization of life and its spreading ugliness and find peace and beauty wherever possible beyond the reach of the pavement. They believe that the mind must keep close touch with nature for its health and inspiration. They believe in human comradeship reaching out beyond political frontiers. They believe that if men walk together on hilltops or in valleys, where long roads lead to open heaths and winding lanes pass through a pleasant countryside, there will be peace in their hearts and laughter on their lips. They believe that men and women will love life better and see it with more understanding and have less need of greed and brutality and intolerance and enmity, if there is this comradeship of tramps walking through each other's lands.

The Youth Hostels in England, Wales, and Northern Ireland are linked up with those in Germany, Sweden, Denmark, and other countries. Already in the English hostels one may find some of these foreign boys and girls on "tramping" holidays through our countryside. It is the beginning of a movement which may help the world forward and create a society of hikers all over Europe who will not be thinking in terms of national egotism or political passion, but will have a secret password of their own to the friendship of other men and women. It is a new brotherhood and sisterhood in the spirit of that saint who preached a sermon to the birds and had love in his heart. It's a new order of squires and maids who will extend the realm of chivalry and safeguard beauty. They will uphold the right of liberty in this comradeship of the open road, the winding lane, and the greenwood tree. What a good and gay adventure, to go walking from hostel to hostel with these lads and lasses!

I spent an hour or two at one of them the other day, on a hill above the village of Holmbury St. Mary, which lies in a country-side still so lovely that one forgets the menace of ribbon develop-ment and all its horrors of petrol pumps and cinemas and factory sites, which have spoilt so many green fields during recent years.

Here there are still old farmsteads and fields where the harvest ripens. Here are field paths which go through leafy woods where, in spring time, bluebells grow thick, and primroses gleam in patches of pale gold. The foxglove grows tall in the hedges; there are clumps of loosestrife and meadowsweet under the elderberry blossom. On the heaths above Peaslake the heather spills its purple over the sandy soil, and the bracken is tall and green. For miles around the hills are purple in the evening light. There are views where the eye looks far over a woodland scenery with not a house visible, nor any roof, because they are hidden under the waves of foliage. From the valleys come the sounds of life: a bell ringing, a dog barking, the chink of a blacksmith's hammer; and standing by a thicket one may hear the nightingale with its fluting ecstasy of love, not apprehensive of the jerry builder.

The youth hostel is newly built. I came to it across fields, not sure of its whereabouts because I lost the lane which leads to its front door. I knew its architect, a young man by name of Lobb, which seems to me a good name for the builder of a youth hostel. Wasn't it the name of a Barrie character who was a reincarnation of our English Puck?

In an adjoining field there was a party of young campers. They had carried their own tents—pup tents, as the Americans call them—and were putting them up for the night. A girl among them was busy over a campfire. A good smell came from her frying pan, and as I passed she stood up with the evening sun behind her and gave me a smile of greeting which was very friendly, so that the words of an old song came singing through my mind:

> *"Madam, will you walk—*
> *Madam, will you talk—*
> *Madam, will you walk and talk with me?"*

In the hostel at eight o'clock that evening there was a pleasant scene. These young tramps—about thirty-five of them, I think—were getting ready for their evening meal. Some of them were already sitting down to it, at small tables in the big common room, which was a very cheery place with brightly coloured furniture and spotless woodwork. Around the walls a woman artist whom I happen to know had painted a fresco in the style of Kate Greenaway with a modern touch.

Some of the girls wore breeches above bare legs and strode about like young Rosalinds on their way to the Wood of Arden. Others, not so slim and boyish-looking, were like the girls of a musical comedy or the sturdy wenches of Innsbruck. It's not every girl who can wear shorts without self-consciousness. The young men with them had no affectation. They were a good type of English student out for a walking tour. One of them had a guitar to which he gave tune now and then, accompanied by a humming chorus from his comrades.

I sat down at a table with two of the girls and entered into conversation with them. They had walked over from Dorking and were very hungry, but their sausages didn't seem to be frizzling with that rapidity which they had expected. We went to have a look at these sausages in the kitchen, where there is room for enough cooks to spoil the broth if they didn't look after their own pots. The warden's wife pointed out a gadget on the electric stove which would speed up the disinclination of a sausage to get brown and crisp.

I had a chat with the warden's wife, who prepares an evening meal for those who don't want to cook it themselves.

"What kind of a crowd do you get?" I asked her.

She looked at the company of tramps and laughed.

"Every kind of type. They're all very intelligent and very well mannered. It's not often we have the slightest trouble. Tonight there are too many for intimate conversation—I have to keep busy—but often on a weekday evening we sit around and have good talks. They think a lot about most things. You would be surprised what a lot they know about books and art and history and nature study. And their minds are open. They have no use for intolerance or narrow prejudices. Most of them have an international outlook and are keen on peace. Of course, they're rather bewildered, poor dears, about this strange world of today—who wouldn't be?—but they're not worrying. They like this comradeship and this adventure of hiking. It does them any amount of good to get away from bricks and mortar and the artificial life of the cities. They're all nature worshippers."

I looked over at a young man and woman sitting at a separate table. The girl had very fair hair, in neat little plaits. The young man would not have looked out of place on the Zugspitz in Bavaria.

"What nationality?" I asked.

She thought they might be Danes. This hostel had only been opened a few weeks, but already they had had Danes, Swedes, Germans, Norwegians, and Americans.

It was the warden who introduced me to a German. He was taking some photographs of the hostel, but after taking another view of the common room, he accepted one of my cigarettes and was glad to talk.

"You English people don't realize your own happiness," he told me presently. "In Germany I found it impossible to be happy. There is always a sense of apprehension and—in my case—of fear and insecurity."

"Why in your case, particularly?" I asked.

He smiled and shrugged his shoulders.

"I am not completely Aryan."

"Jewish?" I asked.

"A touch of Jewish blood. Enough to make things very uncomfortable."

He spoke about the life in Germany. There was much to be said, he thought, for some aspects of the Nazi régime. He ap-

proved of the Labour camps for the unemployed. The Nazis had
some good ideas. But they exaggerated the discipline, the rigid
organization, and the suppression of free opinion. There was
an outward unity in Germany which seemed astonishing to
outsiders, but it wasn't very real, he thought. If Hitler died,
Germany would fall into its old divisions again. There were
vast numbers of Germans who disliked the Nazi régime intensely
but didn't dare to express their views. The whole thing was held
together by the personality of Hitler, who undoubtedly must
possess some genius, but had the fanaticism of the madman who
thinks he is God, or held up by the hand of God. There was a
great deal of nonsense about the Nazi ideals. The new paganism
advocated by Rosenberg and others was just idiotic. No man of
sense could possibly believe in such stuff, and there were, after
all, masses of Germans who were men of sense. Unfortunately
Germans were not distinguished by a sense of humour. The
other day he had met two Nazis in London. They had put on
all kinds of badges and walked very erect, with their stomachs
out, because they thought the eye of the world was upon them.
There are certain types of Germans who do not look very heroic
or anything but ridiculous, especially when they take themselves so seriously.

This young man was a handsome fellow, with very bright
humorous eyes.

"In England," he said, "I find the common folk kindly.
Policemen, bus conductors, people in the East End, are all helpful and kind, not because they think of it, but because it comes
natural to them. The other day I was sitting on the grass with
my wife—I have brought her to England—and two people came
over and offered us a rug to sit on because they thought the grass
was damp. That was kind of them. And everywhere I go I find
the English people so happy without knowing their happiness.
They are not afraid of being killed if they express political
opinions contrary to the majority. They can say anything they
like. There's real liberty here. One can breathe freely. The
English don't get passionate or violent about abstract political
ideas or the economic situation. They do their job day by day,
and adapt themselves to conditions very easily, whereas in Germany people think out a plan and put a frame round it and

make a social revolution—which goes all wrong. We're always beginning a new plan—which goes all wrong! But the English, without any plan at all, make things go right. It's instinctive. It's a kind of self-discipline which they have acquired through the centuries. They don't want many laws. They make their own order. And they are easy-going, and humorous, and good-natured, and take things as they come. Now look at this little crowd here. How happy they are! That is why I would like to stay in England. Because when I go back to Germany I know that I shall have to hide my real opinions and keep a guard over my mouth, and look over the right shoulder to see if anyone is listening. I shall not be happy. There is no happiness in Germany unless one is in favour of the Nazi rule, which is very intolerant. I do not want to go into a concentration camp. I shall always be afraid that I shall be pushed into one. England is not like that. England is a pleasant and peaceful land."

I looked round again at the company in this youth hostel. The young man with the guitar was tuning up. I joined the second dinner at the long table. A young man next to me talked about Russia. A friend of his had just come back and was much disappointed with what he had seen. Two of the girls described a visit to a youth hostel in Heidelberg. Further down the table they were discussing a new novel by an author whose name I didn't know.

When I left the hostel the young man with the guitar had his instrument slung over his shoulder and was walking down a country lane with two comrades.

It was a night of stars. Myriads of them twinkled above the tunnel of the lane. The dew was falling, and there was a sweet smell of hay coming from the fields across the hedge. A rabbit scuttled across the path. On such a night as this in August, twenty-one years ago exactly, a war began which had called for the service and sacrifice of English youth, and the youth of all those nations who thought they hated each other or had some quarrel to the death. What good had it done? What problem had it settled? What happiness had come from it for any people? Now, when I went home there was news over the wireless about another war brewing. Italy was sending its young men to be stricken with fever and dysentery, all manner of disease, on the frontier of Abyssinia. "We need more babies!" said Mr. Mussolini, who gave a bounty for full cradles. "We must expand or burst," said Mr. Mussolini in another mood. He was sending his fleet of bombing planes by way of Egypt. English statesmen had expressed their sympathy with Italy's need for expansion—only to be gained by the invasion of other people's lands; but now, faced with the danger of this Abyssinian war, which might have many repercussions, they were working feverishly at Geneva for some kind of formula which at least would play for time. If Italy took a knock from the Ethiopian, Germany and Austria might move down towards the Brenner. Anything might happen to touch off the powder magazines in Europe, if the gates of Janus were opened again in Rome.

It would be a pity if that young man in a green shirt and shorts, with a guitar on his back, were called away from the Surrey lanes to hear the devil's orchestra of war while he lay in a ditch under high-explosive fire like those who had gone twenty-one years ago—his father perhaps among them. In Italy there were millions of young men who were on their way to deserts and rocks under the blinding sun of Africa, who would regret the guitars they had strummed to their girls in the shade of an albero.

6. The Public School

The public-school system goes on, in spite of the socialization of England. Eton, Harrow, Winchester, and the others, cling to their old traditions and continue to educate the sons of well-to-do parents in the firm belief that there is still place in life for young gentlemen wearing the right clothes at the right time, with healthy views on the importance of sport, and the spirit of "playing the game" in private and public life, with the accent of their class, sufficient knowledge of Greek and Latin to quote a tag or two as the sign of caste, and enough general knowledge to fit them for the army or the professions after the requisite period of special swotting.

Sometimes I have my doubts on all this. Not having been a public-school boy, I have none of the emotional reverence for that type of education or for its special code of morals and manners, though I have no class prejudice on the subject. My doubt is on the general question of whether it is advisable to maintain the pretence of an aristocratic caste—this specialized education —for "the sons of gentlemen," when the privileges and prerogatives of caste have broken down to such a degree that the public-school boy finds himself handicapped in the economic struggle in an arena open to those who know a little shorthand and typewriting, or to those who have had a more specialized training in subjects which the world of today needs most: a knowledge of mechanics, chemistry, scientific agriculture, industrial organization, and administration. It is pleasant for youth to have learnt the odes of Horace, or to have read the essays of Steele and Addison, or to have a fair idea of the Wars of the Spanish Succession. It is very pleasant for youth to handle a cricket bat with skill and style. It is a lovely background to life when it is a memory of the playing fields of Eton or the chapel at Winchester or the reddening creeper on the walls of Harrow. School friendships made in such places, the code of good form learnt there, the sensibilities and tastes and ideals planted in young minds, have a lifelong influence which may be the most valued possession of their owners. But do they fit men nowadays for the new conditions of a world—at least, a nation—from which most barriers of birth and rank have been abolished and in which hereditary privilege has been mostly disestablished—if that is true?

Scholarships now carry the clever boys of the elementary schools to the universities. Even without those advantages, self-educated men, or students of the London School of Economics and other institutions within the reach of poor scholars, may attain the high places. When J. H. Thomas, once on the plate board of a railway engine, is Secretary for the Dominions, when Ramsay MacDonald, a Scottish peasant's son, has been Prime Minister of England, when the Labour party has been in power and filled the highest offices of state, no one may pretend that this country has still a ruling class holding by right of class or caste the keys of place and power. When one asks the way of a policeman in London and gets the answer with a public-school accent, that accent is no longer the sign of social distinction or

THE ICKNIELD WAY

of economic privilege. When the young mechanic who takes a look at the internal mechanism of one's cheap car may have been educated at Winchester, or when the young man who offers to sell one a car from a showroom in Piccadilly hands one his card whereon is printed a name of noble origin, the game is up, it seems, for any system of education in which the training is exclusively and intensively directed to the reproduction of snobbishness. The time has gone when the young gentlemen from Eton or Harrow had places waiting for them in the army or the Church or the estates of the landed gentry. Now that India is going to be self-governed, the Indian Civil Service no longer offers an active career to young men of administrative ability and the old school tie.

They did their jobs well. They held the scales of justice with strict impartiality between Hindu and Moslem; they administered districts in the interests of the native inhabitants, who looked to these representatives of the British Raj for law and order and help in time of plague or famine. Now they are no longer wanted.

They are no longer wanted, these public-school men, in the colonies which are now dominions, formerly ruled from Whitehall or the Governor's Residence. They are no longer wanted exclusively at the Bar, which is open to any self-educated fellow who can pass his law final and eat his dinners in the Middle or Outer Temple. One of our most successful K.C.s earned his first wages as a Fleet Street reporter, and reminded me of the fact not long ago, when we waited outside the Mansion House after a great banquet until the cars could be called up. There were several noble dames waiting beside us, and many men in orders and decorations, but the K.C. did not lower his voice when he talked of his old Fleet Street days.

"The first money I ever earned," he said, "was on a news agency when I reported crime stories. The editor—it was Perris, you remember—threw my week's earnings out of the window wrapped up in a bit of paper. They amounted to seven-and-sixpence. I was 'on space' at the time."

I see a thousand signs around me that the public school has no longer an exclusive entry to the professions or the places. Are they not anachronisms in this modern way of life? Is it not perhaps a cruelty or a folly to preserve their atmosphere of old tradition, their forcing house for young minds into the mould of what their masters still think is the perfect form of English character—good at games, nicely behaved, steeped in the spirit of Henley, Kipling, and Rupert Brooke, ready to die for England in any war arranged by a Conservative government, ready to die with a heroic smile and the familiar words, "Dulce et decorum est . . ."—convinced that England is the greatest country on earth, that the British Empire is created by the will of God in order to bring the blessings of civilization to the coloured races, that the Church of England by law established is the only true faith for a gentleman, that all foreigners are of lesser breeds, that an English gentleman with a public-school education is the most perfect specimen of humanity (with a few lamentable exceptions, because of course there must always be some dirty dogs), and that there is a distinction in clay as well as kind between the Upper and the Lower Orders.

I remember a conversation on these lines between two of my friends in my little house in London. One of them, who was the son of an Elder Statesman of the Conservative party, denounced the public-school system as an iniquity. He had been to Eton. The other young man, of less famous parentage, defended it as the training ground of fine character and splendid achievement. He had been to Clifton—which the Etonian refused to admit among the public schools. The conversation became very heated at half an hour after midnight.

It was with such questions in my mind that I paid a visit to a famous school, not enormously far from my country cottage. It is Charterhouse, once domiciled in the old grey buildings near Smithfield where I went to see one of the Poor Brothers, as I have told in this book.

It was a summer day in June, with a blue sky overhead and a warm sun on the fields, where haymaking was beginning. The scent of the hay was sweet in my nostrils, as it was, hereabouts, when Chaucer's young squire came along the Pilgrim's Way to St. Martha's on the Hill, with fellow travellers who told old tales as they went. The cuckoo was shouting in the copse by Compton.

I drove through deep lanes, overhung by the heavy foliage of

tall elms, with a tracery of sunlight and shadow across the roads.
Foxgloves were growing tall in the hedges, and the elderberry
blossom was like snow on the bushes. A thousand different wild
flowers grew in the hedgerows, and there was a glint of gold
beneath the meadowsweet and wild parsley. For the way to
Charterhouse lies through a pleasant countryside, not yet spoilt,
though terribly in danger because of a by-pass road which cut
with a clean gash through its loveliness, breaking the heart of
an old lady who tried to defend her heritage against all motorists and devils, and annoying a noble baron whose park was
violated by this highway for the use of road hogs.

I inquired the way to the main entrance of the school of one
of the Charterhouse boys, who was riding a bicycle. He was
kind enough to turn round out of his way—which was probably
towards a tuck shop—and ride ahead of my car to show me.

"Good form," I thought. "That boy has nice manners.
There's something to be said for Charterhouse."

There was a lot to be said for Charterhouse. I had met old
Carthusians, as they call themselves, in many parts of the world.
At first I used to wonder why so many men I met knew the
lanes and fields round a tiny village where once I lived. They
had gone bird's-nesting on the heath. They had known the
Jolly Farmer. Many of them were officers in a World War, and
laughed a little and sighed a little when they talked of these
places, which they wanted to see again and mostly never did.
They were old Carthusians.

The day I went to their old school was given up to a pageant.
They were having a dress rehearsal when I arrived, as was explained to me by the sergeant porter who undertook to find
the head master for me.

We walked through the big archway, past the new chapel
by Gilbert Scott. The school buildings, ivy-covered and stately,
are in a noble setting. Beyond them the playing fields stretch
away, smooth and green, to a vista of tall trees, heavy in foliage,
and to the surrounding hills of Surrey. The first and second
eleven were playing cricket, and I stood to watch them for a
few seconds.

"We have some good pitches," said the sergeant porter
proudly. "A bit fast today after the dry weather."

I stood a moment or two to watch the first eleven. It was a good scene. Those tall boys looked fine in their white flannels, and the game was like a ritual—a mystery play—as they crossed for an over and took their places in the field again. It is an affair of grace and elegance, this game of cricket, when watched by foreign eyes used to the rowdy violence of baseball or other forms of national sport. It is very English, they think, in its spirit and code.

The sergeant porter discovered the whereabouts of the head master. He was watching the rehearsal of the pageant, from which he led me a little way for a quiet talk under the trees.

"This is my last term," he told me, with a moment's sadness. "I have had a longish innings. I've been here for twenty-four years."

Fletcher of Charterhouse is a famous name all over the world among old Carthusians. He was the head master of the boys who heard one day in August that their elder brothers were wanted for a war. "Your king and country need you," they were told, and they didn't need telling twice. Afterwards the time came for some of the elder boys at Charterhouse. The younger brothers went after the elder brothers, and didn't come back. Their names are written on a roll of honour.

"How do you compare the present vintage of boys with those of the pre-war years?" I asked.

Fletcher of Charterhouse glanced over at the crowd of boys sitting on the benches above the pageant ground, and a smile softened his thin lips.

"They're all right. We're back to normal now. There's nothing wrong with this lot. For a time after the war the boys were nervy and difficult. Some of them were inclined to be cynical and hard. The war left its mark on them. It cast a shadow over them. Now we've got beyond all that."

"You don't find any sign of degeneracy or effeminacy?" I asked. "I've heard pessimists say that the modern generation of boys are weaklings."

"Have a look at them," said the head master drily. "I don't think you will see any sign of that."

He thought that on the whole they were of good quality.

There was a nice spirit among them. They had good manners and plenty of character.

He allowed me to question him about the need of public-school education in modern life. I felt rather like a lady I know who once asked the reverend mother of a convent whether she thought that nuns ought to be abolished. But Fletcher of Charterhouse was quite willing to discuss this argument. No doubt he had been arguing it out for twenty-four years.

"There will always be a need of good manners and good tone. We don't want to level everything down to the lowest common denominator. We ought to aim at levelling things up. And that is what is happening. The boys who come to Charterhouse now are different from their predecessors. They come from less luxurious homes. Their parents are not so wealthy and have to economize. I have tried to keep fees down as much as possible, and there's one thing I can say with confidence: it's much better for the boys. My experience is that a boy does well in inverse proportion to the income of his parents."

I made a mental note of that phrase. It seemed to be worth remembering by those who regret the passing of wealth and aristocracy by income tax and death duties.

"Do they fit into the economic situation?" I asked.

"On the whole," he said, "they find their places."

Only about a third go up to the universities, and he was inclined to think that was a very good thing for those who had no need of an academic career but were destined for business. It was better to start in early, instead of wasting time and finding it more difficult afterwards to get into the collar.

The modern boy, he thought, was distinctly nonmilitant. There had been quite a row in the school last Armistice Day because a certain canon had given an address which the boys misinterpreted and thought it was an attack on the Germans. They made protests about it and thought it was "bad form," especially on Armistice Day.

"It's rather interesting," said the head master, "that Charterhouse was the first school to hear an appeal on behalf of the League of Nations. Gilbert Murray was here on the eleventh of November, 1918, and gave us a talk on the subject before the Armistice was announced."

He took me over to the pageant ground, and I stayed for an hour or so watching the rehearsal. On the benches behind me were rows of boys in old costumes. I looked at their faces and saw in them the line of heredity back to Elizabethan England and beyond. An orchestra of ladies was going strong, under the direction of a man who was keen on his work. In front of us was a canvas screen representing old walls with a gateway, through which the actors came and went. They were performing a masque bringing to life again old scenes in the history of Charterhouse, from the days when the monks were turned out of their monastery by orders from the King.

The monks went through the old archway, singing their last chant before they went to the scaffold or the rack. Then came the Founder of the School, old Thomas Sutton, who had made great wealth with his merchant argosies and now left it so that old men might have a home in Charterhouse and young boys learn good books within its walls. Famous Carthusians came and told their tale: Lovelace, the poet cavalier; Crashaw, poet, mystic, priest; Addison and Steele, the fathers of the English novel. With them was the immortal character Sir Roger de Coverley, who was born in the imagination of Addison himself and still lives as the type of an old English gentleman. John Wesley came back to die in Charterhouse. Thackeray has the vision of Colonel Newcome when he revisits the school. Havelock—an old Carthusian—is seen at the Relief of Lucknow. And last of all among the famous men who were sons of Charterhouse is the figure of a man still living. It is Baden-Powell who founded the order of Boy Scouts.

The orator with the silver voice of youth gives praise to him:

> "*The legend of a living man remains*
> *Who, youthful yet at threescore years and ten,*
> *To manly service trains the sons of men.*
> *In our own copse he learned the tracker's art*
> *Wherewith to unlock the door of boyhood's heart,*
> *Called the world's youth to adventurous brotherhood*
> *And generous effort for the common good.*"

The boys who took the parts of Addison and Steele played with a sense of comedy and style. Their voices came ringing across the green. One of them was fighting against a tragic memory, very recent in its agony. Another boy, his friend, had taken one of these parts until a day or two before. He had been drowned while bathing in a dangerous place. But the remaining boy went on with the play in the spirit of the school, in the spirit of men from this school whose comrades fell on the Somme while they went on towards Bapaume or Bazentin. "Carry on, there, men! Carry on!" was their watchword.

The orator who wove the thread of plot between the scenes, in blank verse which was pretty good, had a fine, fresh voice. The chorus sang like the choir of Canterbury, which melts the heart of man. Whatever prejudice one might have against the public-school system, or any private belief that its day was done, one saw the living tradition of it that day at Charterhouse.

I took tea out of doors with the head master and his wife. Some guests arrived. One was a young peer who is also a poet. The captain of the school came up and handed round things without self-consciousness. I had a little conversation with him, and he told me that the elder boys were keenly interested in international affairs.

"What's their point of view?" I asked.

"Thoroughly cynical of pacts and pledges," he answered with a smile. "Can you blame them?"

I couldn't. It was on a day when Mussolini, who had signed the Kellogg Pact with a solemn pledge to abandon war as an instrument of policy, was calling new classes to the colours for the invasion of Abyssinia. It was about a year since Germany had denounced the Treaty of Versailles and proclaimed conscription. Japan had captured Manchukuo. France and England had failed to fulfil the pledge to disarm. Everybody had broken pacts and pledges.

Mrs. Fletcher spoke a little about the latest brand of boys as far as she knew them at Charterhouse.

"There's no brutality in them," she said. "They're gentle and chivalrous. I daresay my husband told you about the row on Armistice Day. They hated to think the German dead were being insulted. There is nothing weak about them, but they hate intolerance and cruelty."

"Good for them," I said, and for a moment my mind flashed

back to Stalky and Co., that company of boys who inflicted Red Indian tortures on each other, and to a hundred other tales of schoolboy brutality and a system of cruelty inspired by flogging masters, venting their sadism upon the bodies and souls of youth.

For centuries school life has inflicted infernal torments upon sensitive boys, and only the strong survived those torture chambers of bullying and beating without permanent wounds of the soul. Even now, men I know look back upon their school days with hatred. I met one the other day who told me he had had only one happy hour during all his school career, and that was when a relative took him out to tea. He must have been a sensitive plant beyond the ordinary. It was not often as bad as that, but it was very bad for the undersized and the timid and the shy boys, and worse still, perhaps, for the bullies themselves, who were hardened in their brutality. At the public schools of today, there is still, I have no doubt, a bully or two among the boys, and a brute or two among the masters. Human nature hasn't changed completely. But ideas have changed. There is more sympathy between young and old. There is more realization of the harm that can be done to the mind by injustice and rough handling.

"There is one thing," said Mrs. Fletcher, "which the boys hate above all: that is snobbishness. They would curl up if anyone alluded to them as 'young gentlemen.'"

Yet, all the same, Charterhouse was turning out young gentlemen with the speech, manners, and code of an aristocratic caste. Whether they liked it or not, they were moulded to that tradition. Unconsciously, perhaps, they were steeped in it and would never escape its influence.

When I took my leave of the head master, I walked through the playing fields again, where the tall trees flung long shadows across the grass. There was a small crowd in the corner of one field, and I stopped to find out what interested them. It was a boxing match between two youngsters of thirteen or so.

"Seconds out of the ring!" shouted the referee.

The seconds desisted from fanning the two boys, who went for each other like gamecocks, giving and taking some hard knocks.

On the grass a number of boys were on their stomachs with their knuckles under their chins, watching this combat. Behind them stood other boys, gravely observing the head punching. One boy was taking his punishment like a man from a more scientific fighter.

"They are gentle," Mrs. Fletcher had said, "but there's no weakness in them." Well, this was a Spartan training all right, and that little scene might have happened in Georgian England, when young gentlemen were taught to put up their fists.

I walked into the chapel of Charterhouse. It was very cool and quiet there. I was alone, but in my mind's eye I could see the boys' heads bent in this far vista where the sun came through tall windows.

In the porch I read some words which stayed in my mind, so that I can now quote them:

"You who enter this chapel
Think of the Carthusians
Who died for their country and remember them.
Quit you like men. Be strong."

There are many critics of the public-school system. My philosophical doctor in London is against the herding of boys away from home influence and apart from girls. He believes in coeducation. The old school tie comes in for a lot of ridicule. The moulding of minds to one code and pattern is deplored by those who exaggerate, perhaps, the plasticity of the individual boy. Snobbishness, long the curse of the English, was instinctively produced in these institutions. The arrogant Englishman abroad, contemptuous of all foreigners, was the product of the public school. But the worst features of this form of education are, I think, being modified by a wider outlook among the masters, and a change of view and class among the boys themselves. Snobbishness is going out of fashion. Arrogance, at least in England, is at a discount and is laughed at by the modern generation. There is a lot to be said for the spirit, the tradition, the tone, of such places as Charterhouse. The beauty of their surroundings and their buildings is an antidote to that ugliness which is entering many minds as well as many places. Good form has its value in a social state tending to become careless of manners. Even democrats and haters of class privilege like H. G. Wells have come to admit that we must establish some intellectual aristocracy, some order of educated minds, not drawn from one class, but from all, to counteract the degradation of the mass mind to its lowest common denominator by newspapers and other agents of vulgarity which succeed by mass production.

An Eton boy came to supper in my cottage and talked intelligently about these things. He had just finished his last term and told me that, to his own surprise, he was sorry to leave Eton. There were times when he had hated it. He had been bullied by his house master because of socialistic ideas he had held for a time. He had got into trouble with this Tory-minded man because he had put up a resistance to joining the cadet corps. He had "loathed" some of the boys. Yet, for all that, he had felt a sudden pang of regret at having to leave. On the whole he had been happy, as he now admitted to his own surprise. There was something about Eton which had got hold of him. Life there was not rough. On the other hand, they weren't pampered. Apart from those episodes with a rigid-minded house master the boys had a fair amount of liberty to develop their own character.

This boy was against early specialization. He believed in getting a general education first. Although he had hated Latin, he thought that it was good to get a grounding in it. Classical studies seemed at the time to be rather futile. But now he thought they taught one to think and were to some extent the foundation of the best kind of intelligence.

"Of course, there's a lot of nonsense talked about Eton and other public schools," he said. "We're not turned out as 'leaders of men.' I dare say it's going to be hard to fit in to the right job. All the same, I suppose it's better to get a good general education rather than learn shorthand and typewriting or even engineering and chemistry. It doesn't do to think only of the material side of things, like getting and making money."

I watched him as he sat at my table in a little old farmhouse with low beams. He had no affectations. He was very simple and straightforward. His manners, which were good, did not require any effort. They were part of himself. He talked well about the weakness of the League of Nations and the final test of collective security brought up by the Italian threat to Abyssinia.

"If we do nothing about it," he said, "collective security fails, and it's no use pretending that there is any chance of international law and order."

I listened to him with interest. Eton, it seems, is thinking very much like Bermondsey. But this boy had a style and a poise not easy to get in a central school or even in the London School of Economics. He had been an intellectual rebel in his house, but Eton had given him something worth having, something very indefinable, but not without value in modern life.

7. *The Man with a Vision*

I went to see a man who had a vision one day in a Surrey garden. It was a strange kind of vision to have in a Surrey garden, where, as a rule, as I know, one's mind tends to be content with one's own little paradise and to shut out as much as possible the ugliness of other people's lives and the anxieties of the outer world. Japan is advancing in China, and the Yellow Peril is coming closer—oh, well, that herbaceous border is looking good with its massed colour. Mr. Anthony Eden has gone to Rome to restrain Mr. Mussolini from making war on Abyssinia. Nothing to be done about it—but the flower beds are in need of weeding. The morning newspaper is filled with stories of crime, tragedy, and human folly. Voltaire was a wise man when he said one must cultivate one's own garden. There are two million unemployed in Great Britain. Rather distressing when one comes to think of it. In a Surrey garden with its smooth-mown lawns and clipped hedges, one is tempted to forget the ugly facts of life. Here is beauty. Here is peace. Why worry?

But the man I went to see was a little worried by his own good fortune. After a life of business adventure, here he was surrounded with all the good things that life still gives to men if they are lucky. He was startled by the wonderful beauty which had come to him. Could the eye of man see anything more enchanting than this view from his terrace, looking beyond the vistas of emerald lawns and a glory of flowers, to a happy valley with clumps of trees heavy in foliage, and to the distant hills with their wooded heights? No, when I stood by his side outside his Tudor-looking house, built of old timbers and weathered bricks, and looked across his gardens to that English landscape, I knew that mortal eye could not see anything more lovely, more pastoral, more peaceful.

He is a man of nearly sixty, with silvered hair and sun-browned skin, and the face of a soldier, though he is an engineer and a printer and a business man in many ways of enterprise.

Somehow, he told me, it seemed selfish to have so much of all this—it's good, isn't it?—and not to share it with others less fortunate.

He shares the beauty of his garden—one of the noblest in Surrey and therefore in the world—by opening it to the public several times a year. But he wanted to do more than that. He wanted to do something for the unemployed in England and to put himself at their service.

It was when the vision came to him. Surely those fellows in the north—far from the comfortable prosperity of the south—ought not to be left to rot their lives away without people caring or lifting a little finger to help them. The government was doing nothing. Nobody was doing anything in a real dynamic way. Surely it was about time something was done by people like himself in gardens like this. . . . That catmint along the flagged path was a fine colour. The bees were having a good time in the honeysuckle. A gardener was mowing the tennis court where, presently, young people would come for a game.

We sat together in his study, where the afternoon sun came streaming through a casement window.

"I went up to town," he said, "to see the Ministry of Health. 'What's the worst place in England?' I asked. . . ."

They told him it was a place called Jarrow, beyond all doubt.

He left his Surrey garden and went up to Jarrow.

Yes, it was a bad place. There couldn't be worse for human tragedy. It had a population of thirty-eight thousand. Nearly all of them had been dependent for livelihood on Palmer's great shipbuilding yards, with their steel works and blast furnaces and timber yards. In 1924, because of world depression following a world war, the steel works had closed down. Palmer's, famous in the history of shipbuilding, was sold for breaking up. Eight thousand men were unemployed and had no means of supporting their wives and children. Year after year they were out of work, these skilled men, these men of sturdy, independent spirit, who had been robbed of their craft. Everything had gone from them. Jarrow was derelict. No sound came from the abandoned yards where once there had been the clink of hammers. The fires were out in the furnaces. They would never be relighted. Practically the whole population was dependent upon poor relief, and boys on the threshold of manhood had no chance of work nor had ever done any. Oh, people were sorry for them. Journalists wrote emotional copy about Jarrow. And that's where emotion ended.

"They were very suspicious of me when I first went up," said Sir John Jarvis, as I sat with him in his study looking out to his garden. They had had too much sentimental sympathy. They didn't like people coming to stare at their misery. Their pride wasn't broken.

He went into their homes, in rows and rows of mean little streets. They were without comfort or sanitation. Some of them were overcrowded, whole families of them in two rooms. There was no beauty there as in a Surrey garden.

But a vision was in the mind of this visitor. It was a vision of giving hope to these people. He would start by getting them to paint up their houses until new houses could be built. He would get them to grow things and make things. Now that their old industry was dead he would try to start new industries. It would be impossible to bring back life to Jarrow. These people must be got back to work somehow. Of course, it would need money. There were people with money in Surrey—people who lived in beautiful surroundings and in all comfort. Why not get Surrey to adopt Jarrow? People only wanted a lead. They weren't really selfish. They were only limited in vision by their herbaceous borders.

The owner of Hascombe Court invited the Mayor of Jarrow

to stay with him for a week-end and questioned him for two days. He was a retired schoolmaster who loved those Jarrow folk among whom he had worked and was eager to serve them still. He found time between answering questions to walk in this Surrey garden with its noble trees and spreading lawns and that view beyond.

"I never knew there was such beauty," he said. "Up in Jarrow we only dream of things like this."

He was quite sure that the Jarrow men would coöperate in any scheme which might give them work. All they wanted was work. It was having nothing to do, nothing to look forward to, which was breaking them down.

Sir John Jarvis put his ideas before the Surrey folk. It was not to be a scheme of charity but of reconstruction. He wanted money from them to start employment which would begin by reconditioning the homes by the men's own labour as a test of their willingness to lift themselves out of this Slough of Despond.

There are people in Surrey whose names appear on all lists of donations for national appeals. But money came from people who had never subscribed before, cottage folk and farmhouse folk and old ladies in little old houses and shopkeepers in village stores and working men's clubs and the British Legion. Thirty-five thousand pounds was subscribed, and four hundred pounds came from the pennies of school children.

The owner of Hascombe Court—this man with a vision—had to get into touch with government officials. They urged him to go slow. The government had a plan. He ought to wait and see what they were going to do.

"Certainly," he said, looking at his wrist watch. "It's now four o'clock. My train goes at five o'clock. I'm quite willing to wait until then."

If he had waited for what the government was going to do for Jarrow, he would have waited until now.

He gave reality to the vision he had had in his Surrey garden. At least he made a good beginning with the generous help which came to him. Business firms provided material which the Jarrow men needed for furbishing up their homes. They repainted them inside and out. Timber was provided for building a sports pavilion and club house, at which they worked with enthusiasm.

"Is there anything more you want for this pavilion?" asked the man who had got this going.

Yes, they wanted something else. A fair-sized Union Jack to run up on a flagstaff.

They were still loyal. They hadn't gone Red under stress of poverty. During Jubilee Week Jarrow hung out its colours with the rest of England.

They have cleared away some of the old slum quarters and built new houses with bathrooms and everything needed for decent life. They have been busy on allotments making things grow.

These were the first steps only in the scheme of reconstruction. Sir John Jarvis had new ideas for providing these Jarrow men with work and wages, including the building of an open-air swimming bath, the laying out of children's playgrounds away from the roads, and the construction of a new estate, with bowling greens for the men and tennis courts for the younger people, to be made by their own labour and for the prevailing wage. In all these projects it was decided that the fund would pay for the labour—the men working a five-day week in short hours—and the Corporation of Jarrow would provide the material with the aid of free gifts.

An old lifeboat was fitted out with a motor and made a seaworthy fishing boat. It was named *The Good Hope*, and every catch of fish was to be shared between the fishermen, the nursery schools, and the unemployed. Things were beginning to move in Jarrow because of the vision which had come to the man at Hascombe in Surrey. They were no longer abandoned. Someone had given them the most priceless gift of life, which is Hope.

"We have only made small beginnings," said Sir John Jarvis, as I sat with him one day of June, with the afternoon sun chasing long shadows across his lawns. "The big ideas I have are all to come. But when my wife and I went up to Jarrow a week or two ago, to receive the freedom of the Borough, we had a reception which was very touching. The people made a great fuss of us. They had painted their walls red, white, and blue and hung out flower baskets. The women folk gave open-air tea parties in the back lanes, and we were cheered all along the way."

He showed me a book presented to him at this time. It was

beautifully bound and illuminated, with an enamel design on the cover, and was the work of three ladies of Jarrow who still keep up the tradition of such work, which was famous in the world of learning when the Venerable Bede was born there in the dawn of Saxon civilization, fourteen hundred years ago.

"Anyway, they are grateful for our help," said Sir John Jarvis, "but as yet it is hardly more than a promise. We have a long way to go yet before Palmer's Yards are humming with industry again and all the men are at work on good wages. But that is going to happen. I'm getting on with the plans. It's more than a dream."

It was a dream which was coming true, but the dream came first. We want more such dreamers as this silver-haired man who looked like a soldier but in whose eyes there was the light of enthusiasm and faith.

I listened spellbound to his words. In them was the promise of work and wages for sturdy men with women folk and children who have known despair. In this man's mind were ideas which might reach farther than Jarrow and solve the problems of other distressed areas. They might even wipe out those figures of two million unemployed which soil the picture of English life.

"It is a question of finding new industries to replace the old," he said. "If Jarrow has gone as a shipbuilding yard, it can come back as a shipbreaking yard, for scrap iron to be made into steel. I have a plan for Jarrow which will make it a great steel-producing centre. In the old days we were taught that English steel was the finest, because the iron ore and coal lay together. Now the ore is giving out and we have to get it from abroad, but Jarrow is on the waterfront, accessible to ships bringing ore from Spain and Norway and Sweden. I am having trouble with vested interests, but I shall overcome them."

He had lately travelled three thousand miles by air to study industrial works in Germany and other countries and had seen marvels of efficiency and invention.

"England," he said, "must readapt herself to new conditions. We became a great industrial country before any other nation, and now we are inclined to rest on our laurels while others are forging ahead and making new experiments and trying out new adventures. That is what we must do. If necessary we must build new towns and abandon old ones less adapted to new industries. We must maintain our skilled labour at all costs and intensify its efficiency. We must compete in the world markets by fine quality and adapt our productions to new necessities. What is being done for Jarrow and what Jarrow is ready to do for itself, by starting new works and rebuilding its industrial life, must be done in other areas, like South Wales and the whole of Tyneside. It is essential to plan on big lines and to think adventurously, instead of being tied up in red tape and hesitating to take a step forward. Our men have the old quality. These men of Jarrow have proved themselves to be responsive to leadership and a helping hand. We have had a certain amount of human failure, of course—that's inevitable. But our percentage of success is high whenever we have found a job of work for these men to do. This work calls to the best spirit and the inexhaustible good will of people who want to know how they can best help their fellow men. People have given me more than money. They have given their service. They have wanted to coöperate in self-sacrifice. With such a spirit in England we can do anything if we set our minds to it, and get out of our gardens and our individual interests."

So spoke this man who, in a lovely garden, had wanted to share good fortune with others and had wanted to take something to the most unfortunate place in England, which happened to be Jarrow.

"Now that you have found your way here," he said, leading me towards his flower beds, "come again. We have so many things to talk about."

I drove back through the field country, with old villages, old churches, cottages and farmsteads, remote, it seemed, from ribbon building, roadhouses, and by-passes, with their new vulgarities. Here was a patch of old England, unspoilt and very deep in beauty. It would have been so easy for Sir John Jarvis, the owner of Hascombe Court, to retire from the world into this private paradise as the reward of long labour. He is fond of his garden. He plays a good game of tennis. His house is noble and full of comfort. His park is a quiet pleasance. Its air was drenched with the sweetness of flowers. He was High Sheriff of Surrey in that prosperous county. But one day he thought of men and women up there in the north, unemployed, haggard, hopeless, and unhappy. His mind reached out to Jarrow, and what he thought has made a difference there.

8. The Dramatist

An interesting character has lately become a neighbour of mine. By lately I mean two years or so ago, since he bought an old cottage in the centre of the village. It seemed impossible to me that such a man should settle down happily to village life without even a car to keep him in touch with London and the larger world, for at one time he was a man of fashion in direct line of descent from Beau Brummel and Beau Nash and the eighteenth-century gentlemen of elegance. One of the handsomest men in England as a youth and still retaining a fine figure in middle age. It was good to see him walk down Pall Mall or up Bond Street. People turned to look at him. Ladies, especially if they were pretty ladies, had a flutter when he passed. Men friends desired to know the name of his tailor, thinking, poor fools, that they could wear such clothes with the same glory. In New York and many cities of America to which fate took him year by year he seemed too good to be true. Was it possible, the Americans thought, that at last they had met the Complete Englishman—the living embodiment of the English nobleman even to the monocle in his right eye? They talked to each other excitedly after meeting him. He became a legend from New York to San Francisco. Whole colleges of American girls had heart palpitation when he addressed them from the lecture platform. Great audiences in Carnegie Hall, New York, or the Symphony Hall, Boston, stared at him with amusement, admiration, and incredibility. His very trousers were magnificent. In evening clothes he looked as a duke should look but seldom does.

In London and New York he lived with a certain splendour. When he travelled in Europe with his wife and two children it was in the style of an eighteenth-century Milord. He took suites of rooms in the Palace hotels. He distributed largesse with the careless gesture of a prince of the Medici in mediæval times or an American millionaire before the Almighty Crash. In London he lived in a dwelling place of historical distinction where a royal duke had once entertained his drunken friends to exhibitions of cockfighting in his dining room. It was furnished with priceless pieces of the William and Mary period or the days of Queen Anne. He had fine brocades, rare prints, first editions, and when I took tea with him sometimes I was filled with awe and admiration, for he was a fellow craftsman, a writer of words, a spinner of plots—a novelist like myself—and by some miracle had got away with it as few scriveners do with the reward of genius, which comes only as a rule to financial gentlemen, cotton spinners, munition makers, and merchants. It seemed incredible that he should live in such style out of the proceeds of stories and plays and little words written on pieces of blank paper.

But this good fortune had not spoilt his simplicity of mind or his sense of humour. I remember him winking at me one day and saying, "This is a great game. It can't last." A man of great social charm, with an inexhaustible love of conversation in which his fancy played a thousand tricks with reality, a man who could dramatize the most trivial incident until it became tremendous in its tragedy or comedy, he had at that time a double life, one side of which was kept secret from his friends. Few people ever saw him work. But when, in New York or London, his house was crowded with musicians, artists, actors, writers, Russian refugees, dollar princesses, or English aristocrats, in search of a drink or a meal, he would slip away to a quiet study, shut himself out from this social world, and far into the night live in the world of imagination, more real to him, more amusing, more exciting, than the living crowd whom he used only for his puppets.

It was this remarkable character who walked one day down the village street, looked at the old Norman church with loving eyes, glanced back to see a pretty girl in shorts, went twice round a cottage with low beams on which some repairs were being done, stooped under its doorway, examined its bare rooms, knocked his head against one of the beams, and decided to buy it.

He has been living there summer and winter since then and

is a great addition to our village life. His fine furniture is warehoused except for a few pieces suitable for cottage life. Certain lamentable episodes in the United States, the crash on Wall Street, the closing of the Harriman bank, affected his financial resources, as it did those of other and richer men. Some of them shot themselves through the head, others fell into despair, but this Englishman walked into a Surrey village as though he owned the world, laughed at life's little ironies, bought a writing block at the village stores, opened it at the first page, and began another novel—was it his fiftieth?—as though just beginning his first, with the same enthusiasm for a new plot, the same sense of drama, as when he wrote his first play, and with an unconquerable spirit of youth.

The villagers stare over his hedge. Before he came there was a tangle of weeds. Now his garden has smooth lawns which he mows himself, and trim flower beds over which he stoops to see the latest wonder of petalled beauty. Through the trees behind his cottage there are glimpses of fields where the harvest is ripening as I write these words. Beyond his hedge on the south side there is the rectory garden and glebeland, with a glimpse of the church tower through the foliage of tall elms. A young woman from the village does for him and thinks him wonderful, as truly he is.

Now and again people descend on him from town—his old friends. They are enchanted by his fairy-tale cottage with lattice windows and roses growing on the walls like a stage set. They are amused by his collection of brass horse ornaments used by old ploughmen and carters to avert the evil eye, which hang on his beams. They study his Dighton prints of English gentlemen in top hats with trousers strapped under their boots and high-collared cutaway coats. They listen and laugh at his conversation, witty, whimsical, boyish, with enormous enthusiasms and enormous prejudices. They see him chirp to his canary and hear of its tricks. They walk with him in his garden and admire his almond tree clothed in blossom when the spring comes or his hollyhocks, stocks, Sweet Williams and other old-fashioned flowers. And then they say to him with an air of stupefaction: "Surely you must get bored down here! Surely you can't stay here all the winter! You, of all men!"

He laughs at them. He is never bored for a single second. He has endless adventures of the mind. He finds village life extraordinarily amusing. After all, he is on the telephone. After all, there is the wireless, which he turns on at lunch time and switches on at odd hours to pick up magnificent music in Leipzig, Stuttgart, Milan, Vienna, and London. He listens to the accounts of the Boat Race and Wimbledon, and the passing of the *Mauretania*, and the cheers in the Saar when Hitler is speaking, or Mr. Baldwin at an agricultural dinner, or Mr. Winston Churchill on India, or Sir Frederic Whyte on the world situation, or Mr. Raymond Swing speaking from New York, or Mr. Percy Philip from Paris. Is it possible to get bored when all the vibrations of the world are pouring into this cottage, and when other vibrations reach him, as he truly believes, from the Other Side—vibrations which bring back the faces of those whom he knew when young, who have now passed on, as they say?

Every time he appears in his garden for half an hour's work to keep his lawn and himself in trim, some friendly soul looks over the hedge and talks to him. The rector, a tall man, once in the Guards, gives him a cheery greeting and calls him "young fellow." An old ostler, now retired except for odd jobs in the garden, discusses horses and hunting gentlemen. An old naval man salutes him and tells stories of Jutland and Zeebrugge. One day a party of girl guides desired permission to enter his house and garden and do a good deed. He put them to weeding, and they removed every weed that lurked between the cracks of his crazy pavement. The village maids nod to him with a smile. There is something in his eyes which pays homage to their youth. Lest he should ignore anyone with whom he has passed the time of day in the village shops, he doffs his hat to any girl who passes as though greeting duchesses and high ladies in Hyde Park, where in younger days he met such beauties as Mrs. Pat and Irene Vanbrugh and the Dare girls.

He has strange visitors. They seem to be drawn to this cottage as though they knew a friendly humorous soul was there. A young man came who was tramping through England sleeping under haystacks and in lonely barns. He was a poet. He left three of his poems in return for two glasses of beer and a memorable conversation on rhythm and the colour of words, for he had met a fellow poet. A naval officer, retired, called to exhibit the miracle of a vacuum cleaner for which he was a travelling sales-man—a sign of the times when naval officers have been axed and have to earn a living somehow. A lady farmer rides by and waves her hand to him. Won't he come and play a game of bridge one evening? Why is he so unsociable? Hawkers who were once city clerks ride over on their bicycles which they drop against his hedge, and try to sell him things he couldn't possibly want. Generally he buys them. Often he gives these visitors a glass of beer. They discuss life. They admire his brasses. They go away with a glow at the heart because this noble-looking man has treated them with kindness when in their line of busi-ness kindness is rare.

The telephone rings. The young woman who does for him is astonished at the number of times her gentleman is wanted on the telephone. He is called up from London newspapers. She overhears long and excited conversations about plays, movies, serial stories, wireless talks. The postoffice is kept busy with telegrams, all to do with the literary business. This man who has retired to a small village is still in touch with the great world. They want the things which he makes in his mind. They have a market for dreams. They wish to produce the children of his fancy on some stage or screen.

"We live in a perfect whirl of excitement," says the young woman who keeps his cottage so neat and tidy that not a speck of dust could be seen by the sharpest eye.

He lives under low beams, as I have said. They are so low here and there that even now, after long knowledge of their whereabouts, he crashes his head against them in an absent-minded moment. Several times he has seen stars. More than once he has sat upon the carpet dazed. But he assures me that every time he knocks his head like that he gets the idea for a new plot. He advises all young authors to live in a cottage with low beams.

I see a good deal of him when I am in the country. He comes into my garden before dinner, and we play a game of garden golf. He plays with me as seriously, with the same desperate concentration, with the same style, slightly behind the ball in the Scottish way, as when he played on famous golf courses in England and America, to say nothing of the Riviera. After dinner we listen for a while to the wireless news and entertainment. Then we talk, dear God, how we talk.

Mostly I am the listener, for I cannot compete with this teller of tales—this man of rich and varied experience, this dramatic raconteur, this builder of dreams, this mind which illumines every episode with humour, fancy, vivid flashes of lightning of the spirit, and phrases which startle one's senses by their intensity and dramatic values. He acts his parts, he rises and makes noble gestures. He brings back all the people who have passed his way. He delivers his old lectures and reacts his old plays. One feels the thrill and agony he suffered on the first night of his first play. One is with him in an anti-aircraft station when the Zeppelins came over London and he gave the order for all the guns to fire. He felt sick at the time because of his excitement. One feels sick as he did because he makes it all so vivid.

Then he talks of contemporary affairs, the international situation, the India bill, the government, the social changes in England. He is very passionate in his prejudices. He hates certain politicians with a ferocity which would fade instantly into genial kindness if he met them at his own table. He denounces the idiocy, the villainy of men with whom he would instantly agree if they presented their case to him over a glass of wine. He deplores the degeneracy of English youth, the vulgarity of its manners, the low standard of its intelligence, yet when English youth comes into his garden or mine he is enchanted by its intelligence, its spirit, and its manners. He is a Conservative of the deepest blue, with an emotional loyalty for old traditions. When the B.B.C. plays God Save the King he stands to attention even if he is alone.

Sometimes after one of these conversations lasting late, when I see him off under the stars and return to my little farmhouse, I laugh and wonder what a foreigner would think of such an Englishman—a Frenchman like André Maurois who thinks we are inarticulate, a German like Ludwig who thinks we are unemotional. We are a mysterious people, we English. If any writer generalizes about us he is either a liar or a fool.

9. *The Man with a Gun*

"There's a law against shooting foxes—but I shoot 'em."

The man who spoke these words with a fierce intensity stood ready with a pail to feed a crowd of young turkeys hatched out in time for Christmas and only a few weeks old. On a post near by were some victims of his gun—a squirrel, a jay, and other enemies of fruit growers and poultry farmers.

"They has to be killed," he said, as I looked, perhaps with a little pity, at these dead things which yesterday had been so vital. "It's a battle between me and them. I've no patience with an old lady over there who won't allow a thing to be killed on her land, and lets rabbits, foxes, and all such vermin breed without let or hindrance. How does she think I can make a living with my poultry?"

He had a good poultry farm of many acres, worked by himself and his son, with cutthroat competition in the neighbourhood for miles around, where there are innumerable poultry farms all producing eggs and chickens for the London market.

"We saw a fox in one of your own fields yesterday," said a lady with me.

"Send him over to me," said the poultryman. "I'll give him fox!" He explained the cause of his ferocity.

Not more than a week ago a fox had destroyed twenty of his hens. One morning he found nothing but feathers in a run where there had been a fine crowd of young pullets.

"It's no good wiring," he explained. "We've wired ourselves in everywhere, but these foxes burrow underneath and laugh at it. Well, I got my own back on one of 'em last night. There she was with a litter of young cubs. I emptied a barrel into her, and she jumped ten feet high before she flopped."

"Doesn't the hunt keep them down?" I asked. The hunt meets outside the Bull with a good pack of hounds. The village turns out to see them at the first sound—the old sound which is now dying out—of horses' hoofs coming clip-clop up the village street, as it used to be heard before the coming of the motorcar. At the sight of the hounds and the huntsmen, the Christian

Socialist who sells bicycles and charges batteries has a spiritual struggle, I guess, between his disapproval of all such wickedness and his appreciation of a good picture of English life.

"They don't know how to hunt round here," said my friend the poultry farmer, with great scorn. "I come from a hunting country where they weren't afraid of foxes. Petworth, that was. Old Lord Leconfield was a friend of the farmers. He kept the country clean of vermin, he did. Why, in all the woods and copses round here the foxes play any game they like, and if I didn't shoot 'em I should lose all my birds, and have all my labour for nothing. Now that old woman yonder who won't let things be killed, what sense has she in her head?"

I had a secret sympathy with the lady who gives a sanctuary to foxes, jays, rabbits, squirrels, and other creatures, but in front of the grey eyes of this poultry farmer I hadn't the courage to say so.

He was the descendant of men who had fought the long war against wild nature. Once, not far from here, on the belt of greensand, his ancestors had fought with mammoths whose bones are still found in the quarries. I have the vertebra of a mammoth backbone found in one of them. Later they had fought with wolves. Man, so cunning and crafty in the making of weapons to aid his strength, has won the victory against the beasts. But the fight still goes on against insects and vermin and the cunning fox, and if man ceases to kill, nature will put him out of business, even so close to London as where the fields of Surrey look towards the Sussex Downs.

10. Country Visitors

Into my house and garden come interesting visitors now and then, and these old beams overhead which vibrated through the centuries only to the simple noises made by rustics, now store up vibrations which will startle posterity if it tunes in to them with something more sensitive than our modern microphone. England speaks in my cottage not only when I turn on the wireless with its talks on every kind of topic from every country in Europe—once a week Mr. Raymond Swing, who

lived for a time in this very village, talks to us from Washington
—but when some of my friends are in talkative mood, as they
nearly always are.

One of them, a man of rare gifts, the novelist who lives in the
cottage near the church, discusses every aspect of life with strong
views about them all. He denounces the B.B.C. for its variety
programmes and its lighter forms of entertainment. He denounces the lack of discipline in England, the lack of patriotism
in public schools, the lack of mind and manners in Bloomsbury,
the death of the theatres, for which he is always writing new
plays, the failure of Roosevelt to bring back prosperity to the
United States, and the essential dishonesty of the politicians in
every country. He is very strong in denunciation but is equally
strong in admiration and given half a chance will expatiate
on the glory of cricket, the magnificence of Dutch painting,
the majesty of Wagner, and the charm of Mrs. Patrick Camp-
bell.

An artist comes to sit in my rooms and have a talk. On the
walls hang two of his own paintings to which his eyes stray now
and then. They look well on my walls. But he has most of his
work in his own studio. The patron of art is now departed.
Buyers are few. Artists are poor, if they are not dead of despair.
This one is poor but merry. At least he has a pleasant sense of
humour and laughs at unexpected times with a kind of internal
explosion of mirth. He laughs when someone says a ridiculous
thing as often someone does. He laughs when one of our Elder
Statesmen utters a portentous platitude duly transmitted to
millions of listeners by the B.B.C. But often he is quite serious,
for this artist is patiently pursuing the quest for a reasonable
interpretation of this world's unreasonable bewilderments. In
his own village, twelve miles or more from mine, he has to put
a guard on his tongue among old ladies who have the Victorian
mind, and among retired colonels and other military gentlemen
who are always on the lookout for "Bolshies" and unpatriotic
fellows, as they would call anybody who departs a hair's breadth
from the views of the Conservative gospel as revealed in the
Morning Post. He got into trouble for signing the Peace Ballot.
He has to keep a discreet silence when, in country houses, his
host lays down the law about war being necessary for the dis-

play of manly virtue. He remembers something about the last war. It's not a good memory of his.

Now and again he talks about art, and then there is silence in the room, because he is very good on subjects like quality and tone, and can give one a glimpse of what makes a good picture instead of a bad picture. He is a worshipper of beauty in a time of ugliness but has no arrogance or affectation about it. He talks about art as a carpenter would talk about wood and the technique of making a good job with a ladder or a wheelbarrow. And that is the way in which art is best talked about among those who know something about line and colour. As he said once, there is more nonsense talked about art than about anything else in life, except the ideal form of government and perhaps a thousand other things.

Into my cottage and garden has come once or twice another writing man who lives in another village, where he has an adorable cottage of his own, looking onto a green where village cricket is still played. He has built himself a study of some spaciousness, lined from floor to ceiling with books which I daresay he reads now and then when he is bored with looking how his flowers grow—and that must be seldom—or when he gets time from the books he writes himself—very long books sometimes, so that libraries like Harrod's and W. H. Smith's have to order extra copies because their clients can't read a novel by Mr. Swinnerton in an afternoon or between tea-time and dinner. He tells very funny stories which keep one laughing long after he has gone. He is a marvellous mimic and can imitate the late John Lane or the late Mr. Dent—those famous publishers— with exact portraiture and intonation of voice, allowing for the genius of caricature. But his masterpiece is Arnold Bennett, whom he knew intimately. When he imitates that great novelist, I who knew him well find myself startled by the living voice and mannerisms of our mutual friend.

I am honoured also by a visit now and then from an elderly gentleman who wears a cloak on chilly days and hires a car to come to see me from his country place, which is very grand compared with the dwellings of cottage folk like me, though very charming. In fact, he has two houses and the better is the one next door which he lets in the summer to people who look nice. If they look nasty he has a thousand reasons why they should dislike this house, though none of them are really plausible because it is one of those dream houses which seem to exist only in the imagination of all that is most fascinating in an English country house of Georgian times, as fragrant as old lavender, as lovely as a picture by an old master, until one walks into its rooms with fine old furniture of its own period and into its garden with terraced walks and velvet lawns and flowers which are massed in colour.

Did I say he only had two houses? No, he has a third in London, very straight up and uncomely from the outside, but filled with most astounding pictures by people like Blake and Rossetti and the other pre-Raphaelites, and Sargent, who came after them with his quick bold touch.

But it is in his country house that I like to think of Graham Robertson. He belongs to its spirit, he looks right in his own garden, where there are many pleasant ghosts to walk with him. Among them are the faithful ghosts of his sheep dogs whose bones lie buried in a little sanctuary he has made in a quiet part of his gardens. Sargent painted him when he was a young man, in a long black overcoat, when he knew many famous people and lovely ladies of Victorian England. Sarah Bernhardt was gracious to him, as he has told in a book which I, like all its readers, find enchanting. It is called *Time Was*.

He is a painter, and in his studio are many of his own works, about which he is too modest; but then he is modest about everything, and that is why he had so many friends and makes so many new ones.

I was first taken to his country house by a young friend of mine who flies through the sky when he is not sitting in an office reading other people's books, which he publishes very nicely. The talk drifted to pageants, and I remembered a pageant at Guildford which had made me wet-eyed because somehow it brought back so much of England's beauty, not long after I had seen the ugliness of war, when so many young Englishmen fell in the dirty places. I noticed that my host was amused and perhaps a little pleased by my words. It turned out that he was the author, producer, and chief actor of this pageant.

11. America Looks at England

Into this cottage of mine come now and then friends from the United States, and they are much amused by the cock-eyed windows and its look of being built for Hansel and Gretel.

One of them comes over each year for tennis at Wimbledon, which he describes over the wireless for the benefit of some twenty million people who listen to him in his own country. It was hot at Wimbledon this year, and John Tunis was for five hours in a little box, talking for all that time across the Atlantic. He nearly suffocated, and I helped to revive him next day by giving him the air which blows across my hedges from the Sussex Downs. He is a mere lad, with an ironical sense of humour. To him we English people are very comical at times.

He spent a week-end at a country house party, and he could hardly believe, he told me, that the county folk whom he met there—the old colonels, the hunting women, and a peer or two —could actually be alive and real. They all seemed to him as if they were acting parts in a play by Somerset Maugham. He gave a very good imitation of the queer noises they made when they gave tongue. To American ears the speech of English county folk is an unbelievable caricature of the English accent, as they are pleased to call our native speech, though after all we ought to know best, as it happens to be our own.

Another friend from America sat in my garden this summer with a movie camera which he operated at unexpected moments for the benefit of his class of students—he is a professor of literature and journalism, God help him! in an American university —who will be pleased to see how English authors look and behave in unguarded moments when they are most ridiculous.

He gave us an illuminating picture of American social conditions under the Roosevelt régime, and then he described an incident on his voyage over, when his boat had bumped into another vessel. For a short time the affair looked as though it might be serious, but he paid a tribute of admiration to the behaviour of the passengers, and especially to his steward, a typical English cockney. This man appeared as my friend was hurrying out of his cabin.

"Your life belt, sir," said the steward, holding out that unpleasant article of apparel as if it were a cup of tea which had just been ordered.

My friend from the University of California knew that as long as there are English stewards who remain imperturbable in danger's hour the British Empire will still stand.

Lately over my garden at night there has been a constant drone of engines. It belongs to squadrons of aëroplanes passing towards London to test the aërial defences of that city. There are strange lights in the sky, long belts of white illumination which touch the clouds and move forward as though searching for something up there. The dramatist, going back late to his own cottage after conversation which has roamed around the world and touched a hundred subjects, stands and watches these lights. They thrill him, he says, to his very marrow bones, because once he was in naval uniform commanding a searchlight station in London in time of war. There was a night when he ordered the guns to fire on a German Zeppelin. It was the moment of his intensest emotion—his greatest thrill in life. There are times, I believe, when, although a man of kindest instincts, he would like to have that thrill again. To me, I confess, those lights in the sky are not fascinating. I regard them with a sense of apprehension and horror, having seen something of war at its worst. Haven't we got beyond all that? Are we still practising for the same old grisly game? Is there no chance of security for the babes who are sleeping tonight—among them one small boy like a Saxon prince, sleeping with a fairy tale in his dreams above my porch? Are they to grow up for the slaughter fields?

12. Down by the Sea

I went down to the sea one day, to the other side of those downs which make a faint blue line beyond my garden hedge. It was the holiday season at Bognor. Hundreds of little shopgirls with their boys were on the sands sun-bathing, playing ball games, taking a dip now and then after wading out far to the retreating tide. There were family parties there. Baldheaded fathers were playing at sand castles with their offspring. The babies were having a fine time in the puddles of sea water. At the end of the pier barelegged young women were putting pennies into slot machines and having their fortunes told— Beware of a dark young man!—and competing for prizes with a little ball which bounces up from a bubble of water.

It was a glorious day, almost too hot. The sun beat down fiercely on the promenade with a white glare. There was not a cloud in the blue sky. Not a cloud? Well, for a moment I saw one darkening everything: this holiday season, this happiness of middle-class families, these groups of mothers and children and fathers from the suburbs who are the unconscious models of *Punch* drawings by Frank Reynolds.

My eye was caught by the news bill of a London newspaper. It was posted up at the kiosks. The paper itself was being read on many seats and in many deck chairs. The big black letters of the placard caught my eye wherever I walked that day in Bognor.

WHAT TO DO
IN
AIR RAIDS

OFFICIAL PLANS

There will be, of course, nothing to do in air raids if they are to come again. Those droning engines over my garden had already proved that there will be no effective defence of London or other great cities. Poison gas will float about the streets and creep down into the cellars. Incendiary and high-explosive bombs will make a nasty mess of London palaces, factories, and blocks of flats. But the government was, it seemed, preparing "official plans." The little children will be taught how to wear gas masks as a part of their infant training in this enlightened age; this beautiful period of civilization when the standard of human intelligence is very high indeed, and when "progress" never stands still. What a splendid prospect! What to do in air raids. Official plans. What foresight. What a hopeful future for our new-born babes!

I thought of a friend of mine—a novelist who comes to my London cottage late at night in winter time and taps at my door if he sees a light burning behind the blinds.

"If there is another air raid," he said on one of those nights, "and if there is a cloud of poison gas in London, I shall go out and breathe deeply. Because if that happens life will no longer be worth while, and humanity will be better dead. It deserves to die."

It was Cecil Roberts who spoke those words with which I agreed and agree.

On the way to Bognor that day we passed through the woods of Arundel Park and under the walls of the old castle. There are no more beautiful trees in England than those tall beeches and spreading oaks of Arundel, and the castle, looking from the river Arun, is like one of those dream castles which, as a small boy, I used to see in imagination or in the coloured pictures of a fairy-tale book, inhabited by knights in shining armour and lovely princesses and gallant pages. It is very much of a fake, as one must admit, when one goes through its archways and explores its courtyards and bastions and embattlements. A nineteenth-century Duke of Norfolk, inspired by the sham romanticism of his age, so renovated the castle that one can hardly find an old stone which stood there in Norman time, though no doubt they are there, encased in Portland cement.

I went there one day with a little lady and a big boy. The lady happened to be the wife of the present Duke's land agent and had the use of the keys on days when the public is not admitted and the family is absent. But some of the keys seemed to be missing that afternoon, and we were confronted by gates barred to us with spikes on top. Nothing daunted by a little thing like that, the lady said, "En avant!" She scaled the gateway, made a jest of the spikes, and disappeared on the other side. The boy found the job easy. I was not used to such ways of entry, but I could not show the white feather before a little lady with a gallant spirit. Up I climbed and over the spikes I went, by an effort of will power and unaccustomed muscles. Three times this happened until I breathed a prayer that the keys would fit all other doors. They did, and we wandered for an hour or more in the armoury and other rooms whose win-

DURHAM CATHEDRAL

dows looked over a lovely landscape, densely wooded until the open Downs go billowing to the sea.

The big boy was interested in armour, and I had to cudgel my brains for old knowledge which I had once mugged up on this subject of helmets, cuisses, breastplates, pikes, and halberds.

The present Duke is a young man. I knew his father, the black-bearded, heavy-shouldered man who was premier Duke of England, hereditary Earl Marshal, and Earl of Surrey. He was like the reincarnation of one of his ancestors, that duke who led the Pilgrimage of Grace and lost his head in the Tower of London, or like the earlier dukes who wore black armour and tucked their beards into steel masks and were strong, brutal, cruel men, unless they were softened by their Christian faith and code of chivalry.

Here at Arundel stands the great anachronism of a walled castle still inhabited by a family which owns many thousands of acres of English earth. We have had social revolutions of which the most radical has happened since the war by the taxation of wealth. The roads to the coast are thick with motor traffic, and trippers camp below the castle walls, leaving litter on the grass. But with all our change and our modernity the old lives on. We have many relics of the past, and there is still a little life in them.

13. Manners Maketh Man

There was a conversation in my cottage one evening about English character. It arose suddenly because of the wireless news which reported a debate in the House of Commons about a little English schoolgirl who had written in an essay that England was the finest country in the world. It was alleged— quite untruly, it seems—that the school inspector had reproved her for this jingo sentiment. A newspaper had written fierce and flaming words denouncing the inspector for checking the patriotism of English children. Some pompous gentlemen in the House of Commons had expressed their horror that this noble sentiment should be a cause of reproof. It was a heated debate, while that evening the statesmen of Europe assembled at Geneva were endeavouring to avert a war which might have grave consequences to many nations.

"Ridiculous nonsense!" said a friend of mine who had come in after the evening meal. It was the novelist who crashes his head against his low beams in a neighbouring cottage.

At the other end of the room was a lady who was busy over a piece of tapestry. She pulled through a long thread of coloured wool and spoke with unusual intensity.

"After all, England is the finest country!"

The novelist turned to her and laughed.

"Finest in what way?" he asked.

"In honesty," said the lady, "and in generosity. And in the character of the people."

"My dear lady!" exclaimed the novelist, raising his hand. "Isn't that going a little too far? Haven't we just heard an appeal over the wireless to Bank holiday crowds imploring them not to leave litter about the countryside, not to strew the sands and beaches with broken glass, not to fling lighted cigarettes about and start heath fires? I can't see how we can boast of our national character when such appeals are necessary. All this talk of education and a higher standard among the masses is sheer hypocrisy. There are no manners nowadays. This sprawling democracy is lacking in all consideration for decent behaviour. I get shoved in the ribs when I go to a cinema in London and try to buy a ticket. People shove and push to get on a bus. The other day when I was in a railway carriage and rose to lift down the bag of a woman who was getting out she said, 'That's mine!' as though I wanted to steal it. She hadn't been used to men giving her a helping hand. Life has become a snatch-and-grab business. Young men don't even bother to offer their seats to a lady if she has to stand. That's what they call the progress of democracy! I call it the degeneration of social life."

"All that is rather trivial," replied the lady who was busy with a piece of tapestry.

"Trivial? Good heavens, no! It's all vastly important. Good manners are the touchstone of civilization. In my opinion a bounder, as we used to call a man without manners, is the lowest form of life. The species is becoming very common nowadays.

England, which has produced the finest type of gentleman, has also produced the worst type of bounder, especially when he goes abroad."

He was well away, and I listened to his dramatic accounts of the bounders he had encountered on his way through life. I could not help acknowledging the truth of these portrait studies. I had met their prototypes. He gave an exact imitation of an English tourist in Paris walking down the Rue de Rivoli in plus fours as though he were on an English golf course. He acted the part of an English visitor at Nice, making gobbling noises in his throat because the waitress in the English tea rooms kept him waiting for a toasted bun. He did some excellent caricatures—hardly exaggerated—of English travellers on cross-channel boats, pushing other people's luggage about, monopolizing hat racks, insulting Frenchmen because they failed to understand abominable French, bullying waiters, behaving with an arrogance to all foreigners unjustified by any superiority of knowledge or character.

"I don't want to drag down my own country," he said after this exhibition, "but we must admit that for the Complete Bounder England is an easy first. And I very much fear that the breed is advancing upon us by mass production. We are becoming a nation of nitwits, due to the influence of those ghastly hours of imbecile variety wireless, and the cinema with its gunmen and all its hideous vulgarity. The advance of democracy is the domination of the lowest minds and the victory of Sally the Chewing-gum Queen in every form of art and every department of social life."

It was a Tory Englishman who spoke: a man who instinctively believes in the aristocratic tradition of noble fellows, perfectly tailored, exquisitely mannered, ruling by right of birth and blood over the obedient masses trained to touch their forelocks to their betters.

I felt uneasy as I entered into a laughing argument with him. There are signs of a loss of manners in this England of today. My old carpenter complains of it. There is a danger that popular education and the mass production of newspapers, books, film pictures, and wireless entertainment are an appeal to the lowest common denominator of intelligence. There is that danger against which the lovers of beauty, the scholars, and the thinkers must put up a fight or perish.

14. Old English

I went to see some friends of mine who live in an old house with a good garden. It was once a farmstead, but those who live in it now, like many owners of ancient farmhouses, do not drive the plough or keep cattle in their yards. My friend is a shipping man who drives every morning to the local station, twelve miles away, and goes up to an office from which he returns in winter after dark. His wife lives there all the year round and is never bored, she tells me, as most women would be, because she loves her garden which she has made a lovely picture, and only leaves it now and then to ride over the neighbouring heaths, looking in jodhpurs like a lady in a canvas by Mr. Munnings.

This husband and wife, who are cousins, are both related by descent to a very great gentleman who lost his head because he kept his faith. He was a fine scholar as well as a great gentleman, and he is now a saint in the Roman calendar. His name was Thomas More, Lord Chancellor of England, and his head was carried, it is said, to another old house not more than ten miles away from the one I visited one Sunday afternoon this summer, to take tea with those who have a touch of his blood.

The garden was looking at its best, I thought. A stream meanders through it to fields which provide pasture for a few cows. Against an old barn, no longer used at harvest time, there was a fine array of hollyhocks and delphiniums as tall as the grenadiers of Frederick the Great. There was a glory of colour in the flower beds, and the sun had burnt the grass beyond the shade of tall trees.

At tea-time I sat next to a small girl whom Millais would have liked to paint because of her big dark eyes and her moss-rose skin. There was also a tall boy at table—her brother—who had to leave early to join his ship, getting ready for the King's Jubilee Review.

As I glanced round the room with its old beams, first shaped for this house before the eighth Henry had sent his order to the Tower for the execution of the noblest man in England—that Sir Thomas More, blood relation of these people who gave me tea—I thought how little had changed in such a home these hundred years past, although outside in the big world and the noisy cities everything has changed. A hundred years ago a boy like this would have risen from a table like this to say good-bye to his mother in a house like this, before going back to his ship in Portsmouth harbour.

We talked about the great frost on May 16, which had killed all the fruit in England. There was the usual talk about the neighbourhood to which I had once belonged. We discussed gardens, potatoes, soils and other subjects of interest and importance to those who own a bit of English earth. I ate too many tempting cakes. Opposite was a lady who knew a good deal about the theatre and had seen a play called *The Aunt of England* in which I had a family interest. It was the kind of talk one has over many tea tables, until suddenly it became more serious, on a subject which was casting a shadow over many minds. My host was speaking about the Italian adventure on the frontier of Abyssinia. He knew something about it as a shipping man in touch with Italian transport officers. The situation was already chaotic and disorderly for the young troops conveyed to Somaliland. They had been without water for a whole day under the burning sun. The Italian authorities were trying to distil sea water, but it was a slow process incapable of supplying hundreds of parched men. They had intended to supply the troops with iced wine and had sent over to England for a ship capable of producing forty tons of ice a day—which was quite impossible. Already there was heavy sickness among the troops. Thousands of them were down with fever and dysentery.

"It won't be an easy war for the Italians," said my friend. "With all their aircraft, they can't do much in a mountainous country like Abyssinia. It won't be a walk-over."

He spoke to me gravely about the dangers of this war, if it happened. It might unsettle everything in Europe. In any case, if the League failed to act it would be a blow to all pacts and pledges.

"If it were possible," he said, "I should be in favour of isolation. But is it possible for us to withdraw and stand alone as an Empire leaving Europe to its own madness?"

We walked out into the garden again. I paired off with the husband of the lady who knew a good deal about the theatre. He was a man of youngish middle age and bore a famous and noble name in the history of English law. We sat under a tree from which we could see the deep blue of delphiniums and lupins and the silken patterns of antirrhinums. The air was fragrant with the scent of these flowers. The shadows lengthened across the lawns. Somewhere a bell was ringing for church time.

"What do you think of this world?" asked the man with a noble name.

That was a difficult question for a summer afternoon.

He knew a lot about this world, I found. He knew something about Russia, and told me that it was returning to Imperialism, without an Emperor.

"Russia is anxious to avoid war in the West," he said. "What keeps her nervous is the fear of a Japanese attack. In that case Germany might move towards the Ukraine. It's the old struggle of teeming populations for food and raw material."

He seemed to think those movements were likely to change the future map of Europe and the world.

"What do you see coming?" he asked. "In what direction are we moving?"

We discussed the possibilities of a move towards the socialistic state, or forms of state worship and discipline, subordinating the individual and creating a kind of ant life for men and women obedient to the law of the ant heap. He regarded that with horror, but it was happening in Russia, in Italy, in Germany. It might be forced upon nations for self-preservation as a means of efficiency and economy. The future fight would be to save the individual soul.

He put many of our modern troubles down to the excess of population and the restrictions on emigration.

"Birth control may do something to check the pressure of peoples," he said.

We talked about England, and he saw no remedy for unemployment, except by well-organized schemes of land settlement on a big scale within the Empire.

"The Dominions don't encourage it," I answered. "I happen to know that because I wasted a lot of time trying to work out such a scheme. Australian Trade Unionists don't want emigration from England. They have labour troubles of their own and take a narrow view. Even Canada has shut her gates because of a drift to the cities and much unemployment."

"The Dominions will have to be bribed," said my friend calmly. "They will take our men all right if we put up the money."

The shadows lengthened again. We spoilt the scent of flowers by smoking cigarettes. It was very pleasant in this English garden.

"Apart from unemployment," said my new friend, "England is still very rich. All the little shopkeepers are making pots of money."

"Explain the mystery!" I begged him. "How can England prosper when Europe is bankrupt? How can we be rich when all our basic industries are in a bad way—cotton, shipping, coal?"

He explained the mystery, but I could not follow his explanation. It was something to do with the spinning round of money from one pocket to another. He seemed to know quite a lot about money, but the worst of it is that when I meet such men they talk a language which is double Dutch to the man in the street like myself.

"We may be advancing towards a snag," he admitted presently. "I don't say this prosperity is going to last very long."

I was sorry to hear it. I was rather hoping I had met a prophet of good tidings, at least as regards English prosperity.

"In any case," he said, "money is changing hands. The small people are coming up. The big people are going down. There's no chance for the old landed gentry."

He belonged to that class himself, and it was when we had gone into the house again and were looking at the rooms upstairs, very old and quaint, that he allowed himself a moment's regret and bitterness because of the passing of the old estates.

"One can't help having a bit of a pang when one sees old English mansions pulled down or turned into hotels. Now and then I go back to see a historic house in which I was brought up as a boy. It has been taken over by the National Trust, and I pay my shilling to see it, lining up with the crowd. They've put a car park outside the gates. It's all vulgarized. I confess it makes my heart bleed."

I told him my heart bled all the way from London to Leatherhead because so much old beauty had been blotted out.

"One can't put beauty back. That's the worst of it," said this man who had been brought up in one of the great old houses of England.

Our hostess, the lady who rides on open heaths in jodhpurs, confessed that her bedroom in which we were standing was an ice well in winter, in spite of two fires burning. She froze in her fourposter bed.

We strolled over from this place to a house on the top of the hill. It had once belonged to me. Now its present owner had almost rebuilt it and had added a swimming pool to the garden. He greeted us naked to the waist, having just emerged from teaching one of his small boys to dive. Entirely without embarrassment he gave us welcome and asked me whether I would like to have a swim. I declined, having an old-fashioned shyness in stripping before my fellow men and women. A Frenchman would, I think, have regarded this scene with amazement because of its utter lack of formality. He wouldn't have been able to fit it in with his conception of English life. But does anything fit in with careful studies of England and the English? Our social code is constantly violated by eccentricity, sometimes of a wild kind. Only a few nights later, when I went to dinner in a country house where there was a house party, one of the women was describing vivaciously a visit by herself and some friends to a famous architect. He too had been in a swimming pool and was in a complete state of nature when his guests arrived. He waved a wet hand at them and cried, "Come in. We're all married people here, aren't we?" A most eccentric man, and absent-minded, he invited twenty people to lunch one day, and having forgotten all about that, had no more than a few sausages with which to stay their hunger. The conversation was good, though the food was scarce.

How, then, can we dogmatize about ourselves when we throw up characters like that, clean contrary to the general idea that we are all turned out in moulds, that our manners are stiff and reserved, that we have a very rigid code of good form, that we are unimaginative and unemotional? The French discussing the English, as often I have heard them, believe that we are Puritanical and beyond words frigid, with stiff, unbending etiquette in social life, while they—as they fondly imagine—are free and easy, liberal in conversational intercourse, and informal in their ways. Nothing could be more preposterous than that argument. It is the French who are formal, as anyone knows who has been to a French family gathering. I remember a Frenchman being profoundly shocked because a friend of mine lay on the grass at full length with his arms under his head in the presence of a lady. It seemed to him a grave breach of decorum. I remember being on the sands of a French watering place when a young friend of mine was threatened with arrest by a shocked gendarme because he had undone the button of his bathing costume and let it fall over one shoulder. On the other hand, in England, I once went to a garden party at Hampton Court where my hostess and most of her guests emerged from the river and played tennis to dry themselves in the sun. I wasn't the only man, I am sure, who felt that it was slightly odd to take tea among a party of water nymphs within half an hour of Charing Cross. One of the water nymphs with red hair and lovely limbs saw ghosts on the lawn as clearly as I could see my fellow guests, and told me surprising things about my departed relatives, though I had only just met her. The oddest things happen now and then in English gardens.

15. The Creeping Shadow

There is another garden in which I sometimes go. It lies at the end of a long drive and has the shade of many noble trees. Always when I go there I see games of good tennis played by young people who dash about the court in the hottest sun and then eat an enormous tea provided for them. They are a nice crowd, these young people, and most of them are familiar with places on the Riviera and other happy hunting grounds of pleasure, because their parents were merchant princes who still seem to be doing rather well though they talk about their ruin from bad trade and high income tax.

I went to lunch there one day this summer, and my hostess reproved me for serving on a commission inquiring into the traffic in arms—there was a Vickers at the table—because in her opinion, strongly expressed, if we put a stop to this private manufacture and trade it would be handing over the market to other countries who would have less scruple than ourselves. I argued with her politely. One cannot get angry with a lady whose food one is eating—at least, it is best to keep smiling—and she is a dame who spends much time and money in the interests of crippled children. She is one of those women who have made England what it is, with a strong touch of Elizabeth's steel in their spirit, with no affectations and with strong opinions about everything from the way of making jam to the way of ruling a country. They still exist in country houses and in Belgravia.

Afterwards there was a general conversation in her garden, with occasional dialogues, and sitting there on that summer day this year, I was conscious that there was a sinister kind of drama in this scene and in this talk. The sun was warm upon us. There was the hum of bees in the herbaceous borders. I was among prosperous people in surroundings of perfect beauty and, it seemed, perfect peace. But they were worried. They seemed to look beyond the gardens to a dangerous and unsafe world. They seemed to hear in the silence a beating of drums which were war drums.

One of the men turned to me presently and said in a low voice which no one else could hear:

"I am afraid."

These words, I confess, sent a chill down my spine, because the man who said them was not of a neurasthenic type. One would not have guessed by looking at him that there was any fear in his mind. He was a sturdily built man who had laughed a good deal over the luncheon table. I knew something about him. He had Jewish ancestry. His father had made a great name in the city of London and had been a great philanthropist. This present holder of the name had been behind the scenes of political and diplomatic life. He knew one of our most famous ambassadors well enough to call him Willy. He knew the Foreign Office crowd and had many international associations.

We had been talking of European affairs, and especially of Germany, before he said, "I am afraid."

He knew Germany well. He believed that its people were being ruled by a madman who had in his hands the devilish forces of mechanized warfare which could be set going by the touch of a switch.

"The Germans seem to have a weakness for being ruled by madmen," he said. "Frederick was mad. The Kaiser was mad. Now they bow down to the madman Hitler."

He laughed for a moment harshly and then was grave again.

"Enormous forces are stirring in Europe and the world," he said. "They are below the surface, but we are all living on the edge of volcanoes. It is the preparation for new wars and a new era of the human race. Cruelty, intolerance, brutality, the blind passion of races and peoples are surging up again. Our civilization is just a thin crust over the boiling cauldron."

It was then that he said, "I am afraid."

I could understand his fear. He was a Jew and had believed that civilized peoples had abandoned the persecution of his race, that frightful persecution which has been the blackest blot on Christendom. They had been massacred in many Christian countries. They had been thrust into ghettos, treated like pariah dogs, despised, humiliated, and tortured. They had fled from one country to another to find some sanctuary. Their genius had never been killed. They had given the world great gifts of art, and music, and scholarship, and science. They had, it seemed, broken down the old prejudices and hatred. In England, in Germany, in the United States, Jews had felt safe at last. They had got beyond the cruelties of mediævalism. So they had believed until this man Hitler had arisen. Now it was all coming back again. In Germany Jews were being treated as though they were unclean. Christian women who had anything to do with them were ostracized and brutalized. They were banned from the social life of Germany. They were prevented from trading, doctoring, teaching. They were insulted and persecuted, if they were not murdered or beaten this side of death. As a Jew his mind was filled with horror because of this resurgence of the ancient persecution. But as an Englishman and an internationalist, familiar with the secrets of foreign affairs, he was aware of another darkness beyond the sunshine of this English garden. The rearming of Germany, the failure of the Disarmament Conference, the ineffectiveness of the League, the piling up of armaments in many countries, the challenge of Mussolini to the efforts of the peacemakers, the state of Austria, the whisperings in many capitals and war offices and foreign offices, had given him this sense of fear which he had revealed in that sentence, "I am afraid."

"Sir John Simon was, of course, pro-German," he said. "Our foreign policy has been utterly feeble and vacillating. On Monday we have patted Germany on the back. On Tuesday we have made love to France. On Wednesday we have been polite to Mr. Mussolini. On Thursday—we have no clear line of policy whatever and nobody trusts us, and we don't know what our own game is in any part of the world. The situation in Japan and China is due to our weakness. The little Japanese gentlemen smile up their sleeves and go steadily on with a purpose which one day will menace Western civilization. There is only one policy which may save Western peoples from downfall."

"Tell me," I said.

"A close alliance between the British peoples and the United States of America."

We discussed the chances of that and agreed that at the moment the American people were busy in proposing new laws which would strengthen their isolation and keep them out of any alliances which might involve them in future war.

"England," I said presently, "is doing rather well. Can't we look forward to the future with some optimism?"

It was a man of finance who answered.

"This appearance of prosperity is only an illusion," he said gloomily. "I don't like the look of things. We are only just holding on. If there is another European crisis we shall be in the soup."

One goes into English gardens with a sense of peace. But I find that when one leaves the subject of flowers and the weather there is apt to be disturbing conversation in this year of grace, especially if in these gardens there are people who know what is happening over the hedge. Fear has taken possession of many minds, even in England. It was this sense of fear which I found on a European journey which I made the year before. Its shadow is creeping over the garden walls of England.

16. The Man Who Came Home

Two friends of my friend who lives near the church came over to my garden for a game of clock golf and conversation and a cup of tea. One of them was a tall fellow who had to stoop like an orang-outang when he came inside the cottage. One of his hands—the one he holds out for welcome—is slightly damaged. Something happened to it during a world war. Since then he has played many parts on the American stage, though a complete Englishman, by name of Warlock, which is a good old English name meaning a male witch. As a younger man he was already famous on the English stage, where he played with Oscar Asche and others.

The other man who came that day is a portrait painter who has a studio in London where he gives parties to famous people who admire his pictures but don't buy them. He has a garden to his London house which he has made into a private paradise. Real flowers grow there in spite of the cats, whom he stalks with deadly intent. He was glad to see this garden of mine and had various ideas for improving its beauty. By the time he had done with these ideas I had the conviction that it would be necessary to employ a landscape gardener, perhaps two landscape gardeners, to reconstruct the whole scene. Harris Brown is equally well informed about military uniforms, armour, place names, French, Italian, and Dutch art, and the Red Indians of Canada and the United States.

It was the other man who talked about England. He wanted to keep on talking about England because he had been away from it for a number of years and now had come back to look at it with fresh eyes and a heart which bled when he thought he would have to leave it again because of his place on the American stage.

"What strikes you most?" I asked, giving him a chance.

"The English are a happy people," he said. "That's what strikes me all the time. They're peaceful and cheery and good-humoured. The taxi drivers are never in too much of a hurry to pass a friendly word or two. They like their little joke and are wonderfully civil and polite. The same with the bus conductors. It can't be an easy job. One would think it would try the patience of a saint. But these fellows are always good-natured. They thank one every time one takes a ticket. It's the same in any crowd. The people have a friendliness and a cheerfulness which one can't find elsewhere."

"What else?" I asked, handing him another cigarette as he stretched his long legs in a deck chair.

"England is still beautiful," he said. "I have been motoring about a bit. I find it so beautiful that I want to shout out or burst into tears. It's a beauty which is like an old song. Having been out of the country for several years I just wallow in it and feel as sentimental as a schoolgirl."

"How about ribbon development and the deadly work of the jerry builder?" I asked.

"One can soon escape from all that," he answered. "It's rather horrible, I admit, but when one gets beyond its trail there is old England still untouched and unspoilt."

He talked about the English "accent" as the Americans call it. His ear had become accustomed to the American intonation. The English voice and pronunciation seemed to him affected. Young people spoke as if they were putting on airs and playing in stage characters. Of course they weren't. It was perfectly natural, but that's how it sounded after living in the United States.

"These young people," I said. "What's your impression of them?"

He answered without hesitation.

"They're fine! I see nothing wrong with them. They talk frankly and think frankly. They say things which in my young days would have been considered highly indecorous, very bad form. But they don't mean anything of that kind. I'm all for this new frankness about the problems of life. I listen open-eared to them. Of course I don't pretend that my experience of English youth is very extensive. But I've been in touch with some young people who fill me with admiration and respect. There's no nonsense about them. They look at life seriously and humorously. They're clean and fine and spirited. I don't believe a word about English decadence. Look at England now! It's gone ahead better than any country in the world. It has grappled with its difficulties and mastered them. It's our character, I suppose, that has done it. There's an essential honesty in England, and we adapt ourselves to each day as it comes without making plans which don't work out."

A young German I met had made the same remark. He didn't believe in working to a plan. The English, he said, made the best of things according to circumstances. Perhaps we are wise, after all, in our policy of muddling through. It may be better than a Five-Year plan, or a social revolution which turns everything upside down before it falls into economic ruin or plunges into a river of blood.

17. They Lived in a Castle

One never knows what romantic or eccentric character hides behind an English mask. That revelation came to a French interpreter during the World War. He told me that he had suffered agonies in the English mess to which he was attached because of the conversational inhibitions of the English officers. Here they were in the middle of a war in which all faith was being challenged, all gods thrown from their altars, all ideals dragged down to the level of ape life. God Himself seemed to be challenged by the creatures He had made. Yet these English officers, who were about to die like gentlemen in due course, never talked of anything but trivialities: the mechanism of a machine gun, the jolly good show they had seen at the Empire on their last leave, the habits of the lesser tits and the love affairs of butterflies. The French interpreter, who was a man of intellect, wanted to scream now and then. He desired intelligent talk about religion, philosophy, art, and the profound mysteries of life. The Colonel set the tone and the topic and never got as far as that. The stupidity of the English seemed impregnable. And yet he discovered by accident that one of the officers was a considerable authority on Dante and that another was a musician and composer of no mean talent. One of them had an expert knowledge of French wines. One of them wrote poetry in secret hours.

"You are all in hiding," said this Frenchman. "You seem ashamed to reveal any little talent you may have. You are as mysterious and furtive as the Chinese."

The same remark was made to me by an American writer who had married an English officer.

"I have lived long in England," she told me—her name is Mary Borden—"and I have married an Englishman, but I can't understand what goes on in the mind of an Englishman, if anything goes on. You are as mysterious as the Chinese."

That's what they think of us, these foreigners, and we rather like them to think of us that way.

It seems a kind of compliment. After all, we think, we have secret reserves of intelligence which surprise the world now and then. We're not such asses as we look. We give 'em a shock when they least expect it.

Certainly one can find odd fellows and odd lives in England. One of my friends who married an American girl deliberately abandoned the pursuit of wealth, even as far as a seat in an office, and became—though heaven knows how—the caretaker of a ruined castle down in the west of England. It is a very ruined castle, mostly without a roof. It is not a question of living in a draughty place, because the winds howled through gaping holes in the walls and came moaning through broken masonry only kept up because of the ivy.

My friend and his wife had three rooms or so which they could make reasonably watertight. In one of these the American girl—no longer astonished by anything that might be done by her husband, who is an idealist—painted pictures of French peasants and other subjects which came into her head. She is a real artist. That is to say she has had a good training in the schools but has her own style, sensibilities, and genius. She has the mind of a child who sees life very vividly and freshly and purely, so that there is a primitive simplicity about her pictures which is unaffected, unlike the work of so many moderns.

I went to see this young husband and wife in the ruined castle.

Rye
en Sussex

E. Sander

RYE, IN SUSSEX

They had a small daughter to whom it was all very natural and enchanting because she knew no other kind of place and ruins were just as good to her as a nursery in Park Lane. Flowers grew in the crannies of the stones, and she liked to pick them. With her faithful companion, a woolly dog, she had great adventures where knights and men at arms had marched under the archways. Tourists came on Saturdays and Sundays, and my friend, the caretaker, showed them round and did not disdain a *pourboire* which some of them slipped into his hand. The owner of the castle arrived now and then with friends and expected meals to be cooked for him by this girl to whom he ought to have gone down on one knee instead of treating her as a Patient Griselda. It was all very queer and fantastic. The young husband, obsessed with ideas on beauty as though he had been the first to discover it, spent his evenings writing a novel in the style of his wife's paintings, with intense simplicity and something of the touch of Rousseau. He wrote another. No publisher has accepted them. I fear none will. But if I were a publisher I would take a chance with them because they have a queer quality and are different from all other novels. They are like Italian primitives describing modern life.

The castle was not really a success. The last time I saw this couple the young woman was sitting on a high ladder in an immense block of service flats in London, with a central hall and lounge. She was painting a large-sized picture on the wall above the stairs. It represented a London street scene and looked as though it had been painted by a child of genius, as indeed it had been. The people coming up the staircase—provincial folk, business men, suburban ladies—regarded it with surprise and interest. Some of them thought it ridiculous. Others thought it interesting. Some of the art critics came to have a look at it and said good things about it. But I doubt whether it paid for its paint and the journeys up to town. One does not live by bread alone, said the husband of the artist, who is an idealist and a man of dreams. I hesitated to tell him that man does not live nowadays by art alone. But one day I wrote it to him, and he was shocked.

I go about England meeting strange, enchanting people like that. One never knows what odd character one will meet in a ruined castle or an old manor house or a village shop.

The eccentricity of English character, or rather its deep attachment to individualism, still persists outside the crowds of mass production and standardized habits. There are people still in England who live exactly as though they were back in the eighteenth century before the time of electricity, bathrooms, motorcars, and other unnecessary adjuncts of this modern and vulgar world. I know a man—he is pure Plantagenet in his strain of blood—who lives in an old house which is called a castle, where there is no other light but candles. I went to dine with him one evening, and it was like going back two centuries and dining with a Georgian gentleman in an old mansion quiet in its park. The house was filled with historic relics and treasures, though the master of the castle is a poor man. There was a tattered banner which once belonged to Charles II. On the panelled walls was a portrait by Vandyck of Henrietta Maria, the wife of Charles I, and other portraits of seventeenth- and eighteenth-century men and women. The library is filled with old books in rare bindings: books which one had to hold with both hands, noble books, not made nowadays, with big pages and broad margins and fine print. My host—this Plantagenet whose ancestors had served all the kings of England and was allied to them by blood—pulled out some of these tomes and showed me their splendour of printing and binding.

At dinner there was conversation about hunting and shooting and wines and food. Another man was there who could hold his own on such subjects. His name was Horace Annesley Vachell, whose books are well known. Before the port went round our host rose and took one of the silver candlesticks from the table and in a very courtly way led his lady wife from the dining room to her drawing room. It was a way of darkness with this one candle lighting it. Over the port, which we drank solemnly as port was drunk in the eighteenth century, with respect for its flavour and bouquet—no one dared to smoke, of course, lest those qualities should be hurt—this big, heavy, handsome man at the head of the table told us some of his adventures of youth. He had been out in Australia. He had owned thousands of acres—hundreds of square miles, I believe—of Australian land up by Queensland. He had trekked enormous distances with

great herds of cattle. He had led a wild life with nature and a
few comrades. Now here he was again sitting at the head of his
table by candlelight which flickered on the portrait by Vandyck.

Some little time ago I went to stay in another old house in
which English history had passed. It dates from the thirteenth
century, which is quite a long time ago, and it is in the Close
of Canterbury Cathedral, of which its present owner is a Canon.
I was the guest of the Canon and his son, the latter a friend I
had known in wartime as a cavalry officer in the 1st Royals.
Now he is Warden of an institution in Canada called Hart
House, which is the centre of intellectual, dramatic, and musical
activity in that Dominion. It's an interesting job which he has
made important by his personal influence and quality of character. The name of Bickersteth will be remembered in Canada
by young men who are destined to be its future leaders.

He comes home every other year or so, like a homing bird,
to this old house and to the mother who is proud of him. She
is the mother of English sons who have all done well, and
especially in a great war when one of them was killed. Another
of them was a padre at that time with the London Division, and
I used to meet him now and then between battles in which that
division was cut to pieces time and time again. The men confided in him. He knew their minds as few others. He suffered
because of their agony. They were a gay crowd, this London
division. They had many cockney jesters among them. They
were the humourists of the British army, like all London men
in other divisions. But humour wore a little thin before the end
came. The endless casualties, the constant slaughter, the weight
of odds against the living in each new "show," was too long
an ordeal. This padre invented fairy tales as long as he could
to keep their spirits up. The war would soon be over, he said.
He had heard on good authority that the enemy was weakening.
He gave them what spiritual comfort he could, and in his own
heart wondered what God had to do with all this shambles of
youth. Now he is the head of a public school in England, after
a similar position in Australia.

This English family, brought up in an ecclesiastical atmosphere, steeped in the spirit of all that is most beautiful in the

English Church—those lovely anthems in Canterbury and other cathedrals, the glory of English architecture and stained glass— educated at public schools and universities, belong to a class and type which produced some very noble characters. They have one possession which will, I think, be famous in later history. It is a diary written by the four brothers on war service, in the form of letters to their father and mother. At home, the mother added a history day by day of what was happening in England. I have read parts of this narrative, bound in many volumes. It is a wonderful record of the war as experienced by one English family.

With my friend I wandered about Canterbury and touched its old stones. Once he took me into the Cathedral when it was locked against the outside public. We stood on the steps where Beckett was killed and tried to see that scene of martyrdom by tuning in our minds to its vibrations. In the utter silence, in the cool, dim light down the far vista of the great nave under those tall columns of a white forest in stone, where so many kings and princes and saints and heroes and prayerful folk have bent their heads through all English history, one might see ghosts. We went down into the crypt, and my friend told me that two choir-boys vowed once that they had seen the figure of a man in armour. They were very much frightened. It was here that Edward the Black Prince used to come and kneel before an altar. A little light turned on by a switch glimmered over that altar as I stood by one of the thick Norman columns and felt a slight shiver down my spine, not of fear, but of emotion, because in this shrine one stood so close to the past. In Canterbury Cathedral the spirit of England speaks with its long tale of life, its endeavour and achievements, its tragedies and victories. One must be made of stone not to feel stirred in one's spirit in such a place.

It was in Canterbury week that I stayed there, and I went to see the famous cricket match. It was unbelievable. Had not things changed since the war? Had time stood still here in Canterbury week? There were the marquees of the Guards and other regiments. There were bands playing Gilbert and Sullivan. Here on the green were the old characters of England, exactly the same as in years gone by before aëroplanes and poison gas and motorcars and other inventions which have spoilt the peace of life. The players in their white flannels moved in the ritual of the game. It was like a slow-motion picture. It took an hour, I think, for one of the batsmen to score two runs.

In the refreshment tent I was introduced to local inhabitants —old gentlemen and ladies, pretty girls and young men. The old ladies and gentlemen were glorious, I thought. They might have stepped out of the pages of Thackeray. There, surely, was Colonel Newcome with his white moustache. There was Pendennis. Queen Victoria would have been delighted with this company. She would have known them all as good English types of great respectability and virtue, very loyal, behaving with that decorum upon which she insisted. Their sons would be ready to die for her on the outskirts of the Empire. She would decorate some of them with the Victoria Cross. Canons and minor canons in their gaiters made little darts to the buffet for cream buns and ices. The ladies looked languidly at the cricket under their parasols. Some of them were very lovely ladies who looked as though they had just stepped out of the canvases of Millais and Leighton. Heaven alone knows where they go to after Canterbury week. I do not see them in London. They do not appear at cocktail parties in Chelsea. In Canterbury one finds England as it was before the by-pass and the petrol pump.

But Hugh Walpole finds sinister psychology even in cathedral towns. If he tells the truth, the soul of a canon may be encrusted with selfishness and poisoned by self-indulgence. The very peaches on the old walls are so many temptations to his sensuality. Doubtless the devil comes to Canterbury among the pilgrims. He goes about like a roaring lion seeking whom he may devour. But I cannot imagine him in one of the marquees during Canterbury week, unless he assumes the disguise of a Victorian-looking gentleman in loose clothes and the old school tie.

18. The Young British Soldier

I went over to Aldershot to have a look at the soldier of today, and as I crossed the Hog's Back and motored down through Ash towards this training ground of the British army, I wondered how these battalions of young soldiers would compare with those others I had known along the Albert–Bapaume road and other places in France and Flanders twenty-one years ago. Twenty-one years? No. That was impossible. Even now it seems to me like the day before yesterday.

And yet it seemed a thousand years—so queer is the working of the brain—since I first went to Aldershot as a descriptive writer of a London newspaper. King Edward, I remember, was reviewing his troops. There was a sham battle of the utmost absurdity, though quite amusing to watch. It was as much like a real battle such as I saw afterwards under barrage fire as a scene of battle at the Old Vic. With a fellow journalist who afterwards became an editor, I climbed up to Cæsar's Camp where the King was taking lunch in his pavilion.

"Halt, who goes there?" shouted a soldier, only visible by the point of his bayonet.

"I'm the *Daily Mail*," replied my fellow journalist.

"Well, get down from this hill or I'll shove a bayonet through your belly," said the sentry, revealing himself above a gorse bush.

He had no respect whatever for the *Daily Mail*.

That was a thousand years ago, it seemed.

I had seen the Aldershot Tattoo as the guest of a Guards officer who invited me to dine in his clubhouse and afterwards sauntered to the show smoking a cigar which he raised an inch every time he was saluted—about sixty times a minute on the road through the camp. The Aldershot Tattoo is more than a pageant. It's a religious ceremony. It's a ritual attended by vast numbers of pilgrims who come to worship the spirit of their race, its glory and triumph over all enemies, its unbroken series of victories over Frenchmen, Indians, African savages, and the lesser breeds. It is the annual celebration of national self-consciousness raised to ecstasy when the massed bands play "Land of Hope and Glory," when the pipers step out into the searchlights, when the ghosts of history in a hundred wars come marching under the stars on that limelit sward. We pretend that we are unemotional. We put up a bluff that we are antimilitarist. We smile when a public orator talks of that Empire upon which the sun never sets—as though that were a special privilege of ours and due to our own nobility. But in spite of eleven million voters for the League methods and its ideals of peace, there's good gate money for the Aldershot Tattoo, and vast crowds surge to this arena in every kind of car and wallow in patriotic emotion between their sneezes on a chilly night. I am one of those who have wallowed. It is impossible, I find, to resist this emotional appeal to one's racial sentiment. It is impossible to remain cool and critical when one's pulse beats to the rhythm of massed bands and one's senses are enchanted by this colour, this beauty of massed movement, this beating of drums in the night. It is all very fine and all very foolish. *"C'est magnifique, mais ce n'est pas la guerre."*

There was another kind of pageant the day I went to Aldershot to compare the present with the past. It was the Aldershot Show: an army affair to which the outside world doesn't pay much attention. The crowds watching were mostly soldiers and soldiers' wives and soldiers' children. There were the usual musical rides. Soldiers dressed as clowns rode bareback. A comic motorcar was brought on for a turn with a comic horse whose back legs had no relation to its front legs. The soldier who played the hind quarters of the beast had a difference of opinion with his comrade in front. It was extremely laughable. After that came some exhibitions of physical training, very meritorious on a day of burning sun, almost as good as a demonstration of such exercises by Danish and Swedish athletes.

I sat down on a bench and talked with two young soldiers who were watching these events with mild amusement. They were both men of the Royal Engineers and, they told me, were just finishing their six years service. After that they would have six years on the Reserve.

"Will you be sorry to leave the army?" I asked, handing over my case of cigarettes.

Both the men grinned. One of them, a dark-eyed fellow with a sallow complexion, exactly like a soldier of France, I thought, answered for both of them.

"Glad to be out."

"Why? Isn't it a good life?"

It seemed to me a good life, there at Aldershot. There were roars of laughter round the arena as a man with a Harry Tate moustache shot his own motorcar. On a summer afternoon the British army as represented here did not seem to be overworked.

"It isn't a real life," said my French-looking friend. "It's like being at school. There are too many pettifogging restrictions for a grown-up man. Discipline all the time and no escape from it. It's seven days C.B. if you stay out late with friends. Childish, I call it."

The other man nodded and agreed.

"Ay. Too much discipline. No sense of living one's own life. It's best to be a civilian with one's own job."

There was a show of ladies' hunters, and it was very pretty, but I wanted to talk to those two men and they were quite willing.

"Couldn't you make a career in the army? Jobs are scarce in the civilian world."

The dark-eyed fellow didn't agree. Certainly he could sign on for longer service. But what then? A pension of two pounds a week at forty.

"Not too bad," I suggested.

He thought it was not good enough. What could a man do on two pounds a week if he had a wife and kids? As a civilian he ought to be earning five pounds and seven pounds a week—with a bit of luck.

"Not easy, is it?" I asked. "Not easy without expert training in some technical work. What are you going to do about that?"

He and this comrade by his side were not uneasy about that. They were spending their last six months in the Army Vocational Centre. It cost them ten bob a week, but it was worth it. They were taught metalwork, and woodwork, and electrical engineering, and brick laying, and plastering, and all manner of trades. If a man were keen he could be fully qualified for a job after six months. Seventy per cent of the men who went through this training found places waiting for them when they came out. It was a good show. It worked well. It was the best thing in the army because men could look forward to decent wages when they went back to civilian life, instead of being at a loose end as they used to be in the old days, joining the down-and-outs.

"What do your fellows think of the chances of another war?" I asked, after further conversation.

This man of the Royal Engineers stared into my eyes, and I saw a shadow come into his.

"Most of us think it will be lucky if we're not called up for war before the end of our six years on the Reserve."

"Is that the general opinion?" I asked him.

"Among all who think about it. Some don't."

"I hope you're all wrong," I said, staring through the sunlight at bareback horsemen careering round the arena.

There was a group of officers and their wives waiting for me. One of them was the colonel in charge of the Vocational Centre which those two lads of the Royal Engineers thought the best thing in the army. He was going to take me to have a look at it.

But we stayed chatting while a soldier's daughter watched another comic turn. An Irish lady with the soft eyes of her race and the merry wit of Dublin as I used to know it before the trouble, introduced me to her husband. She had been away from him for a while, and he had written her a letter to say that he was getting dumb because he couldn't talk to her and deaf because he couldn't hear her talk to him. But that has nothing to do with the British army.

He was an army schoolmaster and knew as much about the youngest generation of recruits as any man alive.

"How do they compare with the old regulars?" I asked.

"Different altogether," he answered with a laugh. "The old soldier was tougher and harder. As soon as he had detrained anywhere he drew a bee line for the canteen. They were a lot of hard drinkers. Things would get smashed up. The present-day soldier prefers a cup of tea. He doesn't care to hang round the canteen. He likes to go with his girl to the local cinema."

"I expect they're an intelligent lot," I said. "The standard of intelligence seems to me to be going up all along the line. It makes one a bit hopeful of the future."

He was not quite sure of that. Anyhow, he had to admit that army education was mostly cramming for the second certificate which the men were supposed to pass. It didn't go very far. Any man who wasn't a half-wit could get through after a six months' course. Of course, there were others keen on learning and highly intelligent. Now and again a few of them were men who could make use of every opportunity.

He thought over this question while we watched the show for a few minutes.

"They are all more imaginative," he said. "The modern soldier has more sensibility than his predecessors. I wonder if that's a good thing. They're probably more apprehensive. Education may not be good for a soldier if it leads to that result. But that's starting a big argument."

There was no time to thresh out that argument, as the colonel in charge of the Vocational Centre was waiting for me. He is a tall man with the hard lean face of a backwoodsman, and humorous eyes, and a dynamo somewhere inside him. Our lives had touched some time before this meeting, though I didn't recognize him. He was a sergeant in the World War at that time and had done a brave exploit at a place called Poelcapelle, which I had recorded, as afterwards he showed me, in a newspaper cutting dated 1917.

"These modern soldiers," he said, "are all pampered. They all want to be mothered, and the army mothers 'em. Why, bless you, they can't walk to a cricket match, even if it's only half a mile. They have to be taken there in a motor coach."

I told him about my conversation with the two men of the Royal Engineers, and he laughed at their dislike of discipline.

"They all grouse like that. You can't say army discipline is too severe nowadays. Everything's done for them."

He was pleased at their praise of his Vocational Centre. That is the child of his heart, apart from a young lady named Pamela, aged eleven or so, for whom he has a high respect.

"Come and have a look round," he said.

I had a look round and must say I was much impressed. There were workshops in which men leaving their time of service may get intensive training in technical work fitting them for civilian jobs. We stayed in the office where there was a big map on which many little flags were pinned, reminding me of other maps when anxious fathers and mothers stuck flags into the pictures of France and Flanders and hoped for the best for some boy along the line of them.

"That's where we have found occupations for our men," said the Colonel.

The flags were clustered thickly round London and other industrial cities. The record of success was higher than what I had been told by the two men of the Royal Engineers, and seventy-nine per cent of those who have done these courses have found good positions.

"But they're a funny crowd," said the colonel. "Many of them are as homesick as babies when they leave the army. Do you think they'll take a job in an unfamiliar part of England, even if it's waiting for them? Not on your life. They want to go back to the old village or the old town, where there's no chance of employment and the young fellows are lined up outside the labour exchanges. They want to see their mummies again. Well, you can understand it."

He took me through the workshops. Sparks were flying in the metal-working rooms where the men were making all kinds of things for army customers, including some decorative weather vanes, one of which now is perched upon my cowshed. The carpenters' shops had some good specimens of woodwork and carving, mostly done by machine tools. In another shed the army was learning the internal mechanism of motorcars and how to fix up the electrical apparatus in small houses, and how to do French polishing and sign writing and stippling and moulding and casting, and other technical crafts for which there is a constant demand in industrial life.

I talked with some of the men, and they were keen on their job. They have to make a sacrifice for this training. Ten shillings a week out of a man's pay is not a small sum, especially if he is married and has a family to keep. But they all said it was worth it, and the instructors took me on one side and spoke well of their students.

"As keen as mustard," I was told. "They know that when they're out of the army this training will make a difference to their life. In these hard times a man without technical knowledge doesn't stand a dog's chance."

The colonel went the round of the workshops, and his keen eye missed nothing. I was amused by a number of mottoes hanging up, and when I commented on them he laughed and admitted that one of his little hobbies was to hang up any good saying he came across for the encouragement of the men and his own amusement. They reveal his own character by their choice: a faith in practical philosophy, action, common sense, and cheerful acceptance of life's little snags. And in these proverbial sayings with a touch of irony and a shrewd humour is the character of the British soldier as I knew him twenty-one years ago in France and Flanders.

A first-class will and a second-class brain will defeat first-class brains and a second-class will.

This would be a very quiet world if those who had nothing to say—said it.

God gave the little squirrels acorns to eat, but He didn't throw them into their nests.

Worry is the interest paid on trouble before it becomes due.

Never forget that the darkest hour is only sixty minutes.

Don't despise the little things—often the mosquito is more bother than the elephant.

If you must ride on the wagon, don't drag your feet.

Hot air can take a balloon a long way, but it can't keep it there.

It's better to give than to lend, and it costs about the same.

Some men's brains commence working the moment they wake and never stop until they start work.

One wouldn't find such mottoes hanging round the walls of German workshops, and if we have any quality as a nation above that of other peoples, it is this shrewd common sense with a laugh in it which keeps us sane.

Colonel Ben Hurst of the Army Vocational Training Centre is one of those men whom one would like to have as a comrade and as a leader on a desert island or in any tight place, or when anything goes wrong with one's motorcar, one's wireless, or one's household gadgets. He is the very type of all that was best in the old Regular army armies which went out to the Somme. Is that type passing? One would hate to think so. I don't think so, because it is of our blood and spirit and comes out always in a time of crisis. There is, as far as I can see, nothing wrong with the young soldier of today, though he prefers tea to beer and resents too hard a discipline, is more sensitive—and less brutal—than the old regulars of pre-war days.

What of the higher command? I was talking one evening lately with a friend in my garden. He had been in the Great War as a boy—"Shy Harry," they called him—and now, for twenty-one years afterwards, he had been reading books about it and trying to get the truth of it. He is ironical when he speaks of the brains of staff officers and generals. He meets some of those generals in Surrey gardens and retires behind hedges bordering close-clipped lawns to laugh at them inside himself, and then to confide his horrid apprehension that perhaps in the next war the same mistakes will be made by the same kind of men with the same kind of brain.

He asked me that question point-blank the other night, when we were talking about Haig's verdict on Sir John French—not favourable to him as a commander-in-chief of a great army.

"Do you think we shall have to suffer from the same kind of leadership if another war happens? What an appalling thought!"

Not having much of a brain myself I am less critical of other people's intelligence. I put up a defence of some of the generals, and he laughed and said I had a kind heart. In this man's soul there is still a bitterness because so many of his crowd in those days on the Somme were slaughtered needlessly, as the survivor thought, by command of the Brass Hats who made their little mistakes and gave the wrong orders cracking their morning eggs in French chateaux. It's an old quarrel. I think perhaps the answer to it is in the motto posted up by Colonel Ben Hurst in one of his workshops:

A first-class will and a second-class brain will defeat first-class brains and a second-class will.

But the cost is rather heavy.

19. Factory Folk

The Windmill Press gave a garden party to authors on the lawns around their factory in Surrey. Being one of their authors I received an invitation and was glad to go. Not that I wanted particularly to see my fellow authors. I am strongly of opinion, as I think I have already said in this book, that authors should be read and not seen. But I wanted to see the press, and the gardens, and a charming young man who takes an interest in my books when he is not risking his life in an aëroplane, like another young publisher I know. It is a strange phenomenon of modern times that publishers should take wings and fly away.

The factory was worth seeing. It is a model, I thought, of what may be done on a factory site without making a blot on the landscape and adding to the squalor and ugliness of industrial life. The Windmill Press looks like an American college, and is not unlike an Oxford college except for the weathering of time. The gardens are beautifully laid out and cared for. On each side of the grass paths there was a flame of colour on this day in June. The lawns were green and smooth. There was a rose garden with all the beauties revealing their loveliness.

Authors, both male and female, strolled about this pleasaunce. The most famous among them were pointed out to other guests and pretended they were not aware of being on exhibition. The younger claimants to fame looked as modest as they might when ladies vowed that they adored their latest works of fiction. So very thrilling—but rather naughty, you know! Cunningham Graham was there, looking like Don Quixote. I had the honour of being introduced to distinguished novelists of whose work I was profoundly ignorant, as they were of mine. I was glad to meet a man named Richard Blaker, remembering one of his novels which made a deep impression on me, years ago.

Presently, after eating strawberries and cream in the shade of the trees, some of us were conducted over the building in which the Windmill Press produces its books. I could hear the purr of the machines. Those great printing presses were turning out works of genius—as advertisement columns in the *Sunday*

Times would tell the world—with incredible rapidity and the efficiency of mass production. They were printing some of those three thousand works of fiction which invade the booksellers' shops each year and provide the raw material for the critical judgment and lively wit of Mr. Gerald Gould and Mr. Ralph Strauss and Mr. Cecil Roberts and other critics. Millions of little words were being impressed upon endless rolls of paper, and it is regrettable that none of them seem to make the world wiser or better. Nations still go to war with each other though we authors are all pacifists. Men and women go on misunderstanding each other though we novelists do our best to reveal the secret places of the heart. Of the making of books there is no end, said Solomon, quite a long time ago. But all the books produced since then have resulted only in a world in which anti-gas drill is in the elementary education of infants, and in which youth in many countries put on coloured shirts, arm themselves with rubber truncheons, and proclaim the sacred right of intolerance.

We stood around the presses, and the smell of their oil reminded me of old days in newspaper offices when such machines printed words of mine written after exciting days as a reporter of contemporary life. My friends used to say that my narratives of fact read remarkably like fiction. Now they say that my novels read remarkably like journalism. I heard the beat and rhythm of the printing machine as an old war horse hears the beating of drums.

But I was mostly interested in the factory girls, because I am always most interested in the lives of people. These girls were amused by the invasion of the garden-party folk. They went on with their jobs with little winks to each other now and then, as though to say: "Funny folk, ain't they? Authors, you know. Lady novelists. Oh, Crikey! and don't they look like it?"

In one long room well lit by high windows looking onto the lawns, numbers of girls were collating the sheets which had come from the press. I stopped to watch them. Their fingers moved with incredible rapidity. Their hands were working with marvellous dexterity and deftness. The sheets were piled up in their right order as softly as snowflakes. Mind and body moved with perfect timing.

"They must get bored!" said a lady at my side. "What terrible monotony!"

"They make a game of it," said one of our guides—a director of the press. "They compete against each other and try to beat their own record."

It was this director who told me something about the character of these girls. They liked working in this country place, surrounded by lawns and flowers in summer time, but nothing would induce them to live in the neighbourhood. They preferred any kind of lodging within easy reach of London cinemas, London shops, and London lights. They like the roar of the traffic better than the twittering of birds, and the crowds down Piccadilly after dark than the quietude of the countryside.

A medical man named Thomas O. Garland has collected some extraordinarily interesting facts regarding the lives and minds of factory girls in England. He is attached as a medical adviser to a large factory employing nearly three thousand girls who come to work immediately after school age. He has succeeded in gaining their confidence and is able to help them over many troubles of body and mind due to an amazing ignorance of physiology and to nervous disorders arising from difficulties of home life and emotional crises in their relation with boy friends. As regards the monotony of their work, he finds that they positively like the repetition of some simple and automatic action, and even make a fuss if changed from one job to another.

A complete compensation with them [he writes in an article on "The Factory Girl" in *Public Health*], is the daydream. Recently a charge hand told me that a girl nearly "sloshed" another because she spoke to her. When remonstrated with, the aggressor explained that she had been having such a lovely time, going on to describe a fantasy she had been enjoying until the girl's remark had shattered it. . . .

He finds that the greatest number of cases of nervous debility and hysteria are due to troubles at home. Great numbers of these young factory girls have to shoulder too many responsibilities for younger brothers and sisters. Being the eldest of the family, the factory girl has to give up the best part of her earnings.

THE SMOKELESS NORTH

Here is an example [writes Dr. Garland]:

Mary K., aged sixteen, who lives at Dagenham, has worked for us since she was fourteen. She is the eldest of six, the other five being at school. The father is a labourer and usually out of work: the mother goes out nursing, if she can get a job. When she is out, Mary, after getting home, has to do her mother's work for her—that is to say, she has to cook her own tea, sweep the kitchen, and put the children to bed. . . . Every morning she gets up at five-thirty and catches a train at six-thirty. She starts work here at eight and gets home at a quarter to seven or a quarter past seven, according to the train she catches. She has been here now for two years, and it is not surprising that she suffers from many small illnesses. Her mother's reaction to her poor health was to suggest that she went for cycle rides before breakfast to get an appetite.

On the other hand, the youngest members of the family, when their turn comes, are often overburdened because their parents are getting infirm, or have lost their work and demand support from these young girls, taking the greater part of their wages. In many cases the mother takes all her daughter's earnings with the exception of a few pence for pocket money, not because of greed or cruelty, but because they are desperately pressed to make both ends meet with a swarming family of children. This doctor who watches over three thousand factory girls, finds tragic inefficiency and incompetence among their mothers. They have no idea of thrift or the economical spending of money. They will buy a piano though nobody can play it. One out-of-work father bought thirty goldfish because he had a glass bowl. They are hopeless in the preparation of food.

These factory girls are overburdened very often by the huggermugger conditions of their home life. They have to sleep in little rooms with younger brothers and sisters. Perhaps there is a baby who cries. Then they are sentimental in their friendships with other girls at the factories, and there are passionate jealousies between them because one girl's friend shows more favour to another or cools off. Presently they look around for boy friends and again feel injured if they don't find one. When found there is a walking-out period which lasts several years sometimes before the "engagement." There are many sex troubles and bewilderments, and, now and again, tragedies.

But on the whole these girls—millions of them all over England —face life gaily and bravely. Many of them have indomitable courage and a shrewd humour which keeps them laughing even if there is not much to laugh about. Many of the best factories now pay a great deal of attention to their health and general fitness. They are provided with tennis courts or playgrounds and get instruction in physical exercises. From a business point of view as well as good citizenship some employers of labour know that it pays to keep their wage-earners mentally and phys- ically fit. They get more work out of them. Not so many hours are lost in small illnesses. We are improving all the time in rais- ing the general conditions of life in England, although still there are many black spots, the worst among them being even now the coal fields in which the miners are getting restless again at this time of writing and appealing to the nation to support their claims for better wages and better working conditions.

In the Windmill Press I had an interesting conversation with one of the financial advisers—as I think he was. He deplored the shortsightedness of the government in not having organized a big scheme of Dominion settlement after the war when hun- dreds of thousands of ex-service men were willing to go. They had met the Australian soldiers, who were paid five shillings a day when the Tommy was getting a shilling. The Australians had told them about the chances of their own land. "Why don't you fellows come out?" they asked. But that chance was frittered away by the dole and by an utter lack of planning on the part of the government.

"We must look more and more to the Empire for future trade," said this business man who had once been a regular soldier. "We shan't get back our export trade in foreign markets. They have established their own industries and put up tariffs against us. Even the native populations in the Empire are a valuable source of custom for our goods. Their standard of liv- ing is rising. The Kaffirs of Johannesburg, for instance, are earning a lot and spending a lot. Our policy should be to in- crease their purchasing power and supply them with the things they want. I'm not a pessimist in the long view. Industry will revive. It's reviving. If we can keep out of another European war——"

He wasn't quite sure that we could keep out of another European war which would ruin everything.

Once again on a sunny afternoon in an English garden there was that shadow of war creeping over the hedges with their clustered roses. Or was it just the shadow of a fear?

20. *Work-Shy Men*

I sat in the porch of a country house having tea with two men who have made a success in their businesses and now take their ease in their gardens. They were both north country men, with the shrewd humour and common sense of that part of England where men as a rule think straight and don't talk nonsense. One of them was a good story-teller and kept us laughing by imitating some of the old women who "did" for him when he lived in rooms. But presently conversation turned to more serious topics, including the conditions of labour and the effects of the dole on English life. The humourist became grave. In fact, he became angry. As an employer of labour he had some hard things to say about the unemployed, or at least a section of them made up mostly, he said, of young men who preferred idleness to work.

I listened to this indictment with some distress because it was made by a man of sound judgment and considerable experience, so that I could not take his words as the vapourings of a crusted Tory denouncing the evils of democracy.

"We are breeding up a bone-lazy class," he asserted. "There are large numbers of young men who regard the dole as their right and would rather make the best of that—marrying on it—having children on it—than go out of their way to look for work."

"I can't believe there's much of that," I told him. "I've been talking to some of the unemployed, and they tell me that the worst part of their tragedy is the frightful boredom of having nothing to do. They would give anything for a job of work."

My north country business friend nodded.

"The decent men are like that. Fine fellows. I'm talking about the young scallywags and the scrimshankers. There's a lot of those. How do you account, for instance, for the fact that with all this outcry about unemployment it's almost impossible to get additional labour for any special job? You can't get bricklayers. You can't get harvesters. You can't get bookbinders—which is a line of my own business, so that I happen to know. Many bookbinders are out of work and on the dole, but when I wanted fifty the other day, do you think I could get them? No, sir. Now I'll tell you a story about an unemployed man who asked whether he could get an odd job."

He told me the story. He had offered the man ten shillings to help him shift some rubbish from one part of his ground to another. The man accepted the offer but was slow in tackling the job. The loads he had to lift seemed to fatigue him.

"Now, look here, old man," said my friend. "I'll do the lifting and you can do the carrying."

Each time he carried the load he was long in returning.

"Work doesn't seem to suit you," my friend remarked.

"Well, I haven't had good food lately," said the man.

That was a reasonable excuse. It modified the judgment of an employer of labour not without heart.

"Go up to the house," he said. "You'll get a good meal of beef, potatoes, and pudding. It won't cost you anything."

But the man said that if it was all the same he would rather have a bite at the local pub. Perhaps the gentleman could give him five shillings in advance of his day's work. The end of the story was that the man took his five shillings, made his way to the local pub, and failed to return.

"There's a class like that," said the north country man. "I'd treat 'em rough. They ought to be put into labour camps and made to work under discipline. Some of the young fellows are the worst. They've never done any work since leaving school, and they don't want to begin. This dole has demoralized thousands. It always makes me angry when I hear people say, "Well, it's my right, isn't it? I pay for it, don't I?" Girls go into hospital and get the best treatment for nothing and have every comfort which could be got in a nursing home. "Well, I pay for it, don't I?" they say, instead of being grateful. They pay sixpence a week. They think that pays for all the expenses. They accept it all as their right and are very hoity-toity when anyone suggests that it's more a privilege than a right."

He told me other stories of the disinclination of the unemployed to get busy on their own behalf, even if jobs were offered them. They reckon up the difference between the offered wage and their dole or poor relief. Perhaps it's a matter of ten shillings a week. "Not good enough," they say. "What, only ten shillings for all that work? It isn't sense."

"We're progressing in demoralization," said my friend. "If this kind of thing isn't checked we shall be a nation of slackers and paupers. It's the death of the spirit. I have nothing but contempt for the cowardly politicians who are afraid to administer the Means test and run away like rabbits when there's an outcry from the masses carefully worked up by the Labour party. What this country needs is a touch of discipline and a touch of hardness. We're getting soft. I wouldn't give any man poor relief or the dole unless he worked for it. No work no wages. No work no food. That's the old law of life, and a very good law for the individual. I can't blame these young fellows after all. It's the system I blame. It's absolutely pernicious in its effect on the moral character of the people."

There is an element of truth in all that. The evil exists. I employed a man a few years ago who lived in a cottage with three sons who were all earning fine wages. He had a daughter who was working. Together this family earned from twelve to fourteen pounds a week. When the father left my employ he applied for the dole.

From all kinds of people I hear similar stories in different parts of England. Against my will I am convinced that there are numbers of cases in which the incentive to work is lacking because idleness is subsidized by State relief. That I agree is the way of demoralization, but I refuse to believe that it has gone very far in undermining the character of the people as a whole. At least, I hate to think so, believing in the sturdy character, the honesty, the will to work, of the great majority among the labouring classes. But it is one side of the picture of English life which in truth one dare not ignore. It will be a tragic thing for England if the younger crowd are brought up to believe that the State will provide for them, at least on a minimum scale, whether they feel like work or whether they don't, and that the struggle for self-preservation is now futile and unnecessary because the State has made feather beds for slack or tired youth. Is that spirit creeping up in England? If it is, it will soon destroy the happiness and prosperity which are envied now by those who look at us with foreign eyes. But in the north I saw none of that, as I shall tell.

21. *Talk in a Train*

It was eighty-two in the shade, according to the weather report, but it felt more than that in Waterloo Station, where I waited for a train to Guildford. Although I had been in London only for an afternoon I was glad to escape from it again. It was sweltering in the streets, with a smell of tar and petrol and stale air. The crowds were hot, sweaty, and fagged. Even the girls in thin frocks with bare arms looked overheated and worried by this humid warmth. City men on their way home after office hours looked tired and irritable. In the third-class smoking carriage where I had a corner seat they settled down to their evening newspapers after mopping their foreheads and lighting up pipes and cigarettes. There was silence as far as Surbiton. Then one of them spoke to a youngish man opposite, who had dropped his paper and was staring out of the window.

"What do you think of this Abyssinian affair? Serious, isn't it?"

The youngish man withdrew his gaze from the window and stared at the questioner—a silver-haired man who looked as though he might be a writer of books—and answered after a moment's intense thought. He spoke with a kind of anger.

"I know what I would do if I had any control of the situation."

"What?" asked the silver-haired man.

"I would keep out of it. We don't want any damned nonsense like a war."

It was the beginning of a general conversation in the third-class smoking carriage. I listened from my corner seat.

"I agree," said the silver-haired man. "All the same, we ought to support the League of Nations and the ideal of collective security."

"Damn the League of Nations," said the youngish man opposite, very fiercely. "I'm not going to be dragged out for war to support the League or its principles. I'm interested in my garden. I have two kids at home. What do I care about the Abyssinians? I don't know where they live on the map, and I don't want to know."

A stout man on the same side of the carriage, who had been perspiring very freely, joined in the conversation. He looked like a stockbroker, I thought.

"It will be absolute madness if the government insists on sanctions, as they call it, against Italy. That means war. Well, they won't get me again! I was in the last. Quite enough as far as I'm concerned. But all these pacifists are howling out for war. They want to take action against Italy to uphold abstract principles and all those pacts and pledges which statesmen signed with their tongues in their cheeks. They would like to drag us into war for the sake of collective security. Lord Cecil and his crew keep writing to the *Times* about it. It's sheer lunacy."

"It's newspaper stuff," said another man whose pince-nez were askew as he looked over his *Evening Standard*. "The newspapers ought to be suppressed. They stir things up."

The silver-haired man laughed slightly.

"All the same," he said, "it's not a newspaper stunt this time. I happen to know that there's grave anxiety behind the scenes. And I don't think we ought to let Mussolini get away with his brutal policy of attacking the unfortunate Ethiopians. It's a violation of all his pledges. It's an attack on the civilized code. We're pledged, too, up to the neck. We're under a solemn obligation to uphold the Covenant of the League. If Mussolini is declared an aggressor by the Council of the League, we must take some action accordingly. Otherwise there is an end of law in Europe, and we all go back to barbarism and anarchy. Collective security is the only way of preserving peace in Europe."

"I disagree," said the youngish man in the corner.

He breathed hard for a moment and stared fiercely again at the silver-haired man.

"The League of Nations was supposed to be an instrument of peace," he said. "I used to think so. Now I'm convinced it's the most dangerous bit of bunk in the world. It would make every war a world war. It would drag us all into every petty dispute. What have we got to do with this quarrel between Italy and Abyssinia? Let them settle it themselves. Let's get on with our own job, which is to increase the prosperity of our own people and keep the peace."

"Yes," said the silver-haired man, "but what are you going to do if——"

"I'm getting out at Claygate," said the youngish man, reaching up for a parcel on the rack.

He got out at Claygate.

The silver-haired man addressed the carriage again.

He took the view that if Italy were allowed to massacre the Ethiopians without let or hindrance from the members of the League, there would be no period of security for the British Empire or prosperity for England. There would be uprisings of the coloured races. Germany would await its chance to follow the example of Italy in breaking all pacts and pledges. If Italy were weakened by a long-drawn war in Abyssinia, Germany would swallow up Austria and advance to the Brenner, where many Germans lived under Italian rule. Other nations would take the law into their own hands. There would be many explosions. Europe would be nothing but a battleground between the warring nations. And the machine had made war a menace to humanity itself. Civilization wouldn't survive.

"All that is beside the mark," said the man who looked like a stockbroker, though he might have been a dentist or a linen draper, or a playwright. You never can tell. "What we have got to do is to keep out of war at all costs. I have a boy at Charterhouse. I don't want him to be choked by poison gas, or blinded, or blown to bits because Mussolini is playing the madman in Abyssinia. Let's keep sane ourselves. There are enough madmen in the world."

"The point is——" said the silver-haired man.

"I'm getting out at Clandon," said the stout gentleman.

He got out at Clandon. The silver-haired man got out at London Road after a friendly nod to the remaining passengers.

The man in the corner whose pince-nez went askew addressed a few remarks to me.

"It seems to me everybody is unduly nervous. It's because so many people remember the last war. They're afraid of another. But it's not going to happen as far as we're concerned unless we're living in a lunatic asylum. I trust our government for common sense. I have a high respect for Mr. Baldwin. And I'll tell you another thing . . ."

He hadn't much time to tell me because Guildford was the next station.

But he told me that in his opinion the English people would utterly refuse to be dragged into another war for the sake of Abyssinia or the League of Nations. He knew many young men. They came to play tennis in his garden sometimes. They would just refuse to fight for any cause but a direct attack on their own country.

"They're not pacifists, mind you," he said. "But they're not going to be jockeyed into any adventure of blood for reasons with which they don't agree. Good-evening."

In my own village there was a lot of talk about this Abyssinian crisis. Men who had served in the last war and who are now labourers and gardeners announced that they weren't going to be caught again.

"They won't get me," said my gardener, who once slogged all the way to Jerusalem.

"No more war for me," said an old regular who is now working on a gentleman's estate.

His son spoke to me at the wheel of a car which he was driving.

"All the older men are against the idea of another war," he told me. "Well, I hope it won't happen. I'm just old enough to be called up. I was nineteen last birthday. Just the right age. I can't say I want to be killed. All the same, if I was called I wouldn't shirk it. I'd have a try for the Royal Air Force. It would be more lively than the infantry."

It was very pleasant in the garden after the heat of London. The windows were still open and the blinds up. I listened to the wireless news. There had been great activity among Cabinet ministers. The government had been consulting the leaders of all parties and the high commissioners of the Dominions. Mr. Ramsay MacDonald had told a reporter that "This is the gravest crisis since 1914."

It was a night in August. It was twenty-one years and three weeks since another night in August when England had been apprehensive of the European situation and when at midnight a world war had begun. Twenty-one years after, with that ruin still unrepaired, with its remembrance of sacrifice and agony and death still in the minds of living men and women, there was still no sense of peace or security. All the nations were arming. The gates of Janus were opening in Rome. The German tribes were proclaiming a pagan creed of force and might. There were smouldering fires in Europe, and terrific forces were stirring under the thin crust above the boiling lava of national passions. Upstairs in a little room with crooked beams a small boy was sleeping in my cottage. I had told him a fairy tale before he went to sleep. I was afraid for his sake. It's such a pity for the small boys of life when they find that fairy tales are untrue in a world of high explosives and poison gas.

22. Peace-Lovers

I think anybody who took the trouble to discover what was passing in the mind of England during the Abyssinian trouble with Italy and the crisis of the League in the beginning of September of this year could have no doubt of the convictions of the common man and woman. They were, I think, moved to generous anger against Italy for its deliberate plans of attack upon an unaggressive people. The cynicism of Mussolini in repudiating all his pledges to the League and the Kellogg Pact shocked them, and the fact that Italy was able to buy all the material for the manufacture of armaments and mechanized warfare while Abyssinia was prevented from getting arms outraged their sense of fair play.

This moral indignation expressed by the English people in newspaper correspondence, in speeches by labour leaders, and in the prayers uttered in the churches, seemed to many foreigners sheer hypocrisy. Italian and French journalists, always convinced of our national hypocrisy, referred back to the Boer War, launched with the full weight of the Empire against a peasant folk; to the battle of Omdurman when we mowed down the Fuzzy-wuzzies; to our conquest of black races in Africa; and to our recent bombing expeditions against Indian tribesmen and Arabs.

One must confess that, looking back on history, not enormously old, our indignation against Italian ambitions in Abyssinia does present a good case to the cynics and the disbelievers in England's moral attitude. But what these foreign journalists fail to understand is that the English people themselves no longer stand for the old jingoism, and that something has happened in their minds—as it ought to have happened in all men's minds—since a world war twenty-one years ago. The lesson of that war's agony, ruin, and futility, has been burnt into the soul of England. It has not left us unchanged. One revelation of its effects upon the common mind was given by the answer to the Peace Ballot earlier in the year, when eleven million men and women—the largest vote ever given on any issue in this country —expressed their belief in the League of Nations and in its principles of collective security for the preservation of peace. I agree with some of the critics of the Peace Ballot that the questions were not quite fairly framed, but be that as it may, there is no doubt that the overwhelming response to the Ballot was a tremendous demonstration against war and a deep conviction in favour of League methods for the preservation of peace.

I had a talk with one of the organizers who had gone canvassing for people's votes on this ballot. He told me that he was vastly impressed by the earnestness and sincerity of the common folk with whom he talked on his house-to-house visits. They confessed their ignorance about some of the points. The women especially were diffident in voting on a problem which they felt was beyond their reach of knowledge, but in the vast majority they were eager to do something which might register their hatred and fear of war and their hope of some better system of international justice which would prevent another massacre of youth. He found in these little homes an absolute belief that another war between European nations would be more terrible than the last because of aërial bombing and poison gas. He found the labouring men and their wives needed no persuasion that the League of Nations was the one institution which might prevent such a horror coming upon the world. They didn't know much about its workings. They had grave doubts about the sincerity of the statesmen who talked at its meetings, but they clung to it as the one great hope of world peace. Eleven millions of them gave their allegiance to this faith. There was no hypocrisy in it.

When for a while there was excited stuff in the papers about the possibility of England becoming involved, I had talks on the subject with my fellow villagers. They refused to be excited. They talked gravely and simply. They talked wisely.

One man, who is a gardener, twenty-one years after walking behind our guns under the sun of Egypt and Mesopotamia, gave me his views as he stood in a potato patch, leaning on his spade. He is a lean fellow with a hawklike face and tanned skin.

"I don't like this talk of another war," he said. "There oughtn't to be a war if the nations stick together and prevent Italy from acting like a mad dog. It's what they promised to do, and I don't see how they can go back on it. There is no hope for Europe if the League lies down under the heel of Mussolini. There won't be any war if we all act together and tell that Italian that he must be a good boy or he'll get it in the backside. But, of course, if the other fellows rat, we can't act alone, can we? It's not for us to play the policeman while the others look on and laugh at us. If there's no united action, then I'm all for keeping out of trouble and making our own peace. We don't want any more war. I don't suppose they would call me up again, but I'm thinking of the younger lads. It's a pity if they should be called on in the prime of youth to lay down their lives because there's no sense in the world. We want to avoid that, if possible, but I don't like the look of things all the same. I can't help thinking that Hitler is waiting to make trouble. Do you think there's any chance of his being at the back of Mussolini? It's in my head that Mussolini has got a trump card up his sleeve. Well, I wouldn't like to fight the Germans again! But what I ask myself when I'm working in this garden is why mankind must always be fighting or under the fear of war? Seems silly! Aren't we old enough to have learnt better? What good does it do anyone? I can't see any good that came out of the last war. It makes me angry when I hear talk about another."

He put his spade under another plant and turned up some potatoes.

"Not too bad!" he remarked. "Still, the frost kept them back a lot."

He spoke for the men of the British Legion to which he belongs in the village. All over England there were, I am certain, millions of men who had been in the last war and were now thinking like that, soberly, wisely, with a wistful hope in the good sense of mankind, with a kind of anger that so soon after a world war—twenty-one years after its beginning—there should be fool's talk about another call to youth for another shambles.

That day I had been to town. A man came into the carriage of a tube train. He was an Italian. There was a mad light in his eyes. He shouted out in the carriage:

"*Viva! Viva! Viva l'Italia!*"

The other passengers stared at him and smiled. A young man opposite me shrugged his shoulders as though to say, "An imbecile!" In Rome that night gangs of young men were shouting, "Death to the League!" Somehow the English people have got beyond this self-intoxication and madness of national egotism. The common man in England today is, I believe, as steady as a rock in his contempt for this particular form of insanity. Or is it possible that by the call of a bugle and the beat of drums, and some flaming articles in the daily press, and some speeches over the B.B.C., he could still be stirred to frenzy for any kind of war other than the defence of his own soil and hearthstone and liberty?

But what about other people's liberty and a cry for rescue from defenceless folk attacked by a bandit nation? There is such a thing as honour, and we are on the horns of a frightful dilemma. Sanctions, yes. But not as far as war. Collective security? By all means. But no separate action by Great Britain. Italy must be stopped and Abyssinia saved. But no flinging of

torches into the powder magazines of Europe. All this has led
to a tragic conflict of thought in the English mind, and as I
write these words a general election is at hand and there will be
a babel of conflicting tongues. But England, I am certain, will
give no mandate to any government which may call its youth
to the shambles, even in the name of "collective security" or
lead the way to Armageddon, even in the name of Peace.

V

Farming Folk

1. Neighbours of Mine

I HAVE a young farmer as my neighbour, and for a time he
used two of my fields for his heifers until their frequent in-
vasions of my garden forced me to withdraw their liberty.
Barbed-wire entanglements failed to keep them out. There was
one young devil who would force his way through the wire
under my very nose, and no sooner had I chased him out than
he would come back again like an impudent schoolboy intent on
robbing an orchard. These beasts became a family excitement.
A cry would go up from the kitchen: "There are the heifers!"
There would be shouts from the gardener and the gardener's
boy. I would be summoned from my study to lend a hand in the
chase. They gave great trouble to the farmer and his assistants—
one of them a fair-haired lass in shorts—because of their constant
escapades. They would make a dash for neighbouring woods, or
be found miles away on highways where they held up the motor
traffic. The fair-haired lass still spends a lot of time rounding
them up and seems to find it a joke.

The young farmer—young enough anyhow to have escaped
the war—is a cheery fellow who seems to like his job. He has
the sandy hair and bluish eyes of a Saxon, though he comes
from the island of Jersey and has a father who speaks Jersey
French. I hear him shouting to his horses in that tongue in hay-
cutting time. He wears leather shorts and a blue shirt open at
the neck, and when I look at him across my hedges I think,
"There's a fellow who enjoys life. There's a life such as God

meant men to live." For certainly it's a good life when the sun is shining over a field of tall grass ready for haymaking and when pitchforks are busy throwing the sweet-smelling hay onto the cart where two strong arms are ready to grab it and build it up until the load is ready for two old horses with hairy feet. It's a good picture of English life.

This red-haired farmer whistles at his work. He is always cheery when I meet him. He has a fine boyish laugh when my lady throws a joke at him across the gate. But it's not always summertime, and it's not all honey in a farmer's life, as well I know. This fellow—he went to a public school before he took to farming—has to get up at five o'clock, winter as well as summer; and on winter mornings before the light is up, when rain is making a quagmire of his farmyard, when there is a frost to bite his ears and numb his fingers, it's not much of a joke to turn out of a warm bed to milk the cows and look after the beasts. Another cow has fallen sick. The sow has overlaid some of her litter. The fields are sodden. The farmer's boots squelch through the heavy clay, which sticks to them in clods. Sometimes he is almost knee-deep in mud and muck. On a small farm like this, where labour is scarce because wages would eat up any chance of profit, there's not a moment's idleness from the time a man gets up to the time he flings himself into bed at half-past nine. Perhaps he will have to get up in the night to look after a sick beast or a calving cow. Not much fun. Not an easy life. Quite impossible for any town-bred man who hasn't farming in his blood and spirit.

"How's the farm doing?" I ask this neighbour of mine.

He laughs cheerily.

"Not much profit in it, of course! Just carrying on, you know."

We discuss the workings of the Milk Marketing Board, the Pig and Bacon boards, the prices of heifers and milking cows.

"Surely," I suggest, "the government has done a lot for agriculture, hasn't it? All these quotas and subsidies and marketing boards must have helped the farmers a lot. What about milk, for instance—isn't that paying you now?"

He laughs again as though I were pulling his leg a little, or labouring under some illusion, shared, no doubt, by town-bred

VARNEY
BOOT MAKER

THE COBBLER'S SHOP, OXFORDSHIRE

men whose knowledge of agriculture is limited to an occasional article in the *Daily Express*.

"One can't make farming pay," he says. "Not on a small scale. One just struggles along, hoping for the best. Take, for instance, the price of pigs . . ."

I took the price of pigs with another neighbour, who breeds quite a lot of them and showed me his new litters the other day, holding up a little porker for the benefit of a small boy who was with me.

"There's no profit in 'em," he told me. "The Pig Board is supposed to protect us from foreign imports—there's supposed to be a quota, you know—but Denmark and other countries are dumping bacon on the market and forcing down prices. They're dropping again. Unless the government does something about it . . ."

The English farmer is always looking for the government to do something about it, and even then he isn't satisfied.

"Bad news!" said a young man who brings round Devonshire cream from his own farm which lies a mile or two away from my cottage.

"Has Italy attacked Abyssinia?" I asked.

"The retail price of milk has gone up to sevenpence a quart. It's a scandal!"

"But surely," I exclaimed, "isn't that what you wanted? Don't you want prices to rise?"

"Not the retail price," he answered. "My customers can't afford it. They take less milk. What good does that do to the producer?"

He is producer and retailer too. He is one of those who voted against the Milk Board, though it had a great majority for its new regulations.

"It's a mad world!" he exclaimed at my gate before setting out on his round again. "The government makes great promises to farmers but lets in foreign stuff at dumping prices. And not only foreign stuff either. The Empire is our enemy. Those Ottawa agreements were dead against the British farmer. We're swamped by cheap meat and cheap wheat. Look at Argentine meat coming in at cut-rate prices. How can the British farmer pay the wages of labour and make a profit for himself? It can't be done! What we want is more protection of the home market. Some of our politicians ought to be strung up. That's my opinion."

I disagreed with his opinion, not because I have great faith in politicians, but because I know that one of them, named Major Elliot, Minister of Agriculture, has put up a brave fight, and a brainy fight, to save our farming community—and has saved it. There can be no doubt of that. Many farmers admit it, though they protest that there is still much need for improvement of their chances and that world conditions are still bearing down heavily upon them.

2. Lean Years

Four years ago I went round England on a survey of farms and farming—not because I have any credentials as an agricultural expert, but because I wanted to get into touch with that side of English life and to find out some broad facts about a class of men who seemed hard hit by the world slump. I wanted to get into their homes and fields, and to get a glimpse of their life and character for a book I was writing. I mugged up the price of wheat and potatoes and cattle and pigs. Anyhow, I was a good listener, and they seemed glad to tell me about their troubles.

Their troubles were very acute at the time. I remember talking to a bank manager in Norwich, one of a banking family who have done the business of farming in Norfolk for generations.

"The Norfolk farmers tell me," I said, "that they are in a bad way."

He looked up at me from his desk and smiled, and raised a hand with a tragic gesture.

"If they say that," he answered, "they are understating the case. They are all bankrupt."

All over England the farmers were in a desperate state, I found. A world economic crisis and a complete dislocation of world trade had forced down agricultural prices to such low levels that farmers were suffering heavy losses on almost every commodity they produced. Many foreign countries, stricken by internal poverty and loss of markets beyond their frontiers, were using England as their dumping ground at any prices they could get. Foreign fruit and vegetables were pouring into Covent Garden, and English growers found their own harvests unsalable or bought at a rate which meant ruin to them.

"I can't see much hope ahead," said one of the farmers I met in Oxfordshire. "Good harvest or bad harvest, we can't get a price for the crops we raise. You see this wheat? I shall get twenty-five shillings a quarter—perhaps. I couldn't make it pay unless I got between forty and fifty shillings. It is the same tale with barley and oats."

I had been walking and talking with these men in their own fields in Oxfordshire, some of the best arable land in England and one of the richest counties in past days. The old farmhouses have stood there since Tudor and Stuart days.

The man who said, "I can't see much hope ahead," was farming three hundred acres of land which have been in his family for three hundred years. The farmers around him told me that he is one of the best in the county and that all through the lean years of recent history he never lost hope or courage. Then heavy rains came and beat down some of his best crops, though they stood up better than on neighbouring farms with thinner yields. A hundred tons of his hay lay rotting. For his good ricks, he told me, he would get, with luck, twenty shillings a ton, which would be sold in London by the dealers at five guineas a ton. But only with luck. There was more hay than beasts to eat it, as another farmer told me.

When I sat in one of these old farmhouses, taking tea with the farmer and his wife, my eyes roved to a picture on the wall. It was a print of Watts's picture of Hope, the blindfolded girl playing a harp with broken strings. This farmer, whose ancestors, beyond all doubt, came over with Hengist and Horsa, did not notice this allegory on his wall. He passed me a piece of bread-and-butter and said, "Perhaps if we can hang on for another few years things will brighten up a bit."

In another Oxfordshire farmhouse I sat at the tea table with the family. On one side of the room was an arched window, dating from A.D. 1250, and beyond the flower garden were the walls and moat of this old manor house. My host, who is one of the best farmers in Oxfordshire, has the same name as the village in which his forefathers dwelt for seven centuries or more; and as I studied his face, clean cut, with an eagle nose, I saw the Norman knight in him. He belongs to a stock which has given England its best blood in history: the blood of knights, squires and yeomen, and farming folk, which we can't afford to lose. He was utterly unlike the stage caricature of an English farmer, with a straw in his mouth and whiskers round his face. He was a gentleman of Oxfordshire, with a noble garden outside his windows which looked away to his broad acres. Probably he could stand the strain of bad times better than smaller farmers without reserves. We discussed the farming situation and were joined in the conversation by his son and daughter, who didn't think much of it, though they kept their sense of humour.

"The long and short of it is," said my Norman-looking friend, "that it's a mistake to grow much wheat in England, whatever the yield. Thirty millers have closed down lately along the Thames Valley. They don't want our wheat."

That was too pessimistic. The levy on flour has given the English wheat growers a fair price for their grain by making up the difference between the world price and the cost of production. Perhaps even now there's not much profit in it, but there can't be the same ruinous loss as in recent years.

The year 1931 was the blackest for English farming. Driving through the ploughlands and pasture lands of Norfolk on visits to some of the farmers, I had the unpleasant feeling that I was back in the war zone, visiting battalions and brigade headquarters before the great offensive of March, 1918, when the British army had its back to the wall. All around me a great harvest was ready for reaping. On thousands of acres the wheat was tall and bronzed. I passed through little old villages with tiled roofs and timbered walls, where there was a sense of profound peace, and from which came the cheerful sounds of the blacksmith's forge. Down the road sheep were being taken to markets. There was no outward sign of any enemy attacking this countryside. And yet, after talking to some of the best farmers, there in Norfolk, some of them farming from two to three thousand acres of the best ploughland in England, I knew that for the past five years, unknown mostly to their own nation, they had been fighting a battle against overwhelming odds of ill luck and that they were in the last ditch. It would be untrue to say that they had their backs to the wall. There was no wall.

It was a tragic situation. Here are some of the finest and largest farms in England, into which these men have put all their fortune and labour of mind and body. Those far-stretching harvests of wheat and oats should have been a source of wealth to themselves and the nation. But on every acre of wheat they would lose five pounds at least. They were losing on almost every other crop, except the finest grade of barley, for which there is still a profit although no great market. There had been a frightful slump in the price of potatoes. It did not pay to rail their cabbages. They dropped four to five shillings a head on every sheep. They could get no paying price for pigs. For five years their capital had been withering away by these continual losses, while their land fell in value to a quarter of what they paid for it. Hundreds of them had no more capital. They had borrowed from the banks year by year to keep these farms going on the barest minimum of labour. They could borrow no more. That was the position they were now facing with despair in their hearts.

Despair is not easily shown by men of courage, especially to strangers. One man laughed, a sudden gust of ironical laughter, when, at the end of our conversation in his farmhouse, he hesitated for a moment and then went to the drawer of an old bureau and pulled out his balance sheet for the current year and read out the net result. We had passed each other years ago in a field of France when things were unpleasant. He was a gunner officer up beyond Arras in May of 1917. Now he read out the result of a peace-time job. Wages, £4,000. Loss, £8,000. It was then that he laughed quite loudly, but it wasn't a mirthful kind of laughter, and afterwards he spoke rather bitterly about the political situation and the causes of this agricultural agony.

"What are you going to do?" I asked, and he gave me the same answer as other men. "I'm going to close down. I shall get rid of my men. I shan't put any field under the plough. I can't afford winter feeding of cattle. So now that I have sold my bullocks fairly well I shan't buy any new stock requiring artificial food. I shall abandon all expenditure, even though it means letting down my land, and I shall hang on as long as possible in a state of siege."

"Things may get better," I suggested.

He shook his head.

"I'm entirely without hope," he said. "Nothing will be done for agriculture. Nobody cares a damn!"

Many farms in Norfolk adopted the same policy of closing down. I met two brothers who had just sold their teams, dismissed their labourers, and put their fields to grass after selling their present crops at any price they could get. They had only a few hundred acres, but there was one man in Norfolk with seven thousand acres. He was doing exactly the same thing—not working his land, dismissing all but a few labourers, and retiring to his farmhouse in a state of siege against this invisible enemy of falling prices and failing markets.

"If this situation goes on," said a farmer, "we shall see the ploughlands derelict and choked with weeds, as many of them now are, and thousands of acres run by a man and a sheep dog—prairie farming—with the ruin of village life and the old graciousness of the countryside."

It was not a sudden crisis which overcame English agriculture four years ago, when things were worst. It was a creeping paralysis. Wartime profits began to wither away in 1926. The ex-officer who had bought a small holding, or a three-hundred-acre farm, at post-war prices, lost all his capital and disappeared. Farms dropped heavily in values. Farmers who held on and took over other fields found themselves without capital to feed them, owing to the drop in prices. They could not afford labour for hedging and ditching, so that all over England good land is becoming foul with thistles and weeds.

In every English county, arable farmers, cattle graziers, and small farmers with three hundred acres or so, with a good balance of crops, were in debt to their banks, and in debt for seeds, machinery, and fertilizers. Their books year by year showed tragic losses. The value of their farms had fallen by more than half. They were unable to pay for labour. There was bitterness in their hearts.

"Nobody cares a damn," said my friend who had walked the Arras–Bapaume road.

3. Good Marketing

There were people who cared more than a damn. Something was done about it in the nick of time. The government and the nation decided to abandon the old principle of Free Trade upon which England had waxed fat in the days of prosperity. Under the pressure of the world economic crisis, abstract arguments and theoretical ideals, and even the sound principles of world trade, had to go by the board for the sheer necessity of self-defence. Every kind of artificial stimulant—tariffs, quotas, subsidies, levies—would have to be tried out, to save the English agriculturists and to cut down imports from foreign nations.

It was our abandonment of the gold standard which really saved agriculture in England. It was an enormous shock to statesmen and politicians. It forced them to adopt remedies and policies in a time of danger, which would have been resisted by the industrial population without that menace of economic disaster. Automatically the fall of the English pound restricted imports for a time and gave a chance to the home market. A national government, with Ramsay MacDonald as Prime Minister, and a sprinkling of Liberal and Labour Secretaries of State, swallowed their old ideals and gave a free hand to the institution of protection in all its forms to the producers of foodstuffs.

Chief credit for the actual job of planning a new system of relief for the farming folk must go to that bright, bold fellow Major Elliot, a live wire, a man of courage and humour and dynamic energy and intellectual audacity. As Minister for Agriculture he adopted drastic measures, very alarming to old-fashioned liberals and economists, who believed, and believe, that these palliatives, this violent departure from the pure gospel of Free Trade, would lead ultimately to a further restriction of world trade, heavy losses to shipping and industry, and a shrinkage of national wealth. Major Elliot didn't care about all that. He was out to put the farmers on their legs again and to assure them first share of the home market at prices which would cover the costs of production with a fair margin of profit. He clapped on duties. He handed out subsidies. He arranged quotas with foreign importers, and he encouraged the farmers to abandon their old individualism and to get some kind of order into their own methods of marketing and supply. Marketing boards were set up for milk, potatoes, pigs, hops, and other produce. They were administered by experts and ingeniously devised to give fair play all round: not easy in a country where farming conditions vary so much in different districts and where many interests clash. All this was not done without violent criticism from the very men it was intended to help, nor without much heartburning and controversy in all the market places of England, Scotland, and Wales. One man's meat is another man's poison. Cheap wheat from foreign sources, ruinous to the wheat growers, was a boon to the cattle men. The Milk Pool might be good for one county and bad for another more favourably placed in marketing its supplies at a good price. It was the safeguard of the lowest common denominator reducing all milk to a low level of price, but with a certainty of finding a market. There was to be a dictatorship of rigid control instead of the private liberty of individual farming as it has been carried on for hundreds of years on English soil.

How far has all this succeeded in reviving prosperity in rural England? I have been trying to find that out lately from talks with farmers. It is very hard to find out. I have never met a farmer yet who admits that he is doing well—with perhaps one exception. If one crop is good, another is bad, because of too much sun or too much rain, or not enough sun or not enough rain. Nature tries to catch him out somehow when he's not looking.

It caught out the fruit growers on May 16 of this year, when a night of frost—in the middle of May!—destroyed their orchards in a few minutes, at least by fifty per cent, and in many orchards by seventy-five per cent, of the promised harvest. Evesham went into mourning. Kent burst into tears. Surrey stared at its fruit trees and despaired.

But worse than nature, it seems, is the malignity of the foreigners. They do their utmost to defeat all these quotas and subsidies. The Dominions reaped a great advantage out of the Ottawa Agreements at the expense of the English producers.

To them it makes no difference if cheap produce comes from Canada or the Argentine, from New Zealand instead of Denmark. Their prices are lowered in just the same way.

As far as I can make out, all these systems of relief by tariffs and quotas, and all the marketing boards for the regulation of prices and supplies, have succeeded at least in averting ruin. The farmers are getting markets, and some of them are paying their way with some kind of margin on the right side. There is not much in it, it seems, even now, for the middling man—the typical English farmer with three hundred acres or so of good earth, of whom there are thousands in the Home Counties and the Midlands. A recent analysis of a hundred such farms in Devon and Cornwall showed that there was a profit of £2 on a hundred acres, allowing a living wage to the farmer and his family. If there were no charge for unpaid labour—that is to say, the farmer's time—there was a profit of something under £50 on a hundred acres. That is not grand, but it isn't bankruptcy. It enables a farmer with a family to live in fair comfort, with good food and a roof over his head, and a motorcar to take him about, and money enough for a wireless set and other little amenities of life. There are many who would envy him.

Those Norfolk farmers who, four years ago, were turning off their labour and selling their teams have received nearly £2,000,000 relief in subsidies and other forms of aid, or about £2 an acre on the 990,000 acres of farming land in Norfolk. It must have made a difference to them, though even now they are not admitting any return to glorious prosperity. By a levy on every sack of flour the wheat growers are now getting the difference between the market price and forty-five shillings a quarter, which is about what they need to make it pay. It is a subsidy which is in violent contradiction to the old principles of laissez-faire and Free Trade. But as yet it has put no great burden on the consuming public, who are still getting their food cheap. And although these methods of relief and protection must in the long run slow down the wheels of our world trade— they have already slowed them down—there are other reasons than those of finance why our farming folk should be protected and enabled to get a fair reward for their labour on the soil.

They are, after all, the best of our human stock, and their industry is vital to us all. The land and those who serve it are, in my belief, the foundation of any secure form of civilization. Part of England's weakness, such as it is and may be, is due to our turning away too much from this good earth of ours and relying too much on machine-made industry and financial operations which have no deep roots in the soil itself and no security in a world of changing systems and ferocious nationality intent on self-sufficiency. Neither spiritually nor physically can we, without hurt, turn our backs on the land and let its fields go to waste and its people drift into the cities, as they are still drifting. We need the country way of life and the stock of rural folk to keep our blood strong and our spirit healthy. All our genius has sprung from the earth. All our greatness goes back to fields and woods and farmsteads. The cities must always be recruited from the land if our nation is to maintain its vigour and its character deep-rooted in the soil. Isn't that true, when one comes to think of it?

Such things were said to me not long ago by an old farmer, standing with his dog on a hillside above his fields. I talked with him for a while about the old days, and his mind went back to the black year of 1879, which he remembered as a boy.

"My father was farming this land," he said. "The crops were laid flat by the rains. The sheep were rotting in the fields. It was a black harvest. But now we are having to face other plagues worse than weather: all this foreign competition and the downfall of prices and the high costs of labour! It's very hard to make farming pay, in spite of what the government is doing for us. I think the whole world has gone wrong, somehow. I don't understand all this talk about gold and exchanges and enmity between nations. I'm just an old farmer who knows something about crops and tries to grow 'em."

He looked down at his dog and patted its head, and when he looked at me again I saw that his eyes were wet.

"I'm an old man," he said. "I've had my innings, which hasn't been too bad. But I'm sorry for the younger men. I'm sorry for England, which we and our forefathers helped to make. Our blood and spirit counted for something in the past. Now it's machinery that counts, and the land is not wanted so much. In the last few years thousands of farmers have been forced to sell up and go. I've no use for mechanized farming, which is the only way that farming pays, and it's no good for men because it takes their labour away."

He was one of the old-fashioned kind—a fine old type with white whiskers and kindly eyes under beetling brows. His face was tanned by wind and weather. But he was bewildered by a world in which he had been left behind.

4. Ploughland and Pasture

It is difficult to find these farmers when one goes to visit them. On some farms it is extraordinarily difficult to find any human being. One avoids a barking dog, looks into empty barns, tramps across muddy fields, searches the horizon for a friendly soul, and seems alone in the world. They are working their land with the minimum of labour, and the men are lost in distant fields. But when found the farmers are friendly and hospitable, and as a rule they insist upon one sitting down to a meal at their tables. Then they start talking, and one gets behind the outward appearances to the hard, and sometimes cruel, facts of human life. For apart from world conditions, they are always up against the vagaries of an uncertain climate, and, until recent help came, a sense of injustice rankled in their minds because all their risks and all their labour found such a poor return. The middleman is the fellow who makes the money. The producer gets the dirty end of the stick.

The type varies very much. In Oxfordshire and Kent and Sussex and Hampshire one finds the old type of farmer with three hundred acres and an old house. He is still intensely traditional. He has deep sentiment for this land which he works. In many cases it belonged to his forefathers. I have been to farmsteads where the same family has worked the land for seven hundred years. It is no wonder that they look askance at bright young gentlemen from agricultural colleges who tell them the latest scientific theories and urge the need of abandoning old methods. They are intense individualists. They have no instinct for coöperation with their neighbours, now being forced upon them. They resent the newfangled way and all this mechanization. Many of them are still simple men, not good at keeping accounts, slow of speech, with no time to keep up with modern ideas or the nimble wit of a younger generation. They belong to Hardy's characters, hardly touched by the rush of motor traffic outside their very gates, hardly altered by the social revolution in the post-war world. They are more close to Shakespeare's England than to this time of jazz and the internal combustion engine.

In the marshes round Rye—that relic of old England—one meets men whose minds haven't been touched by all that rush and roar. One meets them still in Wiltshire which was once the heart of England, when here at Avebury all the roads of England led to a circle of giant stones put up for worship by our neolithic ancestors, the downland men. Afterwards Alfred fought the Danes here, and many scenes in English history passed through the Vale of Pusey and up Roundway Hill, where the Royalists, under Wilmot, beat the Roundheads under Waller.

I saw some of these old ghosts in my mind's eye when I passed by the White Horse at Allington, and the big stones at Avebury, and through old Wiltshire villages, out from Devizes and Wootton Bassett, on the way to see the dairy farmers who have now made a milk walk of Wiltshire. These men have that history in their blood. They belong to old farming families. Their forefathers tilled this earth and grazed their flocks on the chalk hills and in the Plain. It is rich soil, good for wheat and all grain, round about Devizes.

"The finest arable land in England," said one of these Wiltshire farmers. "It's a sin to put it down to grass!"

Thousands of acres have been put down to grass in Wiltshire because milk promised to pay better than wheat, with a safer market.

This farmer I was talking to pointed to Roundway Farm, half a mile distant from us.

"Thirty years ago," he said, "that was ninety per cent arable. Now it's ninety per cent dairy. One can't help feeling sorry."

These old arable farmers hate to waste such good earth on grass. They like to see it used for the harvest of tall grain and root crops. In the old days they didn't regard dairy work as farming. They called the dairymen cow keepers, with a touch of scorn. Now, under the stress of necessity, they are all cow keepers, although, with obstinate pride in which there is also sentiment, some of them still hang on to the arable side of their farming and will not desert their ploughland altogether.

So it is in other counties. It was in Warwickshire that I sat at table with a farmer who apologized for being without a collar.

"I was up at five this morning," he said, "and I've just come in from the fields."

Through the windows of his old farmhouse I could see those fields stretching away for six hundred and fifty acres of good English land. He told me that before the government had come to the rescue with a subsidy on wheat he had lost six thousand pounds in ten years. He was one of those men who divide their land between arable and dairy work. It was wheat which had done him down. He quoted the old saying which many farmers have used to me:

"A sack of wheat pays a man's wage a week. Now it needs three sacks and leaves a loss."

"Why grow wheat?" I asked, greatly daring.

At the back of my head was the thought that English farmers cannot compete except by artificial subsidies with the great granaries of Canada. It might be better for them to grow other things and cut out wheat.

He looked at me with mild surprise.

"This land grows good wheat," he answered simply. "It's a sin not to use it. Besides, we need the straw, don't we?"

"How about milk?" I asked, expecting better news.

"There's no real profit in milk," he told me. "The price we get on a year's average doesn't pay for the general expenses of the farm. It's better for those who only do dairy work. I'm a farmer."

It was pride again that was keeping this man to the plough. It would break his heart to give up growing wheat on such good land. But now, with the subsidy on wheat, he is just making it pay again.

5. *The Hop Growers*

I went through the Garden of England—as in Kent they like to call it—just before the gathering of hops. This year the fruit harvest has been damaged by the disastrous frost in May, but there are apples ripening in the orchards, and some of them were being picked. Hops were growing tall on the forests of poles, gipsies were bringing their caravans along the roads, and tramps were sleeping under haystacks at night, impatient for the season's picking which would put some money in their pouches.

I went through many villages of Kent, time-mellowed under tiled roofs, and I seemed to have slipped back into the old days when the oast houses were crammed with a golden harvest of hops and all these fruit gardens and orchards meant a prosperous year for the farmsteads. It looks like that now, apart from abandoned hop gardens here and there, and naked hop poles blown aslant by high winds. There are the old oast houses in thick clusters, looking, to a fanciful eye, like old women with witches' hats. There are the old farmsteads, with their deep barns and their rutty tracks. A mile off the highway and one is back in eighteenth-century England. These Kentish farmers are not much changed in their daily habits since those days, except that they listen to the wireless now and then and go to neighbouring towns in motorcars.

But something has happened to hops. It is now a rigidly controlled trade. The hop growers can only supply so much in quantity and are restricted in the acres they use for this crop. The Hop Marketing Board controls prices and kills competition or overproduction. The nation is not drinking the same amount of beer. Its quantity is too dear at the price of a pint, and the quality is too thin to make it worth while as a drink. Unlike my friend G. K. Chesterton, who, in the heyday of his enthusiastic youth, believed that the more beer a man put down his throat the better he would be in mind and soul, I do not regard this as a national calamity. But it has altered the balance of things in Kent now that there is a decrease of a million barrels a year.

One of the Kentish hop growers explained to me the history which led to the iron regulations of the Hop Marketing Board to prevent overproduction and the slump of prices.

During the war, when there was government control, hops sold for £8 a hundredweight. Afterwards a group of the biggest hop growers maintained a kind of control and tried to keep up the price of hops, until their organization was broken by outside producers who sold their hops for lower prices—any kind of price to get a little ready cash.

Then something else hit the English hop growers. In spite of a heavy duty of £4 on every hundredweight, American hops, grown mostly in Oregon, began to overwhelm the Kentish growers. Whereas it cost £6 a hundredweight to grow the finest English hops, because of the cost of artificial manure, Oregon grows its hops without manure for £3 a hundredweight, and the Irish brewers, who do not have to pay the duty imposed in England, bought more and more of the American hops for their black beers. So did some of the English brewers, mixing the strong tang of the American hops with the milder flavour of our own.

Many hop gardens have been grubbed up and abandoned. Many oast houses are derelict. Old King Beer, who ruled so long in England, has toppled off his throne. It's bad for Kent but good for city populations, who do not beat their wives in mean streets or fight with knives outside the public houses on a Saturday night, as in the old days thirty years ago.

6. *The Miracle Worker*

Incredible as it may seem, I have met a man who has made a fortune out of farming in England. He owns two Rolls-Royces and has travelled twice round the world for his pleasure's sake. Starting as a smallholder forty years ago, he extended his domain until he owned, he told me, thirty-eight farms which were highly profitable. One of his friends told me that he made half a million of money out of them, which is almost unbelievable. Most of this money was made out of potatoes.

I met this remarkable man, this fairy-tale farmer, under the old archway of the White Hart Inn at Spalding in the Holland part of Lincolnshire. Inside the courtyard there were two hundred farmers or so, gathered for market day from the fenlands and the uplands. Outside in the cattle market their men were poking sticks into the ribs of fat beasts while the auctioneer was asking for bids and marking them down at poor prices. Looking less like a farmer than most men might, I was addressed humbly by gaunt-looking labourers who inquired whether I wanted any harvesters. The farmers themselves answered my own inquiries with the greatest civility, and it was one of them who introduced me to the man who had made a fortune out of farming.

In spite of his two Rolls-Royces, he still goes among them on market days under this archway of the White Hart, where for forty years he had made many a deal. He was one of the potato kings of Lincolnshire. Among the other men round him were farmers who had bought some of his land, which he had the good luck to sell when prices were high.

"I have been twice round the world," said the fortunate farmer—an elderly man with the distinguished presence of a Cabinet minister or a bank manager, though he started in a small way, "and, apart from the islands of Honolulu, I can tell you that there is no land so rich as these fenlands of Holland in Lincolnshire."

It is the largest and finest potato-growing area in the world, saved from the sea by the Roman bank or dyke, which still exists, and afterwards, in the time of Charles I, with the help of Dutchmen, who knew all about dykes and dams. Up in northern Lincolnshire and on the western uplands the land is poor and light, suitable for sheep grazing. But down here in the fenlands of Holland the best land used to be as much as £250 an acre. Some of it is still worth a hundred pounds an acre if people have the money to buy it. It is the land of the potato kings of Lincolnshire, once the most envied men in the farming world. One can make a lot of money out of potatoes, it seems. One can also lose a lot. Three years' losses can wipe out a little fortune. It is a costly crop to grow. The most scientific farmers, who produce the biggest and best yields—and these men in Holland adapt the latest scientific knowledge to their farming, so that

CHURCH IN THE FIELDS

their produce is threefold what it used to be forty years ago—spend as much as thirty pounds an acre on their manures and sprays and all forms of culture and labour. Their labour bills are very high because they need a lot of men for lifting and carting and so forth. One farmer I met who has a thousand acres has a wage bill of £8,000. And it is all a great gamble because of the weather and marketing. In 1929 there was an enormous glut of potatoes. The yield was ten or twelve tons an acre instead of about seven or eight at the best. Instead of making a fortune, the potato growers lost terribly. Prices fell away in a few weeks. Thousands of tons could not be given away and were thrown into the dykes or left rotting in the fields.

In 1931 there was a sudden rainfall of nearly seven inches round Spalding and Boston. Seven hundred and fifty tons of water fell to an acre. The dykes filled and overflowed the banks. Fields were swamped. Thousands of tons of potatoes were ruined.

I saw the results of this devastation as I drove through Lincolnshire. Potato fields occupy only a third of the land because it needs a rest, and the potato farmers have to grow other crops —corn, and clover, and mustard, and roots—to make a proper balance and to use their land to advantage. For miles across the low-lying fields intersected by canals, strangely like the Holland of the Dutch, with here and there a windmill, and with villages of red brick in the Dutch style, the wheat lay flat and soaked, and the potato fields were blackened and blighted. On many farms it was impossible to cut the wheat by machines, and the cost of hand cutting was too high to make it worth while.

One of the potato growers in a small way, standing with his back to the wall of the White Hart Inn, told me of his bad luck with the main source of his livelihood.

"I reckoned I had potatoes worth fifteen hundred pounds," he said. "Now anybody can have them for fifteen pounds. I'm down and out."

Since then the potato trade has been assisted by a marketing board and by protection against foreign dumping. It is, I am told, less hazardous, and has a chance of profit.

Sugar beet is grown largely in this part of Lincolnshire, but the subsidies given to the beet-sugar factories and passed on in price to the farmers has been cut until it has very little influence in support of cultivation.

One source of help has been started in Boston, where canning factories for peas and fruit are absorbing large supplies. I went over one of them and saw an endless chain of cans passing through complicated machinery, which fills them, seals them, boils them, cools them, and turns them out ready for the market, aided by the hand labour of a line of girls. This rich fenland of Holland in Lincolnshire grows the finest seeds in the world for root crops, and they are so good that we do an export trade with America, although there is a duty equal to the English price put on these seeds by the United States government.

Another branch of culture profitable in Lincolnshire is bulb growing. In the spring around Spalding there is the same glory which I have seen in the flower fields of Haarlem: vast stretches of tulips and hyacinths in waves of brilliant colour, as though rainbows had dropped out of the sky and lay across the fields.

7. A Man Who Knows

There are many types of farmers in England. In the south and west one meets the old-fashioned type, deeply traditional, hating to change their old methods, simple and rustic men on small farms remote from the hurry and scurry of modern life. They have a dignity, I find, which is rare among city workers. They are without subservience and without class consciousness. With their feet on the earth they look out on life with steady eyes and a simple courage which has helped them to carry on through bad times, now passing, let us hope. Under their old roofs in Tudor and Stuart farmhouses they have given me their hospitality, and I am always struck by their unaffected manners and genuine kindliness in their simple philosophy of life. I have never met those dark, sinister sensualists who appear in the fiction of modern novelists like the Powys brothers, from whose pages one would imagine that our rural character is very bestial and tortured by an eternal conflict of the flesh and spirit. These farmers I have met have a good poise and a shrewd humour. They are shy men, it is true, but I do not suspect anything sinister in their reserves or in their silences. They are not men of glib tongue, and one has to approach them tactfully, but once they believe in one's sincerity they are very ready to tell all they know about this business of farming, and are glad to give one their friendship.

They have a great loyalty to their wives. I have noticed that many times. When I was talking to one of them recently, he suddenly broke a sentence about the price of wheat and looked over to his wife with a smile in his eyes which was pleasant to see.

"We farmers," he said, "are always grousing about something! Conditions are never quite what we want, and of course we've been through a difficult time, but we owe everything to our women folk. They always have the most courage. We couldn't carry on without them. A farmer's wife has to bear an awful lot—hasn't she, my dear?"

"Well, we needn't talk about that!" said his wife, blushing very deeply at this tribute and smiling back at her bearded man.

They had lost their son in the World War. They had been through lean years, but they still carried on and had no bitterness. Here, I thought, in this fine old house whose timbers were cut before Elizabeth was queen, one finds the soul of England and the heart of England at its best, unchanged by all this modern trash of so-called progress. This man and wife have the old loyalties, the old faith, the old courage which gave England her best sons to die—alas!—on many battlefields. Very likely some boy went from this house when beacon fires were lighted at the sight of Spanish ships in the Invincible Armada. Very likely a young man went from the fields outside this door to fight with Harry at Agincourt. Shakespeare might have sat under this roof in Warwickshire and felt at ease with these two people. He would have known them. He could have talked to them about birds and beasts and flowers and crops. Here, away from jerry-built houses and jerry-built minds, one finds old England again and all its sweetness.

But those are the older folk. There are other types, less traditional, more scientific, less rustic. One finds them in Norfolk and other counties. They are the sons and grandsons of men whose minds moved in the old ruts and who talked with the broad speech of rural England. These younger men have been to agricultural colleges or public schools. They are alert and quick to adapt themselves to new conditions. Some of them at first sight are more like city men than farmers. They do not wear straws in their whiskers. They do not wear whiskers. They watch the financial situation as keenly as members of the Stock Exchange. They talk with considerable knowledge of world economics and international finance. They have considerable organizing ability and at a farmers' meeting can put their case as well as any lawyer speaking from a brief. As political propagandists on behalf of protection, subsidies, levies, and quotas, some of these farmers take a lot of beating. Thomas Hardy would not have found them like his rustics in *Tess of the D'Urbervilles* or *Far from the Madding Crowd*. They have moved with the times, though I think they have not yet lost the quality of their simpler fathers, because they are still close to the earth and deal with natural things and have a love for the land.

I learned a lot about present conditions of English agriculture from one of these more modern types. He is a man who went to an agricultural college before he was called up to serve in a World War. He was about seventeen then, I suppose, but like other boys of his age, he wore a Sam Browne belt and was a sublieutenant in Armageddon, of which he saw quite a lot before he was wounded for the last time when he fell back from St. Quentin and kept meeting French troops who disappeared quite quickly. During the war he stood in waterlogged trenches, looking across No-man's Land. He crawled out on night raids. He walked the duckboards through the swamps to Passchendaele. And then one day, marvelling at his luck to be alive, he found himself at home again in a peace-time job, which was farming. His family farms a thousand acres in Warwickshire where three other counties meet. They are mostly graziers, but this man who walked through Armageddon now knows all there is to know about milk, and pigs, and potatoes, and wheat, and other branches of farming. As the secretary of a farmers' union he makes it his job to know, and I found him very illuminating on these subjects, and sometimes humorous

"Now, take pigs," he said.

"Certainly," I agreed. "What about pigs?"

"It's a question of taste and tradition," he told me. "The

English farmer likes fat bacon. He always has done. When he thinks of a pig fit for the market, he thinks of a fat pig. He calls that a pig. But not the Danes nor the English bacon-eating public. City populations won't eat fat bacon. They want it lean. The Danes send over just the stringy bacon which the English city man likes to eat for his breakfast. But the English farmer goes on breeding fat pigs. It would break his heart to send pigs to market looking like race horses."

"I can understand that," I agreed.

"Then there's the question of grading," said this farming authority. "Danish bacon is all of one grade. But English bacon varies from day to day. The retail man finds that he gets a good grade on Monday and a bad grade the following Thursday. That's part of the reason why the pig breeders can't compete with their Danish rivals."

He developed some very interesting ideas about the change of taste affecting the fortune of English farmers.

"The beef trade has been badly damaged by the motorcar," he told me.

"Do you mean the motor traffic is killing all the cattle?" I asked, only mildly surprised at this massacre of beasts as well as the usual slaughter of human beings.

"No!" he said, laughing. "What I mean is that the motorcar has changed social habits and public taste. In the old days the family joint was an English institution. A good sirloin of beef lasted for three days. But now people go motoring about during the week-ends and they won't order any kind of joint. They take sandwiches. Besides, with an increased standard of living people are more finicky about their food, and eat things like poultry, which used to be counted as a luxury. If they eat beef at all, they want rump steak or sirloin. They refuse to order other parts, so that there's a lot of waste in beef. The small household —all these new flats and little bungalows—have caused the swing over from beef to mutton. Housewives like small joints. Beef is out of favour. The low price of cattle is one of the black spots of the present situation. Disastrous! Even then we haven't done so badly as the Dominions."

He quoted some figures. He seemed to have a great head for figures.

"Meat prices in this country—between 1929 and 1932—fell by twenty-eight per cent. In Canada they fell by forty-five per cent: in New Zealand by thirty-nine per cent, and in the United States by sixty per cent. Pretty awful, eh?"

Yes, it was a tragic revelation of a world-wide deterioration.

"Tell me about milk," I said. "The workings of the Marketing Board seem difficult to understand."

He told me about the Milk Board for nearly an hour. He was obviously enjoying himself, disentangling the complications of an intricate system with the gusto of a crossword puzzle enthusiast. It is all very difficult, as we used to say in wartime. But as far as I could get to the heart of truth, it seems that all milk produced in England is divided into liquid milk for drinking, and manufacturing milk for butter and cheese. The price of the latter is fixed by the price of cheese, which is very low, so that the manufacturing milk prices average about fivepence a gallon, which is unprofitable to the dairymen.

The liquid milk varies in price according to the season. It was 1s. 4½d. in the winter months last year and 1s. 1½d in the summer months. But in certain regions, like Wiltshire, sixty per cent of the milk goes into manufacturing, whereas in other counties, like Surrey, it is mainly liquid. Therefore the Wiltshire men would get less for their production than the Surrey men. This is equalized by a milk pool, to which the dairymen contribute about one penny a gallon. This pool is distributed in regions according to the relative amounts of liquid and manufacturing milk. Wiltshire, for instance, gets more out of the pool than Surrey. Each milk producer, therefore, hands over all his milk and receives from the Milk Marketing Board his proportion of the average price. It's something like that, but with many other complications, including a levy on English cow keepers to keep Scottish milk off the English market by annual payments, like buying off the Danes in Saxon times.

After nearly an hour on this subject, I changed it abruptly. I couldn't bear any more about milk.

"What about wheat?" I asked.

My farmer friend knew a deuce of a lot about wheat.

"There was a world-wide overproduction," he said. "During

the war there was a vast increase in acreage in Canada and the United States, and they got wheat growing in places where it wouldn't grow before. Science, you know! But people don't eat more bread nowadays. They make up on vegetables and other things, or tighten their belts in distressed countries. English wheat couldn't stand up against world prices and world dumping. Now the English wheat grower gets a levy to make up the difference between the world price and forty-five shillings a quarter. It's put onto each sack of flour but doesn't make much difference to the bread-eating public. A rise of four shillings on a sack of flour makes a difference of a halfpenny on the loaf. The industrial population can stand that without whimpering."

He came back to cattle—the black spot, as he called it.

"Prices are terrible, in spite of a subsidy. What can we do against all the meat which pours in from the Empire and the Argentine? Last year there was an increase of something like four hundred thousand hundredweights of chilled and frozen beef from the Dominions over the imports for the previous year. There's not much protection about that! We're in an awful mess."

"Taking it all round," I said, "how would you compare the situation of English farming with what it was four years ago, in the black year?"

He thought deeply over a pipe he was smoking.

"Apart from cattle," he answered, "we're on safer ground again. If it hadn't been for the government's action with tariffs and quotas and subsidies, we should all have been ruined beyond rescue. We were literally in the last ditch. Now farming has some chance of paying its way. Some men are doing well."

I was glad to hear it, having a great sympathy with our men on the land. They have a hard life. We literary men and town dwellers are apt to idealize it. We put a lot of sentiment into it, because of the beauty of old farmsteads and a thousand associations of poetry and history. For the men working the land and tending the beasts there is none of that sentiment. They are in the front-line trenches of life. Their toil is never ending. They are deep in muck when weather is foul. There is a lot of cruelty in country life, and the slaughter of beasts is not pretty. Nature is a rough school of men and women. But it has compensations, and it breeds character. All that is strong and hard and simple in our national spirit has its roots in the old earth which is England. These farming folk have been the fathers of our best manhood and our genius, and without that heritage we should be more impoverished than by a slump in prices.

VI

The Front Line of Industry

1. The Battle Line

"THE SOUTH lives on the north," I was told by a man in Sheffield. "All you folk down south live very comfortably and have an easy time with a lot of luxury, while up here in the north men are digging out coal, and working in forges and furnaces, and doing the rough work upon which modern civilization is built."

That's an exaggeration, of course. One has to exaggerate sometimes to make a point. There are lots of factories down south. More are being built each year, because there is a drift of smaller industries to the outskirts of London. The dockers and the factory hands do not live in the lap of luxury as lords of life on the products of slave labour. But there is something in it. In the industrial battle the south of England is behind the line; the front-line trenches are mostly up there in the north. The heaviest casualties are there, all the broken lives flung onto the scrap heap by the invisible enemies of bad trade: machine power displacing labour, and "rationalization," which means profit at the cost of human life. The heavy industries have been hardest hit by a world economic "crisis" which has now become a chronic state. It is in the north that the heavy industries are mainly placed.

"There is a different spirit down south," I was told by a man in Newcastle who had just been spending three weeks in London. "It's almost gay. One is aware of a general sense of well-being and happiness. Life seems easier and softer. There's not the sense of being close to the grim side of the industrial struggle or of being haunted by the menace of unemployment. Things are better now up here, but we're still in the thick of a struggle which is going to be a hard fight still. Well, we're good fighters."

I was aware up north of a different atmosphere, a different rhythm, a different spirit. That phrase, the front-line trenches, stuck in my mind. It's true. The battle line was up there. We in the south, in counties like Surrey and Sussex, are hardly aware of conditions in Northumberland and Durham and Yorkshire. It is a different world. Men and women lead different lives, harder, grimmer, closer to the firing line, and with the effects of this industrial war visible about them.

Here is the power of the machine upon which, as my friend truly said, modern civilization is built. It is infernal in its aspect, to southern eyes, but not without infernal grandeur. If some great artist wants to paint a masterpiece representing Civilization, I advise him to go along the road from Rotherham to Brightside, as a few days ago I went that way. There is a motoring road which goes along a hillside, looking down into a valley and to another hill beyond in a far-reaching panorama. It is a vast picture of gigantic chimneys, furnaces, forges, steel works, factories, and mountainous slag heaps like Egyptian pyramids. Smoke of different colours drifts across this area. At night flames leap up from the depths. Black buildings, massed like the walls of some devil's fortress, rise between the great chimneys and under a cobweb of wires and cables and cranes. No human beings are visible, though there is a great population down there in long streets of little houses under the pall of smoke. Sirens are howling. One seems to hear the beat of engines and the thud of steam hammers somewhere in that valley. Down there they are making everything that is made of metal in this metallic age. Stainless steel is a great industry in Sheffield. At the Ritz and the Carlton in London pretty ladies pick at their food with forks made in Rotherham and Tinsley and Brightside. The clean-shaven young men who are paying for their food shaved themselves with razors made in that valley of steel. Molten metal is running into moulds for many uses of men, including the great guns which defend this industrial civilization and are now in great

demand because civilization seems a little insecure and the nations of the world are passing new orders for the increase of
armaments. They are coming to Sheffield, which is very glad
to have them. The day I arrived there was a rush order for naval
shells, because the gentlemen in Geneva were still unable to
persuade Mr. Mussolini that slaughter of Ethiopians was likely
to lead to trouble.

The Royal Infirmary in Sheffield is a very handsome building. It is much used by a population which is engaged in dangerous trades. It is one of the casualty clearing stations of this zone
of the industrial battle. Molten metal is not as safe as milk.
The machines lop off human limbs now and then. The handles
of knives are made of inflammable stuff in their early processes.
Some girls came shrieking to the window of a factory on the day
I was staying at the Grand Hotel. One of them flung herself
out and fractured her skull. Some xylonite, that stuff which
makes knife handles, had suddenly burst into flame. With all
the care in the world it sometimes happens.

In Durham and Yorkshire and Northumberland the men who
go down the mines never know whether they are coming up
again. In many pits there is always the risk of a gob fire. In many
pits there is the risk of falling roofs, in wet galleries not too well
timbered. . . . They are the front-line trenches.

Trade in the north is looking up, they tell me. There is no
doubt of that. Statistics prove it. In the first eight months of this
year there was an increase of exports amounting to £22,000,000
over 1934. In three years Sheffield, the greatest steel centre of
England, has decreased its unemployed by nearly 25,000. Exports of coal and iron are up by 100,000 tons for the first eight
months of this year. There are signs of new activity on Tyneside.
Unemployment figures are dropping in some of the northern
towns, like Rotherham and Doncaster and Huddersfield. The
newspapers like the *Daily Express* are cheering up the nation
by enormous headlines announcing these good facts, and they
are very good indeed as an indication that England, by some
miracle—a miracle of character and tradition and industry
and sound business—is struggling out of the depths of depression
into which its basic industries had plunged during the recent
bad years. There are victories to record up north. Money is

turning round, and manufacturers are making profits again.
There is no sign of misery in cities like Newcastle and Sheffield,
with their great hotels, their picture palaces, their fine shops,
and streets filled with prosperous-looking people—no sign at all
unless one goes to look for it in back streets. I could paint a very
cheery picture of the industrial north if I concentrated only on
this renewed activity in industry, as I should like to do, and
especially if I emphasized, as I am certainly going to do, the
keen spirit, the real valour of men who refuse to despair and are
very hopeful of the future, which they intend to make good by
their own intelligence and will power.

But I should be lying if I reported that all was well in the industrial north. There are many things which are wrong with it.
While industrialists are making better profits, there is a great
mass of human life there just able to keep above the starvation
line without any margin for the little comforts which make life
good. They have no sense of security. From week to week they
are under the menace of being turned off their jobs—if they
have jobs. There are hundreds and thousands of men who have
no work at all and no chance of work. They will never get it
again. There are towns and villages which I have visited where
nearly the whole population is unemployed. In Durham County
and Northumberland and southern Yorkshire the working
population is fighting a losing battle. They are being beaten
back in a desperate rearguard action. Many of them have given
up hope of any general advance in their standard of living,
which is on the lowest line possible for existence. And yet my
strongest impression of what I have just seen up north is that
of great numbers of men and women who refuse to surrender
in their souls and have a courage which somehow keeps them
going with a patience which I found astonishing and with a
humour which is still unbeatable.

2. *The Abomination of Desolation*

It was a woman in Newcastle who put me right for the tram
on the way to the Central Station, where I was going to take
the train to Jarrow. I wanted to go to Jarrow, not because I

thought it was a beauty spot—I knew it was the worst place on Tyneside—but because I was keen to see what had been done there by that man to whom a vision had come in a Surrey garden, Sir John Jarvis by name.

The woman sat next to me in the tramcar, and we talked on the way to the station. She was middle-aged and plainly dressed but spoke without any northern dialect.

"How are things in Newcastle?" I asked.

"Better," she answered brightly. "But we've had a bad time, you know. Terrible really. But you've no idea how brave the working folk have been. The world will never know that, because it's mostly hidden. The women have been saints. They've kept the homes together somehow—though I can't think how."

She told me that unemployment was still bad. She knew of a firm which had advertised a few weeks before for twenty places vacant. Two thousand people had turned up outside the premises. Some of them had tramped for miles and hadn't the fare to get back again.

"It shows you," she said, "they don't shirk work up here. They want to get it if it's going."

She got off at Westgate Road, and I went on my way to Jarrow. Not many others were going by the morning train. Jarrow didn't seem to be a popular place. In the third-class carriage where I took my seat there were two men in opposite corners. One was a sturdily built man with a thick neck and no collar. The other was a little undersized, thin-faced fellow who sat with his hands between his knees and his head bent. The thick-necked man put down his paper and nodded a good-morning to me.

"Mussolini is a madman," he said. "It's the disease of dictators. They all go mad sooner or later. Someone ought to shoot him like a mad dog."

"How are things on the Tyne?" I asked, after some discussion on this subject.

"Not so bad," said my fat friend.

"Better in Jarrow?"

"Ay. It's better in Jarrow."

The undersized man looked sideways.

"There you're wrong," he said. "It's no better in Jarrow. I'm a Jarrow man. I've been out of work four years, and that's less than most of them. There are only forty men working at Palmer's. There used to be ten thousand. Do you call that getting better?"

"Well, I didn't say it was like paradise," said the thick-necked man.

It wasn't like paradise in Jarrow. I saw that when I walked through its streets with the undersized man, with whom I had become friendly. It was a damp misty morning with a drizzle of rain. Few people were about in the streets of small houses all exactly the same, all very dreary and impoverished looking. Down one street through the mist I saw a number of men lurking like shadows under the shelter of a wall.

"Poor relief," said my friend. "There's few in Jarrow who don't need it."

"I know a man called Sir John Jarvis," I said. "Hasn't he done a lot for Jarrow?"

The man hesitated.

"He's given us hope," he answered. "That's something. But we've been hoping a long time."

"He has given you more than hope, hasn't he?" I said. "He has just bought the *Olympic* for breaking up. Won't that employ a lot of men?"

"Two hundred. That's good, I'll admit. But the population of Jarrow is thirty thousand, mostly out of work. There's a long way to go before Jarrow gets active again."

He led me to a house in a little group of houses built round a courtyard.

"That's where Sir John's agent lives," he told me. "Glad to have met you."

He shook hands with me, and lingered a moment.

"I've nothing but gratitude for Sir John," he said. "He's trying to help. He's spent money out of his own pocket. He's brought some money into the homes. But it's more than one man's job. See what I mean? You'll see for yourself."

I met Sir John Jarvis's agent and was glad to meet him because after two minutes I knew that I had met a good type and a humourist. He had been a petty officer before becoming a lieutenant in His Majesty's navy, and before the day was done

I knew that he was a first-class fighting man, ready for any kind of job which meant the handling of men or boys. But as the agent of Sir John Jarvis in Jarrow he needed a lot of tact because of local politics and a difficult position as an outsider in a community suspicious of strangers, however benevolent their intentions. Jarrow men are proud, and one has to steer carefully between Catholics and Protestants, and between Labour men and Conservatives, and between the mayor and the councillors. Sir John Jarvis's agent has to tread delicately like Agag, and he does it with the breezy way of the navy and a laugh which he takes with him through Jarrow.

He took me to the old racing track, once famous in England for its cycle races. In the cold drizzle of rain a small group of unemployed men were busy making a new football field. They had built the pavilion of which I had been told by Sir John in his Surrey garden. It is out of his fund that they got free meals on their job. I went to a new recreation ground which is being laid out with bowling greens and a swimming pool out of money provided by Sir John and his Surrey friends. I went past many houses redecorated by paint and paper provided from the same source. All good work. All giving activity and wages to a certain number of unemployed men, all bringing a little hope into Jarrow, but not yet touching the essential problem of a thirty thousand population deprived of work by the failure of Palmer's Yards, upon which the entire crowd had been dependent for their livelihood. They are now in the hands of Ward's of Sheffield. That is to say, they are in the hands of the breakers up, for Ward's of Sheffield specialize in scrap heaps. They are only interested in scrap iron, and they will break up a ship or a factory, or a foundry or a steel works, as they are now engaged in dismantling Palmer's of Jarrow. It is this famous firm of Ward's who bought the *Olympic* from Sir John Jarvis, and his friends who guarantee any loss that may arise. It will bring wages, it is hoped, to Jarrow men, amounting to a hundred thousand pounds. Later on it may lead to something bigger—the great hope of new steel works here on the Tyneside where once at Jarrow thousands of men were doing good work and earning good wages.

I went into Palmer's Yards. That is to say, I went into the

Abomination of Desolation. There was a great silence in these old ship yards. No men moved about them. An immense range of sheds and dry docks were deserted and derelict. I gazed up at immense cranes and overhead cables and carriers. Nothing stirred. In one dock was the wreck of a Greek ship with a few ribs left above its keel. It had been burnt out. That is to say its steel plates had been disintegrated by a few men working with acetylene burners. One of them—one of the few living beings I saw in Palmer's Yards—was doing that work on some steel plates in a corner of one of the yards.

I was taken round by two of Palmer's old officials, now working for Ward's. They were both intelligent and friendly men who even now, after long acquaintance with tragedy, could hardly hide the emotion which came to them as they talked about what had happened to Palmer's. One of them was a blue-eyed man and very charming, I thought. He spoke in a kind of casual way, hiding any sentiment, though it was there in his eyes and in his heart.

"This used to be a great place," he said, looking along the line of works as we stood over the skeleton of the Greek ship. "It has a river frontage of nearly a mile and covers about a hundred and forty acres, with Hebburn on the other side. It was more than a shipyard, you know. It was the only place in England where a ship was turned out ready for launching from the iron ore upwards. The ore came to the blast furnaces and was converted into pig iron. That was sent to the steel works over there and made into rolled steel for the ship's plates. We had eighteen miles of railway inside the works. Now it's all on the scrap heap. Quite a pity."

We stood in some empty sheds, and the blue-eyed man held my arm lest I should stumble over some débris.

"I've seen this place humming," he said. "We used to build many ships for foreign nations as well as our own—Japanese, German, Swedish—all sorts. The first iron warship was built in these yards during the Crimean War, and afterwards we built many modern battleships of the Dreadnought class.

"During the war we were working furiously on first-class battleships, destroyers, monitors, submarines, merchant vessels, and every kind of craft. Our erecting shop was a great sight,

The Charter House
Efander

THE CHARTERHOUSE

with the most perfect machinery for dealing with the largest turbines. There was enough power in Palmer's to turn out the navies of the world. Now it's all gone. It's in the hands of the breakers. There's nothing left."

"Why?" I asked.

When I asked that question we were going across some gangway, and the blue-eyed man turned to me and smiled with a kind of tragic amusement.

"Because of something wrong with the figures in a ledger," he answered. "Because money is more important than human life, and credit is withheld from those who supply the goods which other people want."

Standing in Palmer's Works, the only human beings visible in this enormous desolation which a few years ago had throbbed with the prodigious industry of men and machines, we talked about the mystery, the illusion, the fantastic absurdity of money as it is controlled by our present system or as it controls our present way of life.

"Something must be wrong," said this man in Palmer's, "when in some countries grain and meat are destroyed while in others masses are underfed. Something must be wrong with our bookkeeping and credit system when millions of men who are skilled workers, strong and eager to work, are deprived of the chance of labour, though the world needs their products. Isn't it all rather silly?"

I agreed that it was all rather silly. And standing there in Palmer's, where mighty ships had been built, where thousands of skilled men had earned good wages, I felt chilled in spirit because of the great tragedy which had happened here.

I went to see a man who knows the people of Jarrow. It was a priest named Father Maloney, who received me in his bedroom with two spaniels who are friends of his. He offered me a cup of tea and talked of the character of the Jarrow folk.

"You would be amazed," he said, "by their courage. Some of them have been out of work for many years now, but somehow they still keep their spirit. At least they have a wonderful patience and resignation. I sometimes think they have all the Christian virtues, and this time of trial—it lasts too long—has brought out all that fine quality of character and faith more than in the time of prosperity. My Catholic folk keep their faith. It's their one great consolation. It's their one source of courage and patience."

He didn't believe that there was any underfeeding in Jarrow, or at least anything like starvation. But there was no margin of comfort. They were down to the bare limit, living on the dole. Fortunately the children seemed to be keeping up their health and strength. It was a strange thing that, according to health statistics, the Jarrow children were on the whole superior physically to those in other districts more favoured in industrial prosperity. That was partly due to school feeding: two meals a day for children of impoverished families.

"Come and have a look at them," he said.

He took me round to one of the schools. The head master was a keen fellow who had once served the guns in France. Now he was teaching the children of those who had fought with him in the war. It was another kind of battle, against poverty and hardship bearing down first upon childhood.

"We have to divide them up into three classes," he explained, "A, B, and C. The C class is backward. You will see it in their bodies as well as in their minds. They remain in C class all through the school age. You can tell the difference between them and the A class by just looking at them."

I went into the C class expecting to be shocked, but I found these little creatures fairly bright and intelligent. They showed me things they had been making—basket work and woven patterns. Some of them looked a little stunted. Their class mistress spoke to me.

"These boys haven't a chance when they grow up," she said. "There's no chance for boys in Jarrow. That makes me sad when I think of it. The girls are not so hard to place. They go into domestic service."

We went into A class, who sprang up as Father Maloney entered with me and beamed on them. Behind the desk was a woman with the face of a Madonna by Murillo, dark-eyed and beautiful.

"Would you like to hear some of the boys do a little reading and recitation?" she asked.

I was glad to hear the boys of Jarrow. Two of them read with great style and expression. They had good faces with very bright eyes and a look of eager youth. The Venerable Bede, saint and scholar, might have looked like one of those in his boyhood here. It was a boy named Tony, a little fellow, who recited without his book. He had the northern burr in his speech and gave out a heroic ballad with tremendous spirit.

"These boys have no chance," the little schoolmistress had told me. There will be no work for them when they are old enough to work—unless Sir John Jarvis or some other brings rescue before then.

The people of Jarrow are getting desperate for rescue. They have waited so long now. Hope deferred maketh the heart sick. Sir John Jarvis has given them hope, and they are grateful, but every day when they get up for another day of worklessness they ask when things will begin to move. When will the *Olympic* come to dock for breaking up? When will the steel works start again? How long, O Lord?

I spoke with some of the Jarrow men. Not one of them said a word of impatience. One man spoke of his faith as the light in his life. "Christianity helps," he said very simply. "If I weren't a Christian I couldn't carry on." Several of them said, "If we lose our spirit we lose everything. You'll always find a joke in Jarrow."

Somehow I missed that joke in Jarrow.

I was given a message to carry back, not from the workless men, but from a group of business men who sat at a long table and invited me to join them. They belonged to the Rotary Club, and to this moment I am wondering what business they found in Jarrow, where there can't be much doing in the stores and shops beyond the essential needs of life. When I entered the room one of their number was making a very good speech describing a visit to Rotary Clubs in the United States, and as I listened I looked round the table and thought that these Jarrow men might have been in Kansas City, or Grand Rapids, or Scranton, or Middleboro. It was just such a group as I had met in places like that. The chairman introduced me and told the company that I would ask some questions about the state of Jarrow. He would be glad if members would answer me.

I asked a few questions, and one or two members answered.

They spoke well. They were men of education. They paid a tribute to Sir John Jarvis for his efforts on behalf of Jarrow and expressed their hope that his vision would be fulfilled—his vision of a great steel works rising on the desolation of Palmer's Yards. They thought there was a chance of it. They still hoped with all their hearts.

Then the chairman gave me his message. He spoke very gravely, and with a suppressed emotion which was visible in his eyes.

"Tell England," he said, "that our patience is getting exhausted. We wish the nation to know that the patience of the people of Jarrow is coming to an end. They cannot go on forever waiting for the fulfilment of promises. They supported the national government by sending a member to represent them. They will not continue that support if nothing is done to help them in their long tribulation."

Those perhaps were not his exact words. At the table there I could not make a note of them. But that was the sense of the speech and the message which I was asked to carry back with me from Jarrow.

That evening I had a talk with a man who knew what had happened and what was happening behind the scenes in this history of Palmer's Works.

"The story of Jarrow," he said, "is not only a tragedy: it's a crime."

He told me things which convinced me of the criminality as well as of the tragedy. Palmer's Works ought not to have been closed down. Who were the criminals? He named them. They were bankers and trusts and men who deal with an industry, upon which thousands of human lives are dependent, without compunction or compassion, if it interferes with their own combinations and interests. They are the inhuman agencies—a group of men round a green cloth—who do not think in terms of industry and human values but in terms of interest on money or their own profit and powers.

Palmer's was bought up at a knockout price. It was declared to be a redundant shipyard. It was sold to Ward's of Sheffield as a scrap heap. An embargo was placed upon it, making it impossible to set up any shipbuilding works for forty years. Is any body of men justified in English law, or in equity and justice, to ban any tract of English land from setting up the industry for which its men have been trained, for forty years or any other length of time? Is that the liberty for which we have struggled so long? Now, when Sir John Jarvis is trying to establish new steel works at Jarrow, he has encountered sinister opposition. There are firms and trusts who do not want steel works at Jarrow. There are powers who are jealous of such an enterprise, though thirty thousand men and women live on the hope of it and are getting impatient even with hope.

I listened until late at night to a man in whom there burned a fire of indignation. He spoke very quietly but very bitterly. He was a Tyneside man and knew the suffering of the people.

3. The Builder of Ships

In Newcastle-upon-Tyne I had a conversation with a man whose life covers the entire span of the industrial era in England. That seems fantastically impossible, and now that I have written it down I can hear the word "Liar!" murmured by my intelligent readers. Because it does seem incredible that I should have been talking to anyone who goes back as far—farther indeed—than the first iron ships built on the Tyne, and who was a master shipbuilder himself in 1874, and who saw in his own lifetime the whole development of industrial activity on Tyneside, with its forges and blast furnaces and mighty cranes and steel works and dry docks and all that world of mechanical power. But then, Sir George Hunter was born in 1845.

I drove on a wet night to his house, The Willows, and when I was shown into his drawing room by a neat maid I had the impression that I was playing a part in the second act of *Milestones*, by Arnold Bennett. For this room was wonderfully Victorian. It was very large and was furnished in that style which expressed the prosperity of those mid-Victorian manufacturers who amassed great wealth in the 'eighties and sat around on sofas and chairs which were the very best produced by Tottenham Court Road, and collected porcelain which they displayed on overmantels, and bought—as their successors never do—works of art by water-colour artists who lived well on the patronage of their genius by these northern industrialists. They had a reverence for Ruskin until he began to write about economics and made them feel uncomfortable. They worshipped at the shrine of Watts and liked his woolly idealism, though they were hard taskmasters to the men in their steel works and shipyards. So I thought as I waited for Sir George Hunter in his drawing room, until the door opened and he appeared.

"It's very kind of you to come and see me," he said.

He was ninety years old, but he looked not a day older than seventy, if that—a handsome old gentleman with a little white beard and very clear bluish eyes and a delicate transparent skin. His hands, I noticed, were finely shaped and unlike the hands of a man who, nearly eighty years ago, was doing rough work as an apprentice in a Sunderland shipyard.

Some tea was brought in, and we sat together on a chintz-covered sofa, talking about conditions on the Tyneside and world affairs. He spoke quietly, and with a touch of humour now and then, in a beautifully clear voice and with a perfect mastery of facts and figures. Lord! I thought, this old man is a living miracle. His brain is like one of his own engines. It doesn't wear out.

"The fact is," he said, "that for forty years we built iron ships for all the world, and now—we're not doing so. I have built ships for Japan and Germany and many other nations. We shan't get another order from them. Japan is building her own. Our old customers no longer come to Tyneside. That's the new situation. But you're not drinking your tea."

I drank a little tea, and the old gentleman gave me more facts.

"The trouble is that there is not only a decline in British shipping, but the drop is more than relative in reckoning the present figures of world shipping. It's an actual decrease compared with other nations. Since the World War shipping has increased from forty million tons to seventy million, but we are not getting our fair share. The tramp is down by half. In fact, the whole percentage of our steam tonnage has fallen to nearly half during recent years, while that of other nations has increased. It's a pretty ominous thing, don't you think, that firms in this country are actually placing orders with German yards? Japan is going ahead very fast in ship construction. Our difficulty is to compete with the low costs of labour and production which favour our rivals, and especially Japan, which is capturing the Eastern trade."

He talked for some time about Japanese competition and offered to lend me a book on this subject.

"These subsidies given to our shipping," he said presently, "are only palliatives. The great question is—where are our customers? Ah, that's not an easy question to answer nowadays. I confess I can't see it. And how are we going to compete with low costs of labour abroad when we try to maintain a higher standard of living than any country of the world? Have you any views on that subject?"

I had a few secret views. I had a conviction that the miners' wages were too low. I told this to the old gentleman, but he disagreed. In any case, he argued that if the demands of the miners were granted the cost of all shipbuilding would increase by something like a pound a ton. That didn't seem advisable at a time when we were anxious to increase orders and when Tyneside was hard pressed. It would lead to more unemployment and more wretchedness.

"Compared with the old days," said Sir George Hunter, "the condition of the working classes has risen very much. Take the time when a miner or a steel worker was earning eighteen shillings a week, as I remember. He had to bring up and educate a family of six or seven. They had big families in those days. And they had no help from social services. They had to pay for their children's education, and their doctoring, and all the rest of it. They had no dole. There were no panel doctors, or school meals for underfed children. It seems marvellous now that they were able to carry on."

I didn't remind him of the frightful misery and cruelty of the industrial era through which he had lived—the foul conditions and housing of the labouring folk who had built up the wealth of Victorian England.

"In your opinion," he asked suddenly, "what do you consider the best help which could be given to the working classes?"

I answered after a moment's reflection,

"Better housing conditions and cheaper rents."

"I utterly disagree with you," he said with a touch of annoyance. "In my opinion this housing business has been overdone. They pull down houses to build up new ones which are no better. In a few years they will become as bad as the old, or worse. No, my dear sir, the best scheme which could be adopted would be the Family Allowance. It seems to me very reasonable. It would give a chance to the children. An unmarried man earns as much as a married man with a family. The children suffer. But a scheme for family endowment would keep the children in security and with good conditions."

He turned abruptly to other schemes for the prosperity of England. They seemed to him very unsound.

"Take Lloyd George's scheme," he said. "What's going to happen when the money is spent? What then?"

So we talked, or rather Sir George Hunter talked, until, after an hour or so, I took my leave. Before I went he took me into his study to find the book about Japan. His secretary was there, listening to the wireless. There was news about the Abyssinian crisis. Someone was speaking about the Empire. It appeared that the Empire was going to stand by the Mother Country in support of the League of Nations and its covenant which would apply sanctions to an aggressor nation.

The old gentleman of ninety stood listening intently. He had given his attention to other crises in world history. He could remember the excitement in England during the Crimean War. He could remember the Indian Mutiny. He had followed the news of wars in Africa, Egypt, and other countries where British troops had fought for the Queen. Here, at The Willows, Newcastle-upon-Tyne, he had heard the march of men on their way to France and Flanders in a world war. Now, with an old man's poise—is anything very important at ninety years of age? —he listened to this new machine which conveys the human voice and the message of human folly across the world.

"Very interesting," he said. "Mussolini would do well to think again. A very headstrong man, I should say."

I left the house of a man who knew England before the machine age had blasted great tracts of beauty and created a power which, like the Frankenstein monster, is now a menace to mankind because it puts the thunderbolts of Jove into the hands of hooligans and half-wits who are called dictators.

4. New Lamps for Old

In Newcastle-upon-Tyne I came in touch with a group of keen young—or youngish—men who were very anxious that I should not regard their city and county as being down and out.

"Nothing," they said, "makes us more annoyed than hearing Newcastle and Tyneside described as a 'distressed area,' or, worse still, a 'depressed area.' We are neither depressed nor distressed. On the contrary we are full of beans and we're driving ahead to create prosperity."

I was very glad to hear it. I was perfectly willing to admit in the Turk's Head, where some of these young, or youngish, men sat with me, that Jarrow was exceptional as a black spot. The whole of the Tyneside was not like Jarrow, they told me, and I had no doubt that they told me the truth, because if all the Tyneside were like Jarrow it would be desolate indeed.

I sat in another café with some of these keen men who were talking about these things and others. Some of them were newspapermen, and the talk turned for a few minutes upon Abyssinia, as it did in most companies during the summer and autumn of this year. Two of my friends had been in Egypt and Palestine during the Great War. One of them had learnt Arabic and a bit of Turkish, and he was very knowledgeable about international affairs. He had been having a look at the map and pointed out how Italy's boot points down to Africa and how, if Italy took Abyssinia, she would have a straight line down through East Africa.

"After Abyssinia, what then?" he asked. "What about Egypt for the new Cæsar?"

All this had nothing to do with conditions on Tyneside, but as I am writing a book about England and not about the Tyne I cannot forbear repeating something I heard in that Newcastle café. It froze my blood for a moment. A question was asked twice in a low voice by a man sitting at my right hand.

"Have you inquired about woman's views on this subject of a war?"

I heard it the first time, but was unable to answer, as I was engaged in conversation with the two newspapermen who had very kindly ordered a sherry for me. When it was repeated a second time I turned and said, "Not very deeply. Why?"

"My wife," said the man at my right hand, "has rather strong views about it. We have a boy aged twenty-one. My wife says that if he's wanted for a new war—she remembers the last— she will mutilate him with her own hand rather than let him go. Some women are thinking that way."

I felt that chill touch my spine and drank a sip of the sherry.

"Talking about Tyneside," said one of the newspapermen.

I talked about Tyneside with quite a number of men. They agreed on one point with remarkable unanimity: Tyneside had a future. Tyneside was making its own future. Tyneside declined to settle down with folded hands proclaiming its state as distressed and depressed.

"It's fantastically absurd," said one of them. "England can throw her hands up and say 'Carthage has fallen' if Tyneside goes out of business. It's the finest industrial centre in the world. In fact, if you fake the map a little, it is actually the industrial centre of the world. It's the distributing centre for a population of nearly three million. The old Tyne is navigable for ocean-going vessels for fourteen miles from the sea. Tyne Dock alone has shipped more coal than any other dock in the world. It has enough electrical and other power to provide the needs of a vast industry. If the Tyne goes derelict, then England's day is done. But it's not. You can take that from us. If old industries are slacking off then we shall create new industries. We're already doing so."

I made inquiries about those new industries. They are very interesting and reveal a lot of initiative and character among the younger men on Tyneside. They are encouraged and stimulated by an organization known as the Tyneside Development Board. There is a scheme in being for helping inventors to apply their genius to the possibilities of creating new industries, and already it has borne good fruit. During the last few years many

Tyneside men have started works for the lighter industries to counteract—I dare not use the word "depression"—the slacking off of the heavy kind and the slowing down of shipping.

One man named Henderson has set up a foundry for making light castings which had previously come from Birmingham. That was in July last, but he is already making plans to instal further plant. Another has invented a washing machine that gets all its power from the kitchen tap and is now making it for the market, which should be nation wide.

A factory for the manufacture of zinc oxide has captured the world market formerly held by Belgium and Holland. Thirty countries are supplied, and forty per cent of the world exports come from Great Britain. This zinc oxide is used for lead paints, rubber tires, and cosmetics. An old munition factory at Birtley was taken over for this purpose by a keen young man named Norman Dawson, with intelligence and energy which have resulted in the employment of many workers.

Tynemouth is building a new factory which will be used for canning foods. It is already employing five hundred people, and when the factory is extended will employ two hundred more.

In Wallsend two acres of land have been reclaimed for extending a ropery. In order to make this possible a tributary of the Tyne has had to be diverted, and the Wallsend Corporation has reconstructed and widened the approach road. That is one indication, of which I found great numbers, of cases of the coöperation of Tyneside local authorities with industry.

Sir Howard Grubb and his company have booked a twenty-four-thousand-pound contract for constructing a 74-inch reflector telescope to be erected on a plateau five thousand feet high a few miles outside Pretoria. The huge disk of pyrex glass from which the lens will be manufactured will come to Newcastle from New York, and for more than twelve months Tyneside workmen will be engaged grinding and polishing that glass until it conforms to the scientists' requirements.

One extraordinary phenomenon on Tyneside is the recent growth of confectionery firms with all their ancillary services of bottles, boxes, and printing requirements.

I sat for some time with an official of the Tyneside Development Board, who gave me many facts of this kind—all very interesting, I thought, as a proof that there are brains at work in devising new means to employ the labour of a vast population of nine hundred thousand people along Tyneside, among whom are some of the most highly skilled artisans and craftsmen in England.

As a sign of increasing prosperity among the working folk, he gave me the figures of the wireless licences issued in this area. They have risen from 73,000 two years ago to over 100,000 in March of this year.

"You see," he said, "that our population is not so poverty-stricken as people imagine. The wireless licence is a sure sign of prosperity in the home."

I was glad to hear all that, and it is good that England should know it. But as I travelled about Tyneside I was not quite re-assured that all is well up there. I could not forget Jarrow. I have not forgotten that story of shipping told me by Sir George Hunter. I remember his question: "Where are our customers?" There are still seventy thousand unemployed men in Tyneside. But I have a deep admiration for those young, energetic minds with whom I came in touch up there, who refuse to be distressed or depressed and are putting up a gallant fight to make things hum again in this stronghold of industrial energy, as it used to be.

5. Men of Durham

Outside the Labour Exchange in Durham groups of men were waiting to draw their doles, and I entered into conversation with some of them. They were not communicative, being sus-picious of a stranger, but I gathered from them that the labour conditions in County Durham were not rosy. A tall, handsome man with a white moustache, past fifty years of age, I should say, was more conversational.

"I was in the Coldstream Guards," he told me. "What, I ask myself, is the reason why these young fellows don't join the army. It's a good life. One sees the world. It's better than hang-ing about without work. And very likely we shall have another war, so they may as well go now. The Italian situation doesn't look good to me. I expect Mussolini has his eye on Egypt."

He entered into a narrative of his military career. He had been out on the border of Abyssinia. He was of opinion that the Italian army would be decimated by disease. He had many other opinions, expressed in very good English, but he had to cut them short and hurried away with quick steps to get his weekly payment or pension after giving me a salute.

I had an interview with the manager of the Labour Exchange, a bright young man who took a hopeful view of the situation in Durham and his area. Unemployment had gone down by five hundred for two years running. Not an enormous decrease, but not too bad. It showed things were moving in the right direction.

I had an invitation to lunch with the Dean of Durham—a great authority, I was told, on industrial conditions in the north. Before keeping that appointment, made over the telephone, I walked up to the Castle and Cathedral, the noblest sight in all England, I think, when its line of towers and battlements is seen from the valley of the Wear below. I stood a while gazing up at the Cathedral, vast, sombre, and magnificent, as it was built in Norman England and has stood unchanged for eight centuries of history.

In the nave, where I stood presently, I drew my breath in wonderment and awe because of this miracle in stone, with its Norman arches and piers stretching away in far perspective. These stones were laid and carved by men who worked for the glory of God and their faith in Christ, at a time when England was a fierce and warring land, with wolves in its forests and wolf-men in its courts and castles—wolf-men and tiger-men whose hands were on their sword hilts and who came to worship here in armour and chain mail. Richard Cœur de Lion was king when these altars were raised. The Plantagenets were kings when the Prince Bishops ruled this domain. Northumbria was a borderland through which many hosts of men with spears and bows came ravaging and burning. Hunted men came here for sanctuary, hammering at a door with a knocker which still hangs there. The chanting of the monks rose when the Scots came over the border, when great barons of the north were in rebellion against their liege lords, when there were peasant risings, and plagues, and famines, and wars, and slaughterings.

In these cloisters saints and scholars kept the lamp of faith burning when it was dimmed by the passionate forces of national feuds and injustice and all wickedness. They preached the gentleness of Christ to these rough Northumbrians. They toiled over their manuscripts, painting them with infinite love for beauty's sake.

Through the centuries Durham Cathedral has stood above the tumult of history, above the misery of men, through the ages which led to an industrial era when England waxed fat on the slave labour of men and women and children working in the mines over there in a countryside which the eye can reach from the high towers. And now it stands still as those Norman craftsmen built and carved it through another time of change and transition in the story of civilization. Something has happened to the industrial era. There is a new enemy menacing the lives of the Durham men. It is an invisible enemy but very deadly. The strength of men's arms, their skill in craftsmanship, their quality of character are unable to defeat this foe. The towers of Durham are seen by young men who have no work to do though they are on the threshold of manhood, and by men of forty and fifty, very skilled in handiwork, who are too old, it seems, to get work and wages. The machine, invented by men to ease their labour, is now displacing men and throwing them onto the scrap heap of unwanted refuse. . . .

Something of all this came into my mind as I stood very still in the silence of the Norman church.

Dr. Alington, Dean of Durham, and once head master of Eton, received me in his study and was amused when I told him that I had been informed that he was a great authority on industrial conditions in the north. He refused to admit it, but hoped I would not deny the rumour too harshly!

"We have a young man coming to lunch," he said, "who will give you a lot of information with more knowledge than I can claim. He runs the Durham branch of the National Council of Social Service."

The Dean's son, on vacation from Oxford, was interested in my mission of inquiry. He suggested joining in an expedition round the mining centres.

At lunch, in a room which was once part of the monks' dormitory with a high timbered roof, the conversation ranged over many subjects of interest. The young man who was active on social service talked about his job. Mrs. Alington, next to whom I had the honour of sitting, wanted to tell me about the women of Durham, whom she knew in connection with their mothers' union, the largest in England, with twenty thousand members, if I remember the figures rightly. She spoke about their immense courage in hard times, their wonderful patience, their good-humour and intelligence. There were three girls at the table, two of them the Dean's daughters. There was plenty of laughter, raised by the Dean himself, who had a humorous way with him, though simple and unaffected in his family.

Here, I thought, is a picture of English life which a foreigner would like to see. I doubt whether one could find such a way of life in any other country. These people, so charming, so frank, so unaffected, have a background of history and tradition which must soak somehow into their souls.

Here we were dining in a room which was built eight centuries ago, and still haunted, surely, by good ghosts. The Dean led me into two other rooms. One was a bedchamber with a Tudor roof of panelled wood in which James VI of Scotland slept on his way down to become James I of England. Here were old walls and windows which have vibrated to all English history since Magna Carta established our first liberties, so often outraged. These young people who handed me coffee and cigarettes sat in a drawing room after lunch with the invisible spirits of England's turbulent and heroic past. They had the blue eyes of Saxon ancestry, and the Dean himself had the fine features of a mediæval scholar with a modern sense of humour.

It was from this historic background that I set out to the coal fields of County Durham.

6. The Mining Villages

It is surprising how much of the county has been unspoiled by the operations of men and machines digging for the source of power. Durham is still an agricultural as well as a mining county, and the roads wind through a pleasant landscape, well wooded here and there, with arable fields and good pasture. It reminded me somewhat of the Sussex Weald—until that impression was obliterated sharply by the mining villages scattered throughout this countryside.

They are all very much like each other. These rows of little houses, mostly without any gardens, are dominated by enormous slag heaps, like monstrous ant hills, and the result of antlike toil down below. They are ugly and grim, those villages. There is no touch of beauty here, nor of art. The houses built for these people are just square boxes in which to sleep and eat, with little back yards in which the washing may hang. Standing in them, talking to men who used to be miners until they received their last wages, two years, three years, four years ago, I thought of villages in Germany and Austria where each house is pleasant to see, with woodwork carved by master craftsmen and with flower garlands or decorative scenes painted on their whitewashed walls, as at Garmisch and Partenkirchen and Mittenwald. Here, in County Durham, life has been too hard for art. It has been too grim for flowers. Men don't indulge in playful fancy when they come up from the mines where they have been working in narrow galleries with water dripping on their bodies. It is only now, when so many of them are unemployed, and when they are getting a little lead from friendly souls outside, that they are beginning to grow a few flowers here and there and to build clubhouses in which there are a touch of cheerfulness and a few pictures.

"When so many of them are unemployed," I have written. That does not convey the facts I saw. I went into villages in County Durham where, as at Page Bank, nearly the whole male population is out of work, and where young men and middle-aged men and elderly men stand around deserted works and brickyards, listless and very bored, unless they have been encouraged, as now they are being, to get busy with some kind of job on their own, with some new interest in life to fill up their leisure. Round about Bishops Auckland many of the mines have closed down, or are closing down. Men in Escombe and Toft Hill and Sacriston and Trimdon and many others of these mining villages have no hope of getting work and no chance of it. Many of these pits will never open again. Men now working on a few shifts a week are haunted by the menace of being paid

NEAR HUNTINGDON

off and joining the big battalions of the unemployed. Their
women live in the constant dread that the men will come home
one evening with the news that another pit has been closed forever. While I was up there rumours were coming that the Stanley pits were to be closed. They had been kept open, I was told,
to fulfil some contracts coming from Italy. Mussolini had ordered more coal from Durham for ships transporting his troops
to Abyssinia. The Ethiopians were going to be massacred with
the help of Durham coal, but meanwhile Durham men would
draw their wages. Now it appeared Mr. Mussolini was running
short of cash. He owed a million and a quarter pounds sterling
for coal already ordered. The coal owners were cancelling their
contracts. Fifteen hundred men in Stanley would be drawn off
their jobs. Consternation was caused when seven hundred and
fifty men and boys working in the Beamish Mary Pit owned by
the Lambton Hutton and Joicey collieries received fourteen
days' notice. On the same day the notices expired at the
collieries owned by the Holmside and South Moor Company.

"There's no hope for the County of Durham," said a man
who knew the conditions of this mining area and is now helping
some of the men to learn a few handicrafts and the use of the
earth for other things than coal. He spoke very quietly and
gravely as he explained to me the real facts.

"You see," he said, "many of these seams are uneconomical
to the mine owners, and the quota system among other things
has caused them to be closed down. Rationalization, as it's
called, has been hard on the men working at thin seams. Pits
that might have been kept open if conditions were favourable
are shut down in order to work at better seams. And when
they're closed down for temporary reasons there's more than a
chance that they won't be opened again. That means that more
men are utterly deprived of their livelihood. The fact is that
there's a geological fault in the Durham coalfields. West of it
the seams are poor and waterlogged. They have to be pumped,
even if disused, to keep the good mines dry. And coal isn't
wanted so much by our former customers. Oil is taking the
place of coal for power. Other countries are producing their
own coal. I don't see where we're going to get our markets back.

In any case, these poorest pits in Durham are out of business. And so are the men who worked in them."

I talked with some of the miners and was surprised that I could understand them so well. Their dialect was not so difficult as I imagined it would be, and they were glad, I thought, to tell their tale to a stranger.

"There's not much doing," said one of them, standing under the shadow of a slag heap in one of these villages. "Men who are working are not much better off than those on the dole. One goes down there and sweats, and takes a risk of one's life, for wages which don't give a man much of a time, especially if he's married with a family."

"What's the average you can earn?" I asked.

He stared at me thoughtfully.

"You'll get different figures," he said. "It depends on the seam. With a good kibble—that's where the coal is easy to get—and four shifts a week, a man earns about thirty shillings, or maybe twenty-nine. You see, we have to pay for safety gear, and there's always some deduction. One may work four shifts one week and none the next. It's not regular. But if you'll ask other men around this district they'll tell you the same. Thirty shillings or maybe twenty-nine. That's the general average it works out. A married man out of work gets twenty-six shillings, so it's not a fortune if one works. All the same, it's best working. It keeps a man from fretting."

He stared away beyond the slag heap.

"There's young fellows round here," he said, "who have not a chance of a day's shift. They're closing down many of the pits. And it's worse for the older men, who are put off first and won't get another week's wage as long as they live. It's a black shame when men have no kind of hope. That's what's happening in this country, but perhaps it's nobody's fault."

7. Men of Grit

I had a glimpse of life up there in the mining villages where thirty-five per cent, fifty per cent, seventy-five per cent of men and boys are workless. They are all drawing some kind of dole, which gives them a minimum rate of subsistence, just enough after paying the rents to keep them above the starvation line but not much more than that. It's easier down south for unemployed men. They have families who are working on good wages and who give them a helping hand. But here, where everybody is out of work—there are villages like that—there's not much help coming from one to another, although in their poverty they are kind to each other, as I was told a score of times. They don't drink. That temptation is far beyond their reach. Many of them don't smoke, though they were glad to take my cigarettes. They have an endless leisure to fill up somehow, and I confess that I don't know how they get through the days as far as the majority is concerned. The devil of boredom, that worst of devils, must find the doors open.

But some rescue has come to them. It has come partly through the leadership of a young man who came up here a year or two ago, and was stricken by what he saw, and called over the microphone for help on behalf of these men and women. It was the Prince of Wales, who has never rested since in his efforts to organize some national spirit of service up here in the distressed areas, as they hate to be called. Local committees, working in touch with the National Council of Social Service, are doing something to bring a little brightness and purpose to these areas of unemployment. The people down south have not been callous or indifferent to this northern distress. Surrey has supported Sir John Jarvis. Hertfordshire has taken a friendly interest in some of the villages of Durham County. The clerks in Whitehall and the G.P.O. put by some pennies for the miners and their families. The Personal Service League sends up clothes which are cut into garments for the children of the unemployed. All that is good. I saw that this help is being intelligently administered to the very best advantage by many keen and active workers. But all that money is but a drop in the ocean. Twenty times the amount is needed to touch more than the fringe of this mass of human need. These social workers in the north are handicapped all the time for funds. Their schemes to give the unemployed a chance of getting new interests and unpaid work which may keep their minds off brooding thoughts and their bodies active help them to help themselves.

"All this work we're trying to do," said one of the leaders of this adventure in social reconstruction—that young man with whom I had lunched in the Deanery of Durham—"is merely palliative. Needless to say it doesn't touch the fundamental problem of unemployment. What we're after is first of all to teach these fellows how to make the best of a bad business by getting active in ways which achieve a real purpose for themselves and their own group. If they build a sports pavilion, or a workshop, where they can mend their shoes or make a bit of furniture, or learn some useful handicraft, it puts new spirit into them. They feel that they're not on the human scrap heap. They're doing a decent job even if it's unpaid. If they rally up to make a bowling green or a football ground where once there was a slag heap or a refuse yard, they get a real pleasure out of their own physical energy and make something worth while for their community. But they have to be handled tactfully in order to get them going on such work. They don't like the word charity. They're not overkeen on being 'adopted' by the south. These north country men are proud. Any help in providing funds for material is best explained as a friendly interest and the helping hand of comradeship. In most cases we ask them to pay back something for the material they use in boot-mending and woodwork. That keeps their self-respect.

"All this seems to me part of a larger problem which is going to last even if unemployment is reduced. The machine with its increasing efficiency will give men longer hours of leisure, anyhow. A forty-hour week, or less, will leave men with a lot of free time. And what we're doing now, what we're only beginning to do, is to teach men how to use leisure and to get them interested in all kinds of things which formerly were beyond their reach because they weren't taught to do them or were too hard driven. We can teach them how to enlarge their own personality by getting an idea of beauty—flower gardens, a bit of painting, music, wood carving, some touch of creative art—into their home life and hobbies. It's the deadly boredom of unemployment that beats them down. One man complained to me that every day was a Sunday or a Bank Holiday, without a difference between the days of the week. We're trying to lift that sense of the futility of their lives."

"Good work," I said. "Show me how it's being done."

He showed me how it was being done in many villages. At Toft Hill we stood on the edge of a piece of ground which had been a quarry deeply delved. Some men here, working on shifts eighteen at a time, without wages, of course, had done a Herculean task, almost miraculous in six months. They had shifted sixteen thousand tons of earth to level the ground for bowling greens and tennis courts and a playing field. It was earth heavily laden with big stones, and they had used the stones to build a clubhouse which looked like a miniature fortress in its solidity, but as yet without a roof and as yet without the money to pay for a roof.

The foreman of this gang of volunteers talked to me with enthusiasm about the task he had performed with his comrades.

"There hasn't been any slacking," he said. "We're proud of this job. When that clubhouse is finished it's going to be the pride of the county. They'll think a lot of us at Escomb and Page Bank and Sacriston when they hear about this."

He was an elderly man. There was the light of joy in his eyes. Every stone heaved out of that quarry had given him a thrill of pleasure. He was working again. These pals of his were doing some good teamwork for the love of the thing.

"It's the spirit that counts," he said.

These village names have become confused in my mind, and I cannot read the notes I made in a car, but it was at Escomb I believe that the unemployed men had levelled the slag heap which had dominated their village with its ugly mass. They had turned it into a playground. At Sacriston they have built a fine pavilion and a good bowling green. At Page Bank they are running a communal poultry farm, and the men live with their hens and know every feather on every bird. I saw workshops built by the men and provided with tools by this social service scheme for the mending and making of furniture or repairing household breakages, and cobbling shoes, and making toys for the children of County Durham.

"We could do with more help," said my guide, who drove me through these villages and introduced me to unemployed men. "We want more personal leadership and interest. At the best of times this region was neglected by those who profited most by its labour. Too much profit was taken out of the mines. Not enough was put back into the villages to create a healthy and pleasant social life. The owners spent their money elsewhere."

"Some of them were not unknown on the Riviera," said the young man at the back of the car.

We passed a big house with a noble park.

"The house of a mine owner," said one of our companions. "It doesn't look too poverty-stricken."

"It doesn't seem altogether sound," said the young man at the back of the car, "that a miner whose life is not without its risks should earn less than a little lady in a city office who whacks a typewriter between the times she powders her little nose."

We went to a place called Hardwick Hall. It was a very pleasant place—a big house, rather undistinguished, in a fine park of some hundred and fifty acres, with many tall trees therein. I heard its story and its present purpose.

It is the G.H.Q. of the social service schemes in County Durham, and is rented by the National Council of Social Service from Lord Boyne, who charges a nominal rent in return for its upkeep.

"What we do here," said its warden, "is to train the N.C.O.s of the unemployment centres so that they can become leaders of their own groups. They do a short course here and learn something about poultry keeping, and woodwork, and gardening, and toy making, and upholstering, and all manner of things. But the main purpose is to inspire them with the spirit of social service and self-help, so that they can go back to their own groups and pass on the same idea. We give them talks, of course. We get to know the men who are likely to do well as group leaders."

I went through the house and gardens. Everything was perfectly organized as a training school for this social work. The dormitory would have done credit to Chelsea barracks, and in fact there are many ex-soldiers in this company of unemployed men who keep their beds in apple-pie order. The kitchen garden is the pride of the place. It is a walled garden, and fruit was growing on the walls. The cabbages and potatoes were looking well. Every inch of the ground was used by men who, until they came, knew nothing about the earth except the coal that was in it. The pigsties and poultry runs were in model form.

"Some of our fellows have a flair for pigs and poultry," said the warden. "There's a young man here who runs the poultry side of this show with an enthusiasm which has made him an expert. He would do well anywhere on a big poultry farm."

In the County of Durham I was impressed by these social workers. There was no nonsense about them. They were keen practical men, doing their utmost to lift something of the darkness and hopelessness from the unemployed villages. They have a vision ahead of a better distribution of work and leisure, but meanwhile they are getting down to this immediate task.

8. On the Dole

I sat in a working man's club and social centre in Darlington. The secretary of that institution, which is run by the Labour groups, is a man of sixty or so, of a heavy build and with white hair, and hands which had worked as a blacksmith before he lost his job in the Darlington Forge Company, which closed down and threw a great number of men out of work.

There were about thirty men in the room—a long room which was once the Corn Exchange—with bare boards and wooden beams on which, for some reason, there were lots of little flags flying; just to make it look cheerful, I suppose. At one end of the room were a platform and a piano, and the place was heated by a stove. Some of them were playing cards—it was ten o'clock in the morning—and others were reading newspapers. Some of them, I noticed, were doing nothing at all but sitting on wooden benches in a state of meditation or blankness of mind.

The secretary hadn't the faintest idea why I had come or what I wanted, but he was good-natured and, sitting there with hunched shoulders, began to tell me of the club's activities and his own. They had given a seaside holiday to some of the women and children. They rigged up ragged comrades in better clothes. Some of them had nothing but rags for their underclothing. Their boots had worn off their feet. The club was helped by kind friends who sent things along.

"I would like to speak with one or two of the men," I said presently.

I was embarrassed when the blacksmith rose and called out in a stentorian voice:

"Comrades, here's a gentleman from London come to see you. He wants to have a talk with you. He's interested in our club."

The card players looked round. The men who were reading newspapers dropped them and stared at me. The men who were sitting in a state of meditation, or blankness of mind, raised their heads.

"I would hate to interrupt that game of cards," I said. "And I can't speak to everybody at once."

There I made a mistake. The blacksmith insisted that I should speak to everybody at once.

"Gather round, mates," he shouted in his gruff, good-natured voice.

They gathered round on the long benches, and I sat in the midst of them. At first they were just a group of unemployed men, and I saw them as a group. But presently, in the course of conversation which lasted two hours, I began to distinguish separate types and characters.

Opposite on the long bench was a well-spoken man—he spoke the King's English—who had been a chauffeur in private service. Next to me on the right was a long, thin, cadaverous man of fifty-five or so, who had been in the Darlington Forge. On my left was a young man—he told me presently he was twenty-one—in grey flannels and an old sports jacket. He had very fair hair and the fair skin and blue eyes of what the Germans would call in their folly the Aryan race, or what the Americans would call Nordic. Several conversationalists emerged: a sharp-eyed, thin-faced fellow who was sorry for himself and had a grudge against the world; a square-headed, elderly man who put his points with good-humour and rough wit. Nearly all of them, I found, had been employed in the forge, which had closed its gates.

"Ay," said the secretary of the club, as though addressing a public meeting in a big hall, "it was the closing of the Darlington Forge Company in 1931 which flung a lot of human beings on to the scrap heap. Three thousand men lost their livelihood, and there's many as haven't done a day's work since—and not their own fault."

"I was nearly forty years in the forge," said the cadaverous man on my right.

"Is there any chance of it opening again?" I asked.

"Well, there's just a chance," said the blacksmith secretary, and there was a murmur of doubtful agreement.

"They're keeping things in repair. They wouldn't do that unless they thought they might open again one day."

"Too late for me," said the cadaverous man. "I'm getting past work. So they say. It's only the young fellows . . ."

"This new electric welding is no good," said one of the forge men. "They're beginning to find it out. There's ships which went down in the gale last week which would never have gone down if they had been riveted instead of welded. It stands to reason. You get two plates like this. . . ."

He put two fingers together and stared at me as though wondering whether I would understand.

"The electric welding process joins 'em together, like soldering them. Can that stand the strain of big seas? No sir. You might as well join them together with spittle. They're making death ships. That's what they're doing. I speak as a blacksmith. You can't do without forging for steel plates."

"It doesn't matter to most of us if the forge opens again," said the cadaverous man. "Too old at fifty. That's what they say. As far as work goes, there's nothing doing for men of fifty."

"What about men of forty?" asked one of them, sitting away down the bench. "Forty is too old nowadays."

"How do you get on with the dole?" I asked.

That was asking for trouble, and I got it all right.

There was a moment's deep silence. These men seemed to be thinking very hard.

"Twenty-six shillings for a married man," said the blacksmith secretary. "That's what we get. Out of that goes sixteen shillings for rent and rates."

"As much as that?" I asked.

"Not a penny less in Darlington. . . . That leaves ten shillings a week for a man and wife. It's not enough for food and clothes.

There's no starvation, we're told. True. But there's under-nourishment."

"Ay," said the cadaverous man. "One's body goes to pieces. One's strength goes. I'm not the man I was. I couldn't work in the forge now, an' that's a truth."

The man with a grievance wagged his finger at me, and there was anger in his eyes.

"I'll tell you what's happening. Employers of labour are taking on the young lads and rejecting the men of middle age. But what happens to the lads? I'll tell you. They're turned off as soon as they're old enough to have stamps on their card. I have a boy of my own who went into the furniture trade. They've turned him off now that he's old enough to have his stamps."

"Well, what about me?" asked the man who spoke the King's English in an educated voice. "I was in private service as a chauffeur. I'm not eligible for the dole. Now, if I had been driving a doctor I should have got my card because it's supposed to be public service, but not if I was driving a private family. I don't call that fair. It doesn't seem logical to me. And another thing. I had my card for three years because I was working in a garage. I paid the stamps. But because it was ten years ago I'm not eligible any longer. You see how it works in my case. I may say it doesn't work. I don't get the dole."

"Then there's this Means Test," said a man on the bench opposite.

There was a murmur again. They didn't seem to like the Means Test.

"Officials come poking about and questioning one's wife when one's out," said a man, rather better dressed than the others, with a soldierly look due to a little white moustache waxed at the ends.

"Ay," said the secretary sitting exactly opposite me with hunched shoulders. "It's not English. Isn't an Englishman's house his castle? It's an inquisition."

"I can't live with my own son and daughter," said the well-dressed man. "I don't want to drag them down because of my little pension. I have to live alone."

"There's only one thing which will cure this black plague of unemployment," said the secretary, raising his voice as though addressing a public meeting again. "It's a thing which is within the reach of the government. We call upon the government to do this thing. It's to give the working men of England a pension at sixty. That would relieve the situation. It would leave room for the younger men. It would bring more younger men off the dole. It's a simple way out, and if the government is sincere in wishing well to the unemployed, it will adopt this remedy. Pensions at sixty is what we ask."

There was a discussion on this point.

The demand for pensions at sixty did not satisfy a thin-faced fellow who sat next to the ex-chauffeur.

"There's always the gap," he said. "What's going to happen to the men between fifty and sixty? They can't get work. They're turned off at fifty—same as myself."

"Ay, and what about the men of forty?" asked another. "Too old at forty. That's a nice thing to have said to one. I've heard it said until I'm tired. 'We want young fellows,' they say, when I go to look for a job."

The man on my right nudged me with his elbow to get my special attention.

"This overtime business wants looking into. It's a black shame. There are factories in Darlington paying their men for overtime when they ought to be taking on the unemployed. It's to save stamps. Work ought to be spread around."

"Agreed!" said the old blacksmith who looked after the club. "But England turned down the Forty-hour Week at Geneva. That's what England did, while gentlemen in the government profess their anxiety about the unemployed."

"I wish to God I had been born a female," said a young man on the far end of the bench. "It's the girls that have all the luck nowadays. There's six thousand of them have gone into domestic service from Durham County."

"And they oughtn't to be allowed to go," said the secretary. "In my opinion, comrades, it's a dangerous business to let these young girls go down south without knowing the homes they're going to. No girl ought to be allowed to leave Darlington for such work until she has reached twenty-four years of age. Some of these girls have been lost in London. Their own mothers

don't know what's happened to them. There's many temptations
for poor young girls. I'm getting worried about it."

"There's talk of Emigration," said one of the forge men. "If
I were a young 'un I'd go out to Australia where there's a better
chance for a man who wants to work on the land."

"I disagree," said the cadaverous man. "Australia won't take
emigrants, especially from the unemployed class. They have
their own unemployed."

"There's plenty of land in England," said the thin-faced
fellow with a grudge against the world. "What's wrong with
that? Why not grow our own food? We import two thirds of it
from foreign parts, as I was reading only yesterday. There's pigs.
There's poultry. There's market gardens. Some of us unemployed men would do well on a little bit of land. We'd soon
learn, wouldn't we?"

"I'm much afraid there'll be a black winter ahead," said the
blacksmith. "They're closing down more factories. They say
five of them have shut down."

So we talked, and as I sat in this working man's club, warmed
by a stove, with long benches on bare boards, I had a sudden
sense, a kind of idea, that I was in Russia instead of England.
That old blacksmith opposite was very Russian in his type.
These men talking round me might have been in some village
along the Volga. It was not that they were in the least degree
Red. I found them patient and reasonable men, most decent
and excellent men, without a touch of cruelty or malice, but
these scenes somehow reminded me of Russia. It was like a
chapter in a book by Maxim Gorky. But it was in England all
right, up in Darlington.

As unemployed men they saw the black side of the picture.
In a population of 84,000 the unemployed amount to 4,400,
which are better figures than in other places of the north. There
is great industrial activity in this old town on the Great North
Road.

9. Ten Heroes

On the outskirts of a village called Woodland, in southern
Yorkshire, away out from Sheffield, I met a group of men who

were engaged in a gallant little adventure and were very illuminating on their own and other people's lives. I remember them with amusement and admiration.

This Woodland is a pleasant-looking place, unlike many mining villages in southern Yorkshire. The cottages are nicely designed, with a touch of art, and some of them are built round a greensward. It has the aspect of a little garden city, and near by is a Trust House, like those found in Surrey, where one can get a good meal with a waitress who is kind. Not far away is the Broadworth pit, not so beautiful as Woodland on top or below. And over there is the Park Gate pit, which has a sinister reputation, as I am told.

I found my group of men—there were only ten of them—through the garden belonging to a clergyman who is, they tell me, a helpful soul. Through a gate I came to a bit of land running down from a railway embankment. It was the railway company who allowed my ten friends the use of it—it was waste ground, anyhow—for a communal poultry farm. That is the adventure, and when I heard the story of it from these ex-miners it seemed to me a little Iliad in a chicken run.

These men had been heroes of the Great War. Didn't we call them heroes then? I found that out by some chance remark about the Abyssinian affair.

"All of us lot were in the last war," said a big stout-chested man. "We don't want another to interfere with our poultry work."

"I should say I was in the last war! The scars of it are on my body now."

A tall, lean man, with no flesh on his bones, pulled up his trouser legs and showed the traces of machine-gun bullets.

"Well, if it comes to that . . ." said another.

He pulled up his shirt-sleeves and showed the mark of a wound.

"I was regimental sergeant major in the Welsh Fusiliers," said the stout man, who wore nothing but a vest and a pair of old trousers. "The D.C.M. and the Croix de Guerre. Well, I never care about that now. I haven't put my medals up for a long time. But if you want to see wounds, ask that little fellow over there to show you his marks. Fairly riddled he was."

Some lines written by Shakespeare came into my mind:

Then will he strip his sleeve, and show his scars,
And say, these wounds I had on Crispin's day.

It was a Scotsman with a Harry Lauder accent who seemed to be the leader of this group. I chaffed him for coming down south to Yorkshire, and his eyes twinkled.

"In every job there has to be a Scot to look after things."

There was a round of laughter.

"Ay," said the man without any flesh on his bones. "They export men to England, but they don't take any imports. That's the way of Scotland."

"Now see this ground," said the Scotsman. "When we came to it last month it was just a bonny waste of docks and thistles and stones. It was like the stony ground of the Scriptures. Now I daresay you'll agree we've made a good start with it."

I agreed heartily. They had cleared most of the ground and had fenced off parts of it for their poultry runs and allotments.

"We've been through a desperate time," said the regimental sergeant major. "We can laugh at it now, but there were days when we lost heart. You see, we started with a hundred and twenty chickens or so, nice birds, who promised to lay good eggs. You couldn't have seen better birds. The white ladies looked a picture. The brownies were fine and strong. Well, the first knock came to us when we found that their food would cost each man eighteenpence a week instead of a shilling. It got us scared. A shilling a week is a lot to an unemployed man. We couldn't afford the extra sixpence and had to go into debt for it. It's a debt of honour to the clergyman yonder who raised the money for us. Then we were up against it. Our birds went down with a disease called *Trachiata laryngitis*, or something of the kind, though I wouldn't be sure of the right Latin. It was a disease of the eyes. It started in the eyes at first and then ate into the brain, when they dropped dead. Bird after bird dropped dead on us. 'Destroy them!' came word from a professor at the university. But it was destroying our only hope. It went to our hearts. More of 'em got the disease. 'Destroy them!' came word from our professor. Things looked desperate when sixty hens had gone. We felt like weeping. But after that we began to save the birds. If anything was the matter with its eye we plucked it out. The same as recommended in the Bible. We saved twenty birds that way. They're all one-eyed, but it's a queer thing, they lay better than the others with two eyes. Now how do you account for that?"

I could not account for it.

The Scotsman drew me on one side.

"These fowls are just the life of these men," he said. "They spend all their time here and watch each bird as if it were an only child. It's their passionate interest. Well, it gives us something to do and keeps us in the fresh air for hours at a stretch, and we earn a bit by selling the eggs. It's all I can do, anyhow. I've got varicose veins. Just have a look at them."

He pulled up his trouser legs and showed me his varicose veins as the others had shown me their war wounds.

"As long as we can hope to pay off our debt," said the sergeant major, "we shall feel relieved in our minds. Naturally, we're a bit anxious about the future. But we shall put up a good fight to win through. Now look at our birds. Lively, aren't they? See that brown one over there? She has a crossed beak but can eat as well as any of the others. And there's one paralyzed in the feet. Wants a bit of nursing you know."

Presently conversation shifted from the ailments of hens. It drifted to the conditions in the mines of southern Yorkshire and down in the local pits and to their own life on the dole as unemployed men.

"It's the rents that come heavy," said the Scot. "Fourteen shillings for one of those cottages yonder is a lot out of twenty-six shillings for a man and wife. It is true there are some that get let at nine shillings, but there's a waiting list for those as long as the family Bible. My wife and I have to live in half a house, and that's a difficulty, seeing the nature of women. I've had to change three times in a year because women don't get on with each other."

"None of us will ever be employed again," said the sergeant major. "And yet I'm as strong as ever I was."

He looked as strong as Samson.

"Ay," said the thin man whose legs had been riddled by machine-gun bullets. "It's only lads they want now. Machinery cuts the coal, and the young fellows shovel it on to the rubbers—

moving bands, you know—which carry it away. As soon as the lads get twenty-four they're paid off. Older men aren't taken on. The machine is the enemy of man, and that's the truth. It takes away human labour. The strength of a man isn't wanted."

"And what's the good of earning wages anyhow when they're not enough for a decent living?" asked a man who looked younger than the others and had curiously liquid eyes, like those of a deer. "It averages out no more than twenty-nine shillings. The dole is near as good as that. Why should a man take all the toil and risk? A married man can't do well on twenty-nine shillings if he has any kids."

"Call it thirty shillings," said the Scot. "Ay, that's the average since the great strike of 1926."

"It was the ruin of us," said one of his comrades. "They knocked our wages down to nothing and raised the rents on us."

"That's true," said the thin man, "and now they send round officials and ask every kind of question, as one did in my house t'other day. What was I earning before the war? What was I earning after the war? I noticed there was one question he didn't ask. He didn't ask what I was earning during the war—when I got shot up for King and Country."

They stood round me, going into facts and figures, but as men who have no personal interest in wages now that they are unemployed and without the chance of work. It was an academic question with them. They were looking back on the miner's life. Now they were keeping chickens.

"If I was offered a pound a day to go down into the pit again —the pit at Park Gate—I wouldn't go," said the lean man. "It's no life for a man who respects his body and soul. Go into this village when the men are about and you'd think there was a war on. Any number of them on crutches an' hobbling around on sticks and walking up street with their heads bandaged. That's what happens down in the pit."

"Ay, that's true," said the young man with deer's eyes. "In my case it was boils. I still keep breaking out."

I was afraid that he might show me his boils, but he refrained after a moment's hesitation.

"It's not good in these pits," he told me quietly. "When I used to work down there it was in narrow shafts where there

ARUNDEL CASTLE, SUSSEX

was not much air. It got very hot. All the time water dripped
down until my hair was soaked with it and my body was wet.
The water trickled down my shorts. Greasy kind of water which
worked into the skin so that half an hour in the tub wouldn't
wash one clean. It raised boils. That's because one scratches or
keeps rubbing sore parts of one's body. Three times I had the
boils all over my thighs. Doctor said I mustn't go down again.
Then there's always the risk of a blowout. I daresay you read
about those blokes who were copped the other day. One fellow
scrawled a message to his wife before he died. That's a miner's
life. I like hens best. It's fine when they're laying well and one
collects the eggs off them."

The thin man—he was the thinnest fellow I have ever seen—
lamented over the loss of his son aged fourteen and very handy
with the chickens.

"They've taken him away from me," he said, "to put into
engineering. If I wasn't on the dole I would have kept him. He
was a great little comrade of mine. His mother wept her heart
out when they took him away. It's awkward being poor. It
breaks the home up."

"Not that we're grousing," said the regimental sergeant
major with a hearty laugh. "We're telling you these things because you're interested. But this place is our little paradise. It
keeps us busy all day long, and the days are all too short. We're
lucky, we are. This is a champion hobby, and one day there
may be a little profit in it for all of us."

I shook hands with them. After telling me those things there
was a lot of laughter among them. They were not a miserable
crowd. They told me their future plans for taking in a bit more
ground for their allotments. Next month they will fight another
battle with the thistles and the docks and the stones.

"Good luck!" I said with all my heart.

10. Yorkshire Pits

As in County Durham there are pits in southern Yorkshire
which have closed down, or are shortly closing down, because
of worked-out seams, or poor seams, which are "uneconomical"

to their owners. They lie round about the market town of Doncaster, which seems bright and prosperous. Over at Barnsley the coal seam is rich, running six foot thick and worked by machine cutters. But there are other factors in southern Yorkshire which lead to unemployment. One of them is "rationalization," and efficiency of keen business men who cut down overhead charges and thereby—can it be helped?—cut the ground from under the feet of men who thought it was solid and built their lives on it.

So it happened in Pennystone when Cammell Laird's closed their steel works four years ago and put the whole population— 10,000—out of work and wages.

I went to Pennystone and other towns and villages round about Doncaster with a man whom I shall remember not only because of his kindness and charm, but because of his unselfish interest in the lives and happiness of such folk as these. His name is King, and he is secretary of the Advisory Council of Sheffield Social Service.

"You'll be interested in a club they've fitted up in Pennystone," said Mr. King. "It used to be the old pay office of Cammell Laird's. It was taken over by a clergyman named Matthews who was the leading light of this place when it became rather gloomy."

I was much interested in Pennystone and its club. One wouldn't say that Pennystone was beautiful unless one lied. I felt a chill to the spirit when I stood outside the deserted works. A man might lose any natural optimism if he lived six months here without a job to do. But I found an optimist there. It was Mr. Jubb, in charge of the clubhouse, who had lost his job four years ago when there was no more pay in this pay office.

He shook hands heartily and agreed that they had made a fine place of it. With quiet enthusiasm he showed me all the activities at the disposal of workless men. There was, for instance, a good workshop supplied with tools by the social service system. The men used it to the full. They came in to mend the boots of their families, paying back a bit for the leather. They made new furniture out of any old bit of wood, or repaired their own. There was a decent little library of well-thumbed books which they exchanged now and then for similar libraries at Hoyland and other places.

"This is a great thing for the men," said Mr. Jubb, with his eyes alight. "It gives them something to do for themselves and others. There are hobbies for them. A bit of handicraft makes all the difference to a man's spirit. There are many other places round about where this kind of thing ought to be done. I go about preaching the good work."

I understood from others—though not from Mr. Jubb—that there is a certain political opposition to these social service schemes. A few Communists and advanced Labour men regard it as encouraging slave labour. They also regard it as an artful scheme by the bloated bourgeoisie to keep Labour quiet. They would prefer the unemployed to be so miserable that they would rise in their wrath against the Capitalist system.

"Palliatives!" they say, with utter contempt for men who come along and get interested in a hobby or a handicraft. But the men want to mend their boots and don't see why they shouldn't at a cheap cost. They want to make a corner cupboard for the wife and don't see why they are degrading themselves or acting like blacklegs in doing that bit of woodwork. They don't see any political treachery to their class if they come into a good clubroom run by themselves and play a game of billiards on a second-hand table. Anything rather than endless listlessness.

"At Hoyland," said Mr. King, "I want you to meet a remarkable woman."

"I should like to," I agreed. "Is she a female Mussolini?"

"Exactly," he agreed. "All the quality of Mussolini without his blood lust."

On the way to Hoyland he told me the story of the place and the woman.

Hoyland was dependent for most of its livelihood on the pits of Newton Chambers. When they closed down—they were "uneconomical"—fifty per cent of the working population joined the ranks of the unemployed. That is how the situation remains. There were six thousand men of working age in Hoyland. Three thousand of them were on the dole.

"Mrs. Fox started with fish," said my friend.

I was a little mystified.

"There was a fish scheme run by the Society of Friends. It was sold cheap in the mining villages. But the Town Hall and other authorities wouldn't let Mrs. Fox stand under cover because fish makes such a stench in a closed room. In the winter she stood outside with a charcoal stove burning behind her. She was too hot behind and too cold in front. Rather brave!"

"Heroic!" I said, my imagination leaping to the frightfulness of selling fish on winter evenings in Hoyland.

"She runs the social centre now," said my guide. "It couldn't get on without her. She's a marvel!"

I met this marvellous woman face to face and found her very smiling and simple, and devoted to this work of hers, which made her the godmother of three hundred men and two hundred women. I had met her type before—twenty-one years ago. They were the women who ran the canteens in France and the convalescent camps, not above going down on their knees to scrub floors, handing out cocoa and cigarettes to wounded soldiers, scraping the mud off them when they came down from the trenches, keeping them merry and bright as far as men may be kept merry and bright if they're blinded or crippled. This Yorkshire woman had the same spirit. For her the war hadn't ended. She was dealing with the casualties of the industrial battle.

She had a good house. It used to be the Conservative Club of Hoyland, though it seems strange that Hoyland should have Conservatives. Perhaps they lost heart and departed. Anyhow, Earl Fitzwilliam, who lives in his big house at Wentworth not far away—years ago I remember going there when there was a family festival and oxen were roasted whole in the park—has handed it over for a social centre at a nominal rent. It's a fine place for its present purpose, with big rooms which have been turned into workshops and playrooms and lecture rooms and concert rooms. Mrs. Fox runs a canteen which she calls the bar, though no alcoholic liquors are sold. She runs a workroom for the women, who mend and make their clothes out of material bought out of the funds, by Mrs. Fox herself. They have lectures and debates, and billiards, and pingpong, and choirs, and physical exercises. It hums with social activity as far as the men and boys of Hoyland can be induced to take advantage of these good things.

Some of them don't take advantage of them. They're a bit shy or a bit slack. And the old intense, secretive individualism of the English character—very strong up here in Yorkshire— tends to prevent men and boys from getting together for communal exercises and amusements. Many of them prefer to stand at the street corners or sit in their small rooms and back yards. They resent any leadership from one of their own comrades. Bossy, they call it. They have not been trained to teamwork. They are given to inward brooding and their own secret thoughts, and are not easily induced to join a class for learning something or making something. They hate anything which seems to them like interference or charity or catching hold of them. So I was told by Mrs. Fox and her friends, and I could understand it all perfectly, being of that nature myself. But the spirit of this cheerful, laughing, organizing Yorkshirewoman—there are many of them in Yorkshire, I guess—has broken down some of this resistance to social life, and her big roll of membership is a proof thereof.

I was impressed by another place I saw in this district, at Chapeltown, where a monstrous slag heap of the Newton Chambers pit casts its shadow over the miners' cottages. Some of the unemployed there—most of the population is out of work —have made an amusing little club out of some old stables. They have boarded over the floors, kept the draughts out of the timbered roof, put in a small billiard table, and made themselves very snug. Round the walls are some good engravings and oil paintings which must have been the gift of some man of property, and outside, in the yard, they have made flower beds giving a touch of colour to its neighbourhood, so drab and squalid otherwise.

I went to other villages in the mining area, where the population is mostly unemployed by the closing of the pits, or under the daily menace of losing their means of livelihood, as at Corsborough, where the seam is giving out and every miner expects his next wage to be his last. A journey round this area does not leave one with a sense of cheerfulness. One wonders whether this modern civilization of ours is worth the price paid for it by such life as one sees in these dejected villages. One wonders whether our new prosperity, of which we read so much in the newspapers and hear so much from members of the government, is reaching down to the workers in the front line of industry. The south—the lucky south—has not been utterly callous, but perhaps it ought to do a bit more for its hard-pressed comrades up in the north.

And I have come back with an uneasy feeling that the northern industrialists, getting back to full-time production, with their machines working again, with orders coming in, with every sign of renewed prosperity in their great cities, like Sheffield and Middlesborough, are not giving enough support and personal interest and sympathy to that work of social service for which the Prince of Wales made a call when he had been through these areas of unemployment and came back stricken by the thought of them. "They have the dole, haven't they?" I have heard men say. Yes, they have the dole. But that's not quite enough to ease the consciences of the mine owners and the manufacturers, if they have any. They have taken a lot of wealth out of the labour of men who are now discharged. They haven't put much back into those villages and lives. They could do a lot more to brighten up these places. They leave it to a few social workers and volunteers, often from other parts of England, handicapped by inadequate funds and just touching a few groups here and there with a little helpfulness and leadership. But I may be making a false charge. In Sheffield there are public-spirited men who cannot be accused of that. One of them I know has done fine work in a scheme which has brought health and happiness to thousands of men.

11. Plots of Earth

The best thing I saw in the north in social service is the Sheffield District Allotments Federation. That sounds dull, but I found in it all the drama of a great adventure touching the lives of men who have good stuff in them, and offering them an extraordinary gift of happiness. Sheffield is a city built upon hills. It stretches out a great distance with its residential districts and its immense industrial works. On the steep slopes and in the valleys there was a good deal of waste ground. It is this ground which has been turned over for allotments, to men who are willing to work it and grow things in it. Round the city there are no less than fourteen thousand of these allotments, and all of them used by men who have made little paradises of these plots. Three thousand of them are worked by the unemployed, with some of whom I talked.

They were on the dole, these fellows, having been steel workers and factory hands, and men in blast furnaces and forges and engineering shops and cutlery works. Most of them, I thought, belonged to that class which is "too old at fifty," or maybe forty, though here and there were young men who could not get a job. Most of them had never handled a spade or a hoe before they took over these plots of earth. They knew nothing about potatoes except when they had eaten them with fried fish. They had not any expert knowledge of soils and manures. They knew more about steel than they did about beans or cabbages or flowers. But now they are good gardeners. They take a pride in the potatoes they have grown. Each man has made a little Eden out of these strips of English earth on the slopes of Sheffield and its outlying districts.

It was amusing to talk with some of these men, and rather touching. They showed me round their plots with the pride of Surrey ladies in their gardens exhibiting their herbaceous borders.

"It's a pity you didn't come a bit earlier," said one man. "Kitchen gardens don't look their best in autumn. Now a month ago . . ."

Two men were turning up some potatoes, and one of them spoke to me.

"Lovely, aren't they? Well, I put some work into 'em. Watched them from birth as if they 'ad been my own kids. They've done fine on inorganic manure, better than chemical fertilizers."

He stooped down and picked up some bits of brown stuff to show me. It was shoddy torn into strips and put into the soil —a form of manure of which I had never heard, though that's not surprising.

In one group of allotments looking away from Sheffield to the hills beyond I was greeted by a tall old man of sixty, in his Sunday best. Someone had given word that visitors were coming, and he had made himself ready to do the honours in a blue serge suit. He had been a soldier in the Regular army. Now he walked four miles every morning to his plot and four miles back after a hard day's toil.

"I'm sorry you couldn't see Jimmy," he told me presently. "But he was sick for the day. He's a great lad is Jimmy. If any man wants to know anything they say, 'Where's Jimmy?' He's our chief expert on putting up sheds, getting things to grow, and killing any pests which attack the plants."

He spoke to me confidentially, apart from the other men.

"It's grand for them," he said, "on these plots. It gives them an interest in life when everything seems to have slipped. Men on the dole get demoralized for lack of hope sometimes. They go to pieces mentally and physically. They take to brooding and feel on the scrap heap. But when once they get down to an allotment time seems to go fast. Some of them stay up here while there's any light in the day, from first thing in the morning till the sun drops down. It's a grand hobby, and it's worth half a crown a week to them, in things they eat and take home to their families. They never get tired of digging and weeding and looking after every plant as though it were a living pet. They built these huts and glass houses for themselves out of any old scrap and a few bits of glass. Inside these is their private domain. Some of them keep them as neat as ships' cabins. Most of these men, like myself, have left the labour market. They'll never get another job. But this has given them a new lease of life. It makes them happy. In a garden a man keeps happy. And it brings out a man's sweetness. These fellows help each other. They can always give something away even if it's only a sprig of mint."

I went to many of the allotments and talked with many of the men.

"My wife asks me why I don't bring my bed up here," said one of them, laughing. "Well, I never get tired of it. And it keeps me fit. There's something about a plot of earth and growing things which gives a man satisfaction."

All these men give something of their labour and the fruit

of it to the hospitals in Sheffield, to which they send a share of
their vegetables and flowers, never begrudging it, with a generosity which is very noble, I think. And talking with them there
on the hillsides I was struck by the simplicity, the good-nature,
the humour of these allotment holders. They are men of good
tough stock, full of character which is fine and sweet. No bitterness is in their minds, though they have been through rough
times and know the wretchedness of unemployment.

It is to the Society of Friends, "the salt of the earth," as I
heard them called, that a debt of honour is due for this allotment
organization in England and Wales. Four years ago, or thereabouts, they started a scheme in South Wales for helping unemployed miners to cultivate some plots of ground. The government set up a committee to draw up a similar scheme in other
parts of the country. The moneys were provided out of public
funds, and in the season of 1930–31 over 64,000 unemployed
men were enabled to plant their allotments, the total cost being
about £23,000. In September of 1931 the new government,
faced by a financial crisis, dropped their committee and their
assistance, but the Society of Friends carried on the work, and
in September, 1932, the government again agreed to assist them
by grants up to £10,000, on certain conditions. The Friends
made an appeal for £15,000 to secure the government grant,
followed by another appeal for an additional £5,000 for putting
men permanently on the land. The response was splendid, and
working in collaboration with other societies and local authorities there are now over 100,000 men on these allotments. The
whole purpose of the scheme is to help men to help themselves.
They are provided with seeds and fertilizers and garden tools,
bought in great quantities at the lowest cost, and the men pay
part of this back in weekly instalments. It is remarkable that
they have contributed over £26,000 towards the cost of supplies
which amounts to something over £36,000. There are more
than 2,000 societies operating the scheme throughout the country, affiliated to the National Allotment Federation and other
authorities. It is not too much to say that this work is doing
more than anything else to bring health and happiness into the
lives of men who otherwise found themselves hopeless and demoralized. The Sheffield allotments ring round that city with

a girdle of gardens where such men have forgotten boredom and have a hobby which gives a new light to their world. I don't think I'm exaggerating when I say that. It is the truth which some of these men told me themselves.

In Sheffield itself there is the mighty business of an industrial stronghold. It is one of our capitals of machine power. It is the City of Steel, not in its raw state as in Middlesborough, but making the million things of metal used in the world today. Among those are the weapons and the shells with which civilization, this top-heavy civilization of ours, defends its territory, or competes for world markets, or grabs new sources of raw material. There was a rush order for naval shells when I was there, as I have written. Steel manufacture was looking up again. Its shares were rising. There is great activity in world armament.

Standing in the hall of the Grand Hotel, my eyes were attracted by a board with golden lettering. It was a roll of honour for ninety-eight men in the service of this hotel who fell in the World War. I read their names—good Yorkshire names—except eight of them, which were Italian. Eight Italian waiters had gone out to die from this hotel in a war which happened twenty-one years ago. Now the evening papers were talking about a war with Italy, if sanctions were applied. My eye was caught by a paragraph in a Sheffield evening paper:

Tyneside brass founders and dealers in iron and steel scrap are being inundated with inquiries from financiers and speculators anxious to "cash in" on the prospects of war in Ethiopia.

A Newcastle scrap merchant told a *North Mail* representative yesterday that he had received offers for brass, copper and gunmetal scrap from all over the country.

All metals and materials capable of conversion to military purposes are steadily rising in price.

I went out into the streets of Sheffield and saw crowds lining up outside enormous picture palaces with flaming signs. A busy traffic was streaming past. In the lighted shop windows there was a display of all the little luxuries of life. Young girls were studying the autumn fashions. Sheffield was making money, and prosperity was round the corner.

England is doing well by some miracle of character and industry and, perhaps, a little luck. Birmingham is working overtime. Nottingham is very pleased with itself and advertises its prosperity. In a hundred cities the trade reports are very favourable. Apart from those special areas which hate to be called depressed or distressed, England is on the up-grade of industry and commerce. Even her coal output has gone up from 9 million tons in 1930 to over 12 millions in 1935, though pits are closing down in Durham and southern Yorkshire. Money is turning round faster. Our standard of life, in many classes, is very high compared with other countries—the highest in the world, just now. We are a very lucky people, if the luck lasts.

Epilogue

HERE THEN is something of England. Now that I have written this book I am aware of how much I have left out, and how much more I could have written if I had gone on without a limit of length. For every man and woman knows his or her own England and could add different characters and different scenes to those I have described. But here is something of the England that I know myself, and here are the people I have met in their houses and workshops and streets and fields. I have put down the things they have said to me about their own lives. I have given their views in this year of grace. They are authentic talks. I have not made them up out of my own head or coloured them with my own imagination and ideas. I have tried to open many doors and to introduce my readers to odd and interesting folk of all degrees, so that after reading these pages they may know more of the variety of character in this country today and see something more of the spirit of England as it is expressed by many men and women. I hope that this spirit comes through: the simplicity, the good-humour, the kindliness, the courage, the honesty, the patience of so many in the crowds. We are still a nation of individualists, and I think that comes out in this book, in which I have given a portrait gallery of people not yet standardized by the mass production of thought and character. In this machine age, which is killing some of our character and some of our beauty every day, England is still beautiful where one slips away from the roar of traffic and the blight of industrialism; and in these quiet places

where there are still English meadows not yet taped out by the
jerry builder, and trees not yet marked for the ax, and old
houses with old timbers, there are, as I have shown, men and
women still living very deep in tradition. The two worlds live
side by side, the old-world England hardly touched by the
increasing rhythm of the speed mania which is called Progress,
hardly affected by the trash of the mind, the jazzing up of life,
the restlessness, the triviality, which goes by the name of the
Modern Spirit; yet in this other world of bricks and mortar, of
picture palaces, of factories and flats, and electric trams and
chain stores, there is something still very traditional in the
crowds that pass and in the individuals which make up the
crowds. All this modernization is, I find, very superficial. I
mean, it has not yet bitten into the soul of England or poisoned
its brain. As I have written in the first pages of this book, the
crowds who came out into the streets for Jubilee belonged to
Shakespeare's England as well as to King George's. They had
the touch of Chaucer's folk in their blood and humour. In any
time of crisis or tribulation they reveal themselves unchanged
in their courage and sense of comedy, which I believe is the
chief quality—that sense of comicality even in misfortune—
which distinguishes us most from other peoples. The other day
in Wapping, when a big fire blazed and its filthy smoke rolled
for days over many houses, not without menace, observers
spoke of the cheerfulness with which the crowds down there
faced their discomforts and their danger. Foreigners who know
us well enough to take our measure and have no cause to hate
us cannot resist an admiration for our common folk. They find
us, like my friend James Truslow Adams, the American his-
torian, a decent, honest, and orderly folk with a real tradition
of liberty and an instinct for law—self-made and self-obeyed.
Like many others, he is struck by the kindliness of the ordinary
folk in everyday life. And my friend André Siegfried, the
French critic and economist, admires our national good-nature
and simplicities. It amuses him that during some world crisis
correspondents to *The Times* not only write to the editor to in-
form him that the cuckoo has been heard or that an owl is nest-
ing in the Tower of London. Or that they have made a study
of the robin in its bath, but—incredible as it seems—have their

letters printed. He finds that we are closer to nature than his own people in the sense of comradeship with birds, and little beasts, and flowers, and all growing things. There is something of the peasant in all of us, though we have become industrialized. We love the beauty of nature, though we allow it to be destroyed and help to destroy it.

It would be good to write that all's well with England. All is not well when there are thousands of homeless men and boys in the streets of London every night. All is not well when the splendour of our civilization, its glitter and glare, its wealth and power are built upon the labour of men like those miners up north, grievously underpaid for all the risks they take so that they would be better, or almost better, on the dole. All is not well with England when so much of its manhood—even youth on the threshold of life—is unemployed.

The national government is advertising its service to the country. There are a million less unemployed. A million houses have been built. Good! Some share of the credit is due to them. They have steered the ship of State through many dangerous reefs. They have kept a steady hand on the tiller. They have done a good deal for agriculture and something for shipping. But our advance towards prosperity is due mostly to the character of the people, to the intelligence of its business men, to the industry and steadiness and patience of the working classes. More could have been done, I think, for those areas up north where unemployment is a black plague still. Those men on allotments prove that they can use the earth. They are good at poultry and pigs and market gardens. Was it beyond the power and imagination of the government to bring more of them onto the land and enlarge the range of that scheme which was put in hand by a little group of idealists called the Society of Friends? We have the greatest Empire in the world, and foreigners envy our empty spaces. Is there not room enough for some of our younger men, the sons of miners who will never go down to the pits again? Have we no leadership for such plans as that?

Not all is well with England when every week there is a massacre of innocents on the highways, and when every year the casualties of motor traffic are as great as those of one of our battles in a world war. Children are run over and killed by cars as fast as express trains, when they are picking flowers in country lanes, or playing hopscotch in narrow streets. There is a haunting dread in every family that their small boy will be one of the victims of this Moloch on his way to school or the village shop. The Minister of Transport puts up many signs and speaks over the microphone pleading for caution and consideration in driving. He fails in the courage to do the only thing which would reduce this toll of deaths on the roads, which is to limit the speed to twelve miles an hour through villages and any built-up areas. Why all this hurry? What's it all about? What sense is there in this mania for speed at the cost of human life?

England is not without strains of evil and strains of weakness. We have our full share of human folly. We shan't escape the price of it. But there is in the mass of our people in every class a quality of spirit which redeems all our faults. It is a spirit of decency and an instinct of fair play. We find it hard to hate. We have no ruthlessness, no natural cruelty. We are, in the mass, a kindly, whimsical humorous folk. We want to live in peace with our neighbours and cultivate our gardens, if we can get a plot of earth. Among us still, as I have shown in this book, I think, there are many odd characters, many gay crowds, many good companions, many heroic lives, and an inexhaustible reserve of courage, laughter, and good will. We shall need all that quality of ours because, as I write, there is no sense of security in Europe or the world. The tiger nations and the wolf nations are arming to the teeth. The human tribes are on the warpath again. The drums are beating in the jungle. . . .

In England this year there was peace, and I went into its gardens and saw its beauty, and into its streets with gay crowds. One can breathe freely and talk freely, for we still keep our liberties. There is no intolerance in our mind. There is no need to look over one's shoulder in a public place lest a police spy should be listening, or lest a gang of boys should be waiting with rubber truncheons to beat one's brains out. In the old earth of England and in its wind and weather there is some salt which gives us health, and sanity, and strength.

THE END